BIKING
IN METRO HALIFAX

A MONTH-BY-MONTH ADVENTURE GUIDE

CLARENCE STEVENS

NIMBUS
PUBLISHING

Nimbus Publishing Limited
P.O. Box 9301, Station A
Halifax, NS B3K 5N5
(902) 455-4286

Design: Kathy Kaulbach, Halifax
Printed and bound in Canada

Illustrations: Andrea MacIvor pp.1, 129; Bob Dickie p. 45; Azor Vienneau pp. 29, 67, 85, 109, 142, 160, 179, 198, 215.

Canadian Cataloguing in Publication Data
Stevens, Clarence.
Birding in Metro Halifax
Includes index.
ISBN 1-55109-159-3
1. Bird watching—Nova Scotia—Halifax Metropolitan Area—Guidebooks. 2. Birds—Nova Scotia—Halifax Metropolitan Area. I. Title.
QL685.5.N6S73 1976   598'.07234716225
C96-950060-2

Nimbus Publishing acknowledges the financial assistance of the Canada Council and the Department of Canadian Heritage

To my parents, Clarence and Frances Stevens, who I love dearly.

CONTENTS

Preface

Historians tell us that there are more people interested in nature in general and birds specifically than at any other time in the history of our world. Today, there are literally millions of birders in North America alone. The United States Fish and Wildlife Service reports that bird-watching is the second most common hobby on the continent; in fact, North Americans spend millions of dollars every year on birds. As the popularity of birding has grown, so has knowledge about birds and birders.

However, there are still some misconceptions out there. The most common one concerns who is a birder and who is not—I admit sometimes it is easy to get confused. I regularly hear: "I am not a birder, I just feed birds." If you fall in this category, surprise, you are a birder. In fact, people who feed birds make up by far the largest group of birders. In our own Nova Scotia Bird Society, it is estimated that 70 per cent of its members fall into the category of back yard birders. Furthermore, bird society members represent only a small portion of those who are feeding and watching birds in the province. Current estimates indicate that one in every five households is presently feeding birds, or has fed birds in the past; predictions for the year 2000 show that ratio growing to one in every two households.

Most birders are either back yard birders or they start out that way. Then they casually start noticing birds in other places as well. Before they know it, they are hooked and actually go out searching for birds. Even then, some people still deny that they are real birders, but we know better!

Why Bird Halifax County?

In order to fully understand the advantages of birding in Halifax County, we must first look at the whole province. Nova Scotia is one of the best birding locations on the continent. Our coastal positioning means that we regularly see many species that inland areas are lacking. To the north of the province lies the boreal forest, which covers most of Canada, and to the south grows the southern hardwood forest. Where these two great forests meet, there is a relatively narrow band of mixed woodland and here most species from both forest types can be found. Nova Scotia is situated in this productive mixed woodland forest. It also falls in the middle of the Atlantic Flyway, which is the largest migration route in eastern North America. In the fall, birds from Ontario, Quebec, the Arctic, and the four Atlantic provinces all funnel through Nova Scotia on their way south.

Besides our regular migrants, a wide assortment of rare birds are constantly seen in the province. In fact almost every year a new species of bird is added to our provincial list. Birds blown off-course from the west or the north often continue to fly in the wrong direction until they see the Atlantic Ocean looming before them. Being situated at the end of the continent, Nova Scotia is often the place where these lost birds decide to rest and feed before attempting to fly over the ocean or follow the coast southward. Birds blown off the coast of Florida by strong southern gales commonly end up in Nova Scotia because it is frequently the first piece of mainland these birds can find. This also holds true for birds carried off the coast of Europe. Every year European birds show up in Nova Scotia, some as the result of storms and some under their own steam.

Halifax County is fortunately an ideal place for birders to experience and benefit from all of the above occurrences. Halifax County's Eastern Shore hosts a diverse array of bird life that is constantly changing throughout the year. Halifax County is also the home of Hartlen Point, one of the best birding sites in the province. Hartlen Point has attracted hundreds of different species. Each year a greater variety of birds are reported from Halifax County than any of the other counties. This is partly because the highest concentration of birders in the province is in Halifax County. This not only means more eyes to spot the birds, it also means more feeders to attract and sustain bird life. Cities are not usually perceived to be great places to see lots of birds but this is not so for the Halifax region. The Halifax Harbour greatly increases the inner city bird life and makes our Metro area the second warmest part of the province during the winter months, which draws birds in from the cooler regions. Inside the city it is also much easier to find urban-loving birds, such as the Northern Mockingbird. In addition, the city has a greater percentage of introduced species of trees and plants. These exotic plants are often the first recognizable food source to birds that have arrived here from faraway locales.

Scope of this Guide

This guide is currently the most complete and accurate body of information on birding locations and birds found in Halifax County, the geographic focus of the book. However, a decade from now, land use, bird population, and our birding knowledge of the county will have changed. I look forward to your comments to help keep the information current for any future updates of this guide.

Although this book focuses on Halifax County, much of the information relating to when certain species may be seen is either true for the rest of the province, or the times of occurrence in Halifax County are very close to those in other counties. In this sense, the book can be of value to those interested in birds in any part of Nova Scotia.

Book Set-up

A quick glance at the table of contents will reveal that this book is divided into three main parts. The first section contains twelve chapters named for the months of the year and each one contains information pertinent to that month. Every chapter begins with a description of what the birds are doing and types of experiences that one may hope to have during that month. The chapter then discusses in detail some of the specific highlights of that month within two categories: City Birding and Further Afield. The events listed under City Birding occur close to human habitation, be it the city core or people's back yards. Further Afield sections discuss birding experiences one can have by going out into the countryside.

Section 2 explains how to reach the places mentioned in the monthly chapters, providing tips on how to bird the site and indicating what species you can expect to find. Halifax County is divided into birding regions and all locations are organized by which route or highway they are found along.

Section 3 is a complete checklist of all the birds that have been found in Nova Scotia. It explains what species you can hope to see in Halifax County and indicates how common or rare each bird may be.

How to Use this Guide

This guide is designed to be used in several ways. If you are looking for enjoyable reading, the information here is presented with an accessible and entertaining approach to birding. An effort has been made to stay away from technical terms as much as possible.

This guide is best classified as an indoor/outdoor guide. In the home it can be used to help you become more aware of when to expect certain species to pass through your yard or neighbourhood and which of those birds will visit the feeders. If you use the guide for this purpose alone, you will find it beneficial. However, I hope that it will also inspire you to go out and search for other species of birds. One does not have to dedicate a great deal of time in order to have an interesting bird trip; certainly length does not determine the value of a birding outing. Birding can be an all-day event, but it is a pastime that can be easily combined with other activities to take as little as ten minutes. This guide can help you prepare for outings in several ways.

You can open the book to the month you are interested in and choose one of the suggested birding events for that time of year. Or you can use the checklist to discover what species of birds you have the best chance of seeing in Halifax County. You will be pleased to find that 169 of the 446 species listed fall into the commonly seen category. Perhaps there is a particular species of bird you have always wanted to see. In this case, use the index to find information on where and when the bird may be seen. The index can also be used to look up the name of a place you want to visit.

Before you actually go out to identify birds, if you spend a few minutes at home leafing through your field guide, you will find the brief prepara-tion useful. Of course, the ideal approach would be to go through your guide and study each of the birds found in your area. Unfortunately, most birders do not have the time to do this. That is where this guide can come in handy. Depending on where you choose to go in the Halifax County, this guide will tell you exactly what species you are most likely to see and thus which birds you should read about before heading out. It will also give additional tips on how to identify the species you are looking for.

However, I must stress that this book is not a bird identification guide. It has been developed as a companion volume to these guides. The two best ones for our area are Peterson Field Guides *Eastern Birds* and The National Geographic's *Guide to Birds of North America*. If you are relatively new to birding, the Peterson Guide is by far the most helpful. As you become more involved in birding, you will want both, plus others. The purpose of this book is to help people know where to find birds and, more importantly, *when* to find them, as even the best birding spots in the world are quiet at times. You do not have to do much birding to discover how difficult it is to find birds when you are at the right place at the *wrong* time. Read this book and discover how many birds there are to see if you look in the right places at the *right* time.

Once you have decided to go birding, by all means take this guide with you. The valuable information contained within will help you to make informed decisions in the field about what to do if you find yourself in a particular situation; it shares secrets used by experienced birders to locate birds more easily; it can even provide you with helpful hints not found in standard bird identification guides. Some have said that this guide is like carrying your very own birding expert around in your back pocket!

Notes for Visitors

Nova Scotia is one of the safest places in the world to take a vacation and do some birding; however, there are a few precautions to keep in mind. Although ticks are present in the counties west of Halifax County, the latter is still tick free. When birding around lakes, be careful not to touch poison ivy, a plant that is fairly common in the province and can cause a painful rash. In the woods mosquitoes and blackflies can be bad at times, so be sure to carry insect repellent with you just in case. No matter what part of North America you are coming from, and regardless of the season, there is a good chance there will be birds present that you have not seen before. Recent bird sightings for Halifax County can be obtained by phoning the chat line at (902) 852–2428, or in the Friday edition of *The Mail Star* or the Sunday edition of *The Daily News*.

I would like to thank the following people who have in one way or another contributed to the quality of this guide: Tom Adams, Christine Aikenhead, Krista Amey, Doug Beattie, Carl and Kathie Blades, Helen Blake, Dorothy Blythe and the staff at Nimbus, Pat Bonang, Don and Lois Codling, Lynda Conrad, Joanne Creelman, Trip Denice, Bob Dickie, Fred Dobson, Peter Dooley, Michael Downing, B. J. Edmondson, Stephen Flemming, Ian Goudie, Liz Greenough, Diane Henriksen, Dede Hiscock, Dorothy Jackson, Ron Jeppesen, Don Keith, Peter Kerswell, James Kinnear, Petar and Leila Kovacevic, Simon Krasemann, Fulton Lavender, Gwen MacDonald, Andrea MacIvor, Gail MacLean, Robert Mann, Paula McCluskey, Barb McKay, Ken McKenna, Ian McLaren, Cadence MacMichael, Nancy McNair, Scott Merry, Louise Mosher, Rod Murphy, Tanya Neklioudova, Evanne O'Leary, Linda Payzant, Rich Peckham, Roger Pocklington, Heather Proudfoot, Paula Richardson, Vicki Richmond, Joe Robertson, Bev Sarty, Jeannine Shirley, Eleanor Simonyi, Don Shiner, Blair Smith,Clarence and Frances Stevens, Margo Storey, Jessica Tallman, Catherine Tanner, Jim Taylor, Dennis Theman, Mary Vaughan, Shawna Veinotte, Azor Vienneau, Irma Warrington, Neil Williams, and Sherman Williams.

January Birding

....

A Time of New Beginnings

Some people will be surprised to learn that just over a hundred species of birds are present in the Metro area each January. The worst of the winter weather has yet to arrive, so bird populations are still fairly healthy, making this one of the better winter months to do some birding. Two other factors combine to produce great birding opportunities in January: the Christmas Counts and the regular movements of birds. Most of the Audubon Christmas Counts are conducted in late December and early January. These surveys give us a relatively good idea as to what species are present and where.

In the winter, in order to conserve energy, most species of birds will not travel any farther than necessary to find food. Therefore, once a certain species is discovered at a location, it is likely to stay put for at least a little while. This

J·A·N·U·A·R·Y

makes it easier for those wishing to see a particular bird because they can track it down by finding out where it was seen on a Christmas Count.

January is a convenient time to go birding, as many of the species can be seen from the warmth of your car. Unlike the summer, when most of the species are present in the woods, in the winter, open grassy areas as well as any open water are popular with birds. These types of habitats are relatively flat, making it easy to scan them from inside your car. Of course, the occasional excursion on foot will help you to spot additional species. In grassy areas, look for winter songbirds, such as Snow Buntings, Horned Larks, and Lapland Longspurs. These are also good places to watch for hawks and owls. In January, hawks, eagles, and owls may be seen in the daytime, inside and outside the city limits. Whenever there is open water, a great variety of waterfowl may be observed in January, including over twenty species of ducks, up to ten species of gulls, and as many as six species of alcids, or seabirds, including the popular Atlantic Puffin.

In December and January, feeder-watchers should prepare for the arrival of additional winter finches. January is also a popular time of year for birders to start keeping notes on various types of birds.

New Year's Resolutions

The dawning of the New Year is celebrated as a time of fresh starts and new beginnings. We tend to view it as an opportunity to change our lives for the better. Accordingly, we often set New Year's resolutions, which are usually tough, life-changing decisions that we have been putting off. Statements such as, "I vow to lose weight this year," or, "This is the year I will quit smoking," are typical. Just as typically, these resolutions quickly fall by the wayside. So why not try something different this year? After all, a life-changing decision does not have to involve a sacrifice or changing something about ourselves that we do not like. It can also involve adding something positive to our lives. If you have never done any birding, I recommend that you try it. Birding has many hidden pleasures, which can lead to a heightened awareness of the natural world. If you have had a taste of birding and liked it, make it part of your resolutions to set aside some time to look at birds and learn a little more about the various aspects of the hobby.

A New Year's Day Tradition

Many birders like to kick off the New Year by venturing out and seeing how many species of birds they can find on January first. Not only can this be an interesting way to begin the New Year, it can also be a great way to start off the "year list." The year list is simply a list of all the birds a birder has seen in one year. It is a very efficient way to record birding memories. As birders look back over their year list(s), they often recall many of the adventures which they had experienced.

Many people collect things. Whether it is coins, rocks, or salt shakers, collecting somehow fulfils a need. That urge to collect explains why many birders keep a year list. A nice thing about this sort of collecting is that an infinite number of people can "collect" the same bird without depleting the resource in any way. Also, a collection of year lists takes up virtually no space. Some birders like year lists because they can make a common species exciting again. January first is about the only day of the year you would run into a birder who is trying to see a pigeon or a House Sparrow. One of the most practical reasons for keeping a year list is that it helps birders stay familiar with a wide variety of species and keeps their birding skills sharp. Without constant contact, one can begin to forget the pleasant subtleties of each species, such as how warming the cheery nature of a Black Capped Chickadee can be on a cold winter's day. For some, a year list is simply a record of the birds they happen to see that year. Others become more involved in keeping a list, and they try to seek out species to fill the gaps. Either approach has its rewards.

Take Note

When it comes to birds, each year we can expect certain events to unfold. Exactly how and when these events take place varies slightly from year to year, depending upon both continental and local conditions. Some grand events, such as spring migration, are fairly easy to predict and observe, while others are only noticed by those who are aware of the natural rhythms of our area. Careful observers have found that much of what occurs in the natural world is reflected in their own community.

Note-keeping can be especially helpful in discovering many of those intricate changes that take place on an ongoing basis. A few observations can be interesting, but as the number of observations grows over time, so does their value. After a while, patterns will begin to emerge from your notes, and you will be able to predict certain events before they happen. Of course, some people can do the same thing by recalling from memory events of past years. However, without notes, the current course of happenings has a tendency to either dilute past inconsistencies or cause them to be overemphasized.

While you can begin note-keeping at any time, many birders prefer to start in January and continue until December, so their notes are organized on an annual basis. Others prefer to arrange their observations according to the seasons. Regardless of how you choose to do it, you will be surprised by how note-keeping can increase your interest in birds. Whether you choose to make your own notes or to just use those contained in this guide, you will be quickly convinced that the educated eye does see more.

Seventeen years ago, I recorded my first observations of an unknown bird that I saw in my neighbourhood. Since then, I have seen how personal notes and observations have opened a world of enjoyment. They have helped me and others gain valuable insight into and a greater understanding of birds and the world they live in—a world we share with them, yet only vaguely understand.

City Birding

....

Sewer Stroll

By January, dropping temperatures have caused the opportunity for birding in Halifax Harbour to heat up, as waterfowl move in to take advantage of the open water. At least once a year, the Nova Scotia Bird Society conducts a field trip to take in as many of the interesting birding spots surrounding the harbour as possible. Headlands, beaches, sheltered bays, estuaries, and small islands are some of the coastal habitats visited during the excursion. The trip is conducted in January or February, as that is the time of year when Halifax Harbour plays host to a variety of bird life not present in other seasons. During much of our winter, the water in the lakes, ponds, inlets, and small bays is often frozen, causing the relatively warm and open waters of the naturally deep Halifax Harbour to act as a magnet for waterfowl.

Another attraction is the various sewer outlets scattered along the harbour's shores. These outlets attract birds by providing a source of rich nutrients, which directly and indirectly create an abundant food supply around the outfall. A number of the more productive outlets are visited during the Nova Scotia Bird Society's expedition, now dubbed the "Sewer Stroll."

If you wish to conduct your own sewer stroll, hold your nose, roll up the windows, and hang a ring of garlic around your neck! Actually, most people don't realize they are visiting a sewage outlet until some helpful birder points it out. So if you feel uncomfortable about going on a sewer stroll, just call it "a birding tour of Halifax Harbour," and no one will know the difference. The area covered for the Sewer Stroll normally encompasses the entire shore of the harbour, from Hartlen Point to Chebucto Head, and sometimes as far as the village of Sambro. Of course, it is neither possible nor desirable to visit every metre of shoreline, so key spots are selected, places that have proven to host the most birds over the years. The following is a recommended tour of the best places to visit along the harbour and the names of birds you can expect to see at those locations.

There are certain species that will be seen at most or all of the locations along the harbour: the American Black Duck, Herring Gulls, and Great Black Backed Gulls. These species are our three most common water birds and no further introduction may be needed for most people. However, if you are not acquainted with these birds, see "Winter Gull Identification" in January and "American Black Ducks" in December.

Sewer Stroll: The Dartmouth Shoreline

Hartlen Point marks the most easterly tip of the Halifax Harbour, making it a logical place to begin this outing. This point of land is one of the best birding locations in the Metro area and in the province. For this reason, most of the species that can be seen on a typical birding trip around the harbour could also be observed at Hartlen.

However, many of those species are more easily seen at other locations along the waterfront. Three species at Hartlen Point that may be harder to locate in other parts of the harbour are the Glaucous Gull, Oldsquaw, and Black Scoter.

If you do not wish to venture outside the city limits to begin your harbour birding trip, you can start at Cuisack Street in Dartmouth or any of the other locations mentioned in this description. At the end of Cuisack Street is a high hill that gives an observer a commanding view of a large section of harbour water and a small sewage outlet. This location is a perfect spot to scan for a variety of water birds, and if you would like to get a closer look, there is a path that runs from the top of the hill down to the shoreline. This is one of the few places where Black Guillemots are seen inside the city limits on a regular basis during the winter months.

By driving to the end of Old Ferry Road, one can reach the eastern end of Dartmouth Cove. There, the occasional Razorbill or Thick Billed Murre is seen, as well as interesting birds that wander over from the west side of Dartmouth Cove. The west side of this cove is one of the most productive birding spots in the Metro area during the winter. Local birders often refer to this location as the Canal Street sewage outlet, even though the outlet itself is located at the end of Maitland Street. On cold days, this outlet can be scanned with binoculars from the car, but in order to see the greatest number of species, it is best to get out of your vehicle. This is an excellent place to see Common Black Headed, Bonaparte's, and Iceland Gulls. Various species of alcids are seen regularly at this location, as well as many species of unusual ducks that have travelled to this spot from Sullivans Pond.

Sullivans Pond is one of Metro's few fresh bodies of water that stays open all winter, making it a mecca for waterfowl. While technically,

Sullivans Pond is not part of Halifax Harbour, it is always included in any birding trip of the harbour as many of the species of ducks and gulls which gather there fly between the pond and various parts of the harbour. Birds one can reasonably expect to find there are Mallards, Wood Duck, American Coot, Green Winged Teal, American Wigeon, Black Headed Gull (also known as Common Black Headed Gull), Northern Pintail, and Metro's largest concentration of Ring Billed Gulls. There is always the potential for this location to house other surprising birds as well, so check the pond carefully. For detailed help on how to find certain species here, see "Birding Sullivans Pond" in the Places section.

Although the shoreline of Tufts Cove is polluted with tar, oil, and debris, it appears to be a natural gathering place for a great number of Black Ducks, along with a small number of Mallards, Green Winged Teals, and American Wigeons. This is also a good location for Great Cormorants and Black Headed Gulls. Tufts Cove is carefully checked by local birders as this area attracts at least one unusual species each winter. Mew Gull, Eurasian Wigeon and Canvasback are a few of the rarities that have been sighted in the cove. Many of the birds present can be seen from the parking lot on Nootka Avenue that borders the cove. To see all of the birds hidden in the various nooks and crannies, one can walk to the right, along the shoreline, past the tower, to the wharf. From the wharf, it is a three to five minute walk along the road back to the parking lot. The short piece of shoreline to the left of the parking lot is also worth a check.

Sewer Stroll: The Bedford Basin
Most of the birds found in the Bedford Basin congregate at one of three locations. The largest group can be seen from Shore Drive, where the

Sackville River empties into the basin. There, the mixture of salt and fresh water, along with handouts from locals, help to sustain a large group of waterfowl.

This is the most likely location in the Metro area that a person will see a Barrow's Goldeneye. Anywhere from two to six of these rare ducks are present each January. Up close, a male Barrow's can be picked out from the dozens of Common Goldeneyes by the white crescent on his face. At a distance though, the best field mark is the black bar of plumage that extends down between the white of his chest and sides.

Unless the female Barrow's is sporting her all-yellow bill, she can be more difficult to pick out because a birder must rely on subtleties such as bill length and forehead shape. There are two tips to aid in the identification of the female Barrow's: when the goldeneyes are swimming in a line, the female closest to a male Barrow's is usually his mate; and wait until late February, when the female Barrow's has normally obtained her all-yellow bill.

Other species that are often present here in small numbers are Greater Scaups, occasionally Lesser Scaups, Hooded Mergansers, and Common Mergansers. The one or more beautiful Hooded Mergansers present are best seen with the flocks of goldeneyes. The Common Mergansers are usually in their own separate flock or are found as solitary birds. If the Commons are not present at this location, drive east along Shore Drive (towards Dartmouth), until you come to a small bridge and a little cove. Here, Common Mergansers often gather to feed on sticklebacks.

The remainder of the waterfowl found at the mouth of the Sackville River frequently fly over to the sewage outlet at DeWolfe Park. Locally, this park is also called the Waterfront Park; some birders know it as the Mill Cove sewage treatment plant or outlet. It is located at the end of Convoy Run. There, the birds gather around a swirling circle of water that should be viewed first from inside your car. As soon as you get out of your vehicle, the shy Common and Barrow's Goldeneyes generally fly away rather quickly. Besides the ducks, a lot of Iceland Gulls gather here as well as the occasional Glaucous Gull.

The Bedford Basin waterfowl also gather at the seaward edge of the ice sheet to either rest on the ice or to feed along its girth. Where the ice sheet meets the open water, an upswelling effect occurs, creating a more productive feeding zone. Although the size of the ice sheet varies throughout the winter, it frequently spans the harbour, close to Traveller's Hotel on the Bedford Highway. The birds found along the edge of the ice may be viewed from the Traveller's Hotel or the adjacent, currently vacant lot.

Sewer Stroll: The Halifax Shoreline

Along the Halifax shoreline, the first stop of interest is at the China Town restaurant, located near the intersection of Kearney Lake Road and the Bedford Highway. The restaurant parking lot is a good vantage point for that section of the harbour. Winter plumaged Common Loons are regulars there, but the real draw are the Thick Billed Murres. They do not come into the harbour each winter, but when they do, this location appears to be a favourite of theirs.

Fairview Cove, adjacent to the Fairview Cove container terminal, is a somewhat sheltered outlet. It seems to be popular, especially with smaller gulls, such as Black Headed and Iceland Gulls, and the odd time, a Lesser Black Backed Gull will appear. However, the best place to see a Lesser Black Backed Gull is at Richmond Terminals. For over fifteen years, an adult Lesser has spent the winter at this location. In fact, this bird has become so reliable in his habits that he has become the most observed Lesser Black Backed Gull in the province. (Since these birds live for about thirty years, and this guy is so popular, I think someone should give him a name. I vote for "Larry the Lesser.") His favourite perch used to be the top of one of three flag poles that stood together overlooking a small cove, where he fed at low tide. Amazingly, he always chose the same flag post. During high tide, if he was not at "his post," he could be seen roosting on the rooftop of the Volvo plant with the other gulls.

Those flag poles are gone now, and the rooftop of the Volvo plant has been abandoned by the gulls. However, the Lesser Black Backed Gull can still be found feeding in the same small rocky cove located along the access road to Richmond Terminals. At high tide he joins the other gulls that have taken up residence on the rooftop of the Lasmo Building that stands at the end of the access road. These rooftop birds can be easily observed from the shoulder of Barrington Street or the parking lot of the Barrington Commercial Centre, located at 3695 Barrington Street. Some of these same birds can also be viewed from the road leading into Seaview Park.

The second to last stop on the city shoreline is Point Pleasant Park, where two sights of interest along the Sewer Stroll are found. On Black Rock Beach uncommon species of ducks are often seen feeding with the flocks of Black Ducks. On the opposite shoreline of the park is a sewage outlet. There, the observer can see lots of gulls, the Common Loon, Red Breasted Mergansers, and usually one or two additional species of waterfowl.

Horseshoe Island Park is located on the Northwest Arm, off Quinpool Road, near the Armdale Rotary. Again this is a location where large numbers of Black Ducks gather, and often unusual species of waterfowl may be present with them. Wood Ducks, Northern Pintails, and

"Thayer's" Gulls are such examples. (Although the verdict is still out on the "Thayer's" Gull, it is most likely a subspecies of the Herring Gull.)

From this point, the Sewer Stroll generally moves outside the city limits in order to see additional species. If you wish to continue, see the following section for the best locations. With a little bit of exploring, I am sure you will discover other good birding spots along this piece of shoreline. Although the key species are mentioned, keep in mind that many other species may also be seen. These locations are visited frequently by birders as they consistently offer a variety of interesting birds.

Sewer Stroll: From Fergusons Cove to Sambro

The Places section of this book offers directions to destinations mentioned here that you may be unfamiliar with. Birders usually drive slowly along the Fergusons Cove Road and watch for birds on the water. This cove is the best location on this trip to find Horned and Red Necked Grebes. Nearby is the Herring Cove Look-off. Although no birds of particular interest are seen from the look-off, it is usually visited briefly because it offers such a good view of the water.

In January, Tribune Head is an excellent place to see White Winged Scoters and Surf Scoters. Harlequin Ducks are often seen here as well but seem to frequent this location more in February. The "Harlequin Duck" section of February offers additional information.

The Tribune Head sewage outlet can be reached by parking along the shoulder of Village Road and walking up Stonewall Road. Although you can drive on the latter, it is a very narrow lane, making it difficult to park along without blocking the road for local residents. Besides, the walk in is less than two minutes, and this lane regularly has interesting songbirds along the way. Whether you choose to walk or drive, stop where the lane makes a sharp turn to the right. At this bend is a very short trail that gives a good view of the Tribune Head sewage outlet.

The next major stop is the Chebucto Head lighthouse, which stands on the highest point of land along this shoreline, making it a great place to view birds, whales, and other wildlife. This headland also marks the seaward end of Halifax Harbour and the beginning of the open Atlantic Ocean. For this reason, seabirds are often sighted from this headland after stormy weather. In January, bad weather frequently carries two species of seabirds—the Atlantic Puffin and the Black Legged Kittiwake—into inshore waters. At Chebucto Head, it is fairly easy to find Black Legged Kittiwakes; spotting an Atlantic Puffin is quite a bit trickier.

Most people who visit Chebucto in January do not see the puffins because they are either unaware of their presence or do not know how to look for them. Do not expect to see the puffins standing on the rocks as they do on the postcards; they do this only at their breeding colonies. Instead, look for them swimming along and diving from the surface of the water. You have to watch carefully, though, as puffins come to the surface for only a few seconds before they dive again. Each time one resurfaces, it is at a different place from where it dove. Do not be discouraged if you don't see any right away. With a little practice, you will learn how to quickly spot the bird between dives.

Here are seven pointers to remember that will aid in seeing puffins at this location:

1 The best time to go is after rough seas; the puffins are rarely seen there during good weather.

2 When you arrive, scan the water a few times with your binoculars to help you find any species that may be present.

3   Many of the puffins may be too far out for you to identify, but don't worry, smaller numbers are often sighted swimming at the base of the cliff or close to the shoreline, to the left of the lighthouse.

4   Upon finding a bird that you think may be a puffin diving, take your binoculars down and watch the general area until the bird resurfaces. Using your eyes instead of your binoculars allows you to see a wider area of water at one time. With binoculars, there is a good chance that the bird will resurface and dive outside the range of vision. If you cannot see the surface of the water clearly without them, by all means use your binoculars.

5   When the bird dives, start to count the length of time the bird is underwater. This will tell you two things. First, it will give you a general idea of how far the bird may have travelled underwater. Generally, the longer the time, the larger the area of water you must watch. Second, the length of time the bird is underwater has a direct bearing on how long the bird will come up for air—after a long dive you can expect to get a better look at it. The average dive lasts for about one minute but may be shorter or longer, lasting up to three minutes.

6   If the bird is a puffin, expect it to resurface to the right of where you last saw it, as it will be working its way towards the open ocean.

7   Remember that the Atlantic Puffin will be in its winter plumage, so its normally white face will be dusky. In addition, its bill will be slightly smaller and will be just yellow and black, no red. Even in winter plumage, these are nice looking birds. Although the Atlantic Puffin is difficult to see at Chebucto Head, this is the best place in Halifax County to see these birds from land. In winter, enter the Chebucto Head parking lot carefully as it is often icy.

The best way to see the birds in Ketch Harbour, en route to Sambro Harbour, is to drive the East Road and stop at the three or four places along the way where you have a view of the water. A variety of birds may be seen in this harbour but be especially on the lookout for Common and Thick Billed Murres, Razorbills, and Red Necked Grebes. From the main road (Route 349), a large wharf can be seen. It is often worth your time to park at the wharf and walk to the very end. Thick Billed Murres often feed right at the edge of the wharf, providing birders with an exceptional close view.

The same weather conditions that bring puffins to Chebucto Head also produce the occasional Atlantic Puffin on the waters that border Atlantic View Drive. The last stop on the Sewer Stroll is Sambro Harbour. The small body of water that lies beside the parking lot of Sambro Fisheries Limited is always worth a quick check as this sheltered spot often hosts a few species, especially on colder days. West Bull Point Road affords the birder an excellent view of Sambro Harbour. This is the best spot in the Metro area to see a Glaucous Gull—there is always at least one or more of these large white birds present. Along the connecting East Bull Point Road, the tiny Bufflehead is seen on a regular basis.

Agile Masters of the Sky

This is one of the best months to see hawks and other birds of prey, although winter is a difficult time for hawks. Some studies have suggested that as many as 70 per cent of all hawks die during their first year of life, a surprising statistic since most of the birds of prey are thought of as sturdy, swift, and keen-eyed agile masters of the sky. However, the truth is that at birth, hawks inherit the ability to perform split-second manoeuvres at neck-breaking speeds, but they must learn to develop and fine–tune their skills to a high degree of accuracy if they are to survive. When it comes to birds of prey, the females are usually the stronger and larger sex, which generally makes them better hunters. However, these added advantages aren't always a guarantee of success when hunting.

One day I watched a fantastic demonstration of how much skills can differ between individuals of the same species. From my window, I watched as a female Bald Eagle swooped down on a Herring Gull that was paddling weakly in the Bedford Basin. Missing her mark, she made a wide curve and circled back for a second pass. Building her speed, she came in low above the water and screamed by within centimetres of her prey. Not ready to give up on this "sure" meal, the eagle banked, gained altitude, then dropped rapidly to less than a third of a metre above the water's surface, as she expertly executed a high-speed plunge. However, at the last moment, the gull jerked to the right and the eagle came up with two "fists" full of icy water. While preparing for her fourth attempt, her soon-to-be mate, who had been watching the episode from a nearby island, flew in, casually picked up the virtually immobile gull, and carried it away. While both of these eagles were born with the ability needed to survive, only the second bird had mastered this particular hunting technique to a point that it appeared easy.

It is during this learning period that the greatest numbers of hawks die of starvation. In particularly harsh winters, many inexperienced Sharp Shinneds are drawn to places that appear to offer easy pickings, such as bird feeders. However, hunting at feeders brings a new array of problems. The opportunities to hunt increase but the success rate drops, and danger levels increase immensely. The speed of the Sharp Shinned Hawk and its ability to concentrate on its prey are usually assets, but at a feeder, these skills can lead to death because the bird's chances of colliding with glass windows are increased.

Although you can never really hawk–proof your yard, you can help discourage a hawk from developing dangerous habits by placing feeders as close as possible to tree or bush cover.

Hawks in the City Limits

Within city limits, the two most common species of hawks are the Merlin and the Sharp Shinned Hawk. Both species may be seen anywhere in the city, but generally speaking, Merlins prefer not to stray too far from open areas with lots of evergreens. For this reason, the south end of Halifax is often a popular location for these birds. The Sharp Shinned on the other hand, can be found just about anywhere. Both of these species specialize in feeding on small birds, so often they will show up at feeders. The Merlin can capture and kill birds up to the size of a Rock Dove but generally prefers to feed on smaller birds. The Sharp Shinned can catch birds as big as Blue Jays but can rarely kill them; people have seen Blue Jays escape unharmed after being captured by Sharp Shinneds.

Other species of hawks that are occasionally seen inside the city limits during the winter months are the Northern Harrier, the Northern Goshawk, the Red Tailed Hawk, and the Rough Legged Hawk.

Eagles of Metro

Many are surprised to learn that the bird of prey easiest to see in the greater Metro area in January is the Bald Eagle. Eagles can be seen at a variety of locations around town and may show up anywhere that open water has attracted a number of ducks or gulls. However, the three places where they may be seen daily is the Sackville Landfill Site, the Bedford Basin, and the power plant at the Head of St. Margarets Bay. In the Bedford Basin, a favourite perch is a large white pine with a dead top, located at one end of Spruce Island. Also, watch for the eagles further up the harbour, towards Walker's Wharf, or on any of the tiny islands of rocky outcrops exposed at low tide. Often an eagle can be seen sitting on the sheet of ice that forms most years in the basin. Bald Eagles frequently land there to eat a recently caught meal and are often surrounded by a small ring of crows waiting to snack on the leftovers. A circle of crows on the ice is a sure sign that an eagle has been there recently. There are two adult eagles which frequent the basin, and occasionally an immature eagle wanders in. Most of the time though, this immature prefers to hang out at the Sackville dump with the other scavengers.

Owls

The first cold snap or snow storm of the winter causes changes to occur in the bird world and can bring a variety of birding opportunities. Amongst those is a chance for some to see their first wild owl, often from the comfort of their own home. The most commonly seen owl is the Barred Owl, but occasionally a rarer species is sighted.

One cold January day in the district of Halifax County known as Jollimore, Dorothy Jackson was preparing for a quiet and relaxing morning with a good book. No sooner had she started reading, when the local crows decided to make a racket in the back yard. At first she thought they were just having one of their "conferences," as crows often do. However, soon they were making an unusual amount of noise. Upon investigating, she saw a large number of crows swooping and diving at something mostly hidden on the ground, only its two ears were protruding from behind a bank of snow. She immediately thought the crows were attacking and possibly hurting an old stray cat that lives in the neighbourhood.

As quickly as possible, she raced outside and scrambled up the bank to rescue the creature. She was totally surprised when a large bird flashed from behind the bank and flew off with a whole heard of crows clambering behind it. On the snow laid a few blue feathers and a leg, indicating that this bird may have caught and was trying to eat a Blue Jay, when the crows discovered him. The bird must have been very hungry because he returned shortly with the crows in tow, to gain what little nutrition he could.

It was then that Mrs. Jackson saw the bird well enough to identify it as a Long Eared Owl, the rarest breeding owl in the province. The news of its presence was spread quickly throughout the birding community. Crows, too, were busy spreading the word. At one point, Mrs. Jackson started to count just how many had arrived but gave up after she reached forty.

Another rare owl that is reported almost every year in January is the Great Gray Owl. I have gone to see these many times, but in each case all I saw was a Barred Owl. Of course, this does not mean that I do not want to hear future reports of possible Great Gray Owls, as I fully expect to see one someday. If the truth be known, I enjoy seeing Barred Owls. These are very impressive birds to see for both new and old birders. But in the wild they appear much larger than people expect; even the most experienced birders perceive exciting birds to be larger than they are. This is why Barred Owls are often thought at first to be the larger Great Gray. Another reason that a Barred Owl may resemble a Great Gray Owl is that some Barred Owls are much grayer than others. Two good birding tips to remember when looking at an owl that you think might be a Great Gray are to check the colour of the eyes—they should be bright yellow not brown—and the owl should be without the horns on top of its head, which its yellow-eyed cousin, the Great Horned Owl, has.

Winter Gull Identification

The first question that springs to many people's minds when they think about identifying gulls in the winter is, "Why would I want to?" Why not! They are birds after all, they are easy to find, and they're friendly. As well, during the winter months, up to ten different species of gulls can be seen in Metro. Hopefully you have discovered that seeing a new species of bird is fun. So get out there, expand your horizons and learn something new. Who knows, you may even enjoy it!

While immature gulls can be difficult to iden-tify, with their varying degrees of brown mottled plumage, adults are easier to distinguish and thus should be the focus for those just beginning to look at gulls. Here are some tips which may prove useful when attempting to sort out different species of gulls you are likely to encounter in the Metro area.

Our most common gull is the Herring Gull. One can learn how to identify a Herring Gull within seconds—it has light grey wings with black tips. Once you know what a Herring Gull looks like, you can use this bird as a measure for identi-fying the other local species of gulls. Since we have no shortage of Herring Gulls, you can be relatively sure they will be present at just about any location where other species of gulls congre-gate. Watching a group of gulls will make com-parisons of the Herring Gull to other species easier, as this will allow a direct (side by side) as opposed to an indirect comparison, in which both birds are present but not in the same field of view.

Our second most common gull is the Great Black Backed Gull, which is larger than the

Herring, with a dark gray or all-black back and wings. The back and wings of the Herring Gull have been compared to the colour of a dry road surface, while the darker gray of the Great Black Backed resembles the colour of wet pavement or pothole patches.

Our third most common gull is the Ring Billed Gull. The average adult Ring Billed Gull is about one-third smaller than the Herring; it looks like a tiny Herring Gull with a black ring around its bill. If the bird is resting with its bill tucked into its feathers so that you are not sure about its size, it can be identified by the colour of its legs. Adult Ring Bills have yellow legs and Herring Gulls have pink ones

Iceland Gulls are about the size of a Herring Gull or slightly smaller, while the Glaucous Gull is the size of the Great Black Backed Gulls. When in adult plumage, both have gray wings like the Herring but without the black tips. Both immature Glaucous and Iceland Gulls are easy to identify as they are the only all-white or dusky-white gulls normally present in Metro during winter. The Black Headed and the Bonaparte's Gulls are small gulls with red–orange legs. The Black Headed Gull also has varying amounts of dark red on its bill; the Bonaparte's bill is pure black. Both of these species are only about half the size of a Herring Gull. These petite gulls are more like terns than gulls. In flight, they have a very rapid, dainty wing beat and show an easily visible slash of white in the middle of the wing that runs most of the wing's length. When sitting, they show a large beauty mark on each side of their face.

In Metro, Sullivans Pond and the various sewer outlets in the harbour are excellent places to look for both common gull species and the following rarer ones. During or shortly after stormy weather, exposed headlands such as Chebucto Head are excellent places to view the one exception to these rarities—the most sea–loving gull, the Blacked Legged Kittiwake. Kittiwakes look very similar to Herring Gulls as they have light gray wings with black tips. However, the wing tips of the Kittiwake are pure black, unlike the Herring Gull's tips that show white spots. They can also be separated by the leg colour—pink on the Herring Gull and black on the Kittiwake. Since Black Leggeds are seabirds, they will only be seen from headlands, after rough seas or strong winds.

Occasionally, a Lesser Black Backed Gull is sighted. This European gull can be separated from its larger counterpart, the Great Black Backed Gull, by size and by the colour of its legs and feet, which are yellow not pink.

A less common species of European gull, a Mew Gull, has also been spotted in the Halifax Harbour. On average, one of these gulls is seen each winter. The Mew Gull or the Common Gull—the European name for this gull—looks almost identical to the adult Ring Billed Gull, but it has a pure yellow bill with no black ring. In past winters, Mew Gulls have been seen at places such as Sullivans Pond, Tufts Cove, and Eastern Passage Beach but could show up at any location along the harbour.

Further Afield

....

Arctic Ghosts

Birds are the most easily observed wild animals in North America. As a result, more people have taken up bird-watching than any other form of wildlife observation. Although most people who bird-watch like to see just about any type of bird, a favourite bird family is the owls. Birders are generally thrilled when they see an owl; in fact, many people who wouldn't consider themselves birders find a chance encounter with an owl exciting. Although all owls are interesting and beautiful, one of the most stunning is the Snowy Owl.

Snowy Owls are large and round-headed, ranging in colour from pure white males to mostly white immatures with heavy black speckles. The Snowy's white or mostly white plumage, along with its ability to fly without making a sound, have earned it the name "Arctic Ghost" amongst the Inuit. Snowy Owls breed in the high Arctic, and small numbers drift southward during most winters. However, in some years, large numbers of Snowy Owls can be seen after making a mass exodus from the polar region that is generally triggered by a decrease in the lemming population. Lemmings are small volelike mammals which are a popular food for the Snowy Owl and many other Arctic species. Like the Snowshoe Hare, the lemming population goes through a boom and crash cycle, and when the lemming numbers crash, Snowy Owls head south. Although Snowy Owls usually begin to arrive in Nova Scotia in mid-November, they are commonly called "Snow Owls" because they are usually seen in the province after the snow has arrived. It is best to look for them during January.

Snowy Owls are considered one of the most enchanting kind of owls in the world. Unlike most species of owls, they are often active in the daytime and are most readily seen in habitats with few or no trees. They often perch on the ground but also frequently use fence posts and sometimes power poles; trees are rarely used.

A sighting of a Snowy by Gwen MacDonald, Vicki Richmond, and Bev Sarty at Prospect one winter was made particularly interesting by the presence of a red squirrel. As is typical with Snowy Owls, the bird was perched on the ground in a large area of open habitat. For some reason, this squirrel took great interest in the owl and was busily circling the sitting bird and chattering at him. Snowy Owls often eat small rodents, such as red squirrels, so the cheeky little fur ball was taking quite a chance. Whether the squirrel was curious about the odd bird or had a death wish was unclear. Perhaps he was trying to mob the owl as crows often do, or maybe he was just plain "squirrely." Regardless, one thing was clear, the Snowy Owl was not hungry.

Although Snowy Owls are generally seen further afield, do not rule out the possibility that you may encounter one in the city. Lower Water Street in Halifax is not a typical birding spot in the city, nor is it a location one would expect to see anything out of the ordinary when it comes to birds. However, birds can be unpredictable. Such was the case when an immature Snowy Owl was seen, by nearly fifty different people, sitting on the wharf at Purdy's Wharf. Snowy Owls are not city birds; they are birds of the Arctic Tundra in summer, and in winter they drift southward to feed on rodents found in farmlands and other open areas. Perhaps this individual entered the city during the still of the night, and being a relatively inexperienced, immature bird, he did not realize the possible dangers associated with such a place. The owl managed to get through the day with no mishaps, other than frequent harassment by mobbing crows. In fact, the bird was sighted again the next day at the same location.

The Big One that Didn't Get Away

On December 9, 1992, Ron Jeppesen of Seaforth experienced what he considered to be his most spectacular bird observation of all time. While looking out his window at the ocean, he saw an adult Bald Eagle fly about 400 m (1,300 ft.) out from the shore and dive with full force at something in the water. This was followed by a great deal of splashing, and it was obvious that the Bald

Eagle was having a difficult time getting out of the water. Mr. Jeppesen immediately grabbed his binoculars and camera and raced down to the shore. He was thinking, "How does one rescue an eagle that is stranded on the water?" By the time he got down over the coastal rocks, the Bald Eagle had used its wings to row himself into shore. In that short time, not only had the eagle managed to swim to safety, but he carried with him his prize—a full-grown Canada Goose.

Although Bald Eagles certainly have the strength to kill prey as large as a Canada Goose, they rarely do. The majority of their meals are either fish or carrion. What was not surprising about Mr. Jeppesen's story is that the eagle was unable to fly with its prey. Studies show that the average male Canada Goose weighs 4.2 kg (9 lbs.), while the average Bald Eagle weighs exactly the same or slightly less.

Dovekies

Dovekies are tiny black-and-white birds that are at home in the high Arctic and the open seas. Their name is Swedish and translates to "like a dove," in reference to its tiny size. They are also called sea doves, although Dovekies are only about two-thirds the size of a normal Rock Dove. In fact, Dovekies are the smallest birds you will see on the water in the wintertime. The Dovekies have many other nicknames, including ice bird, knotty, and pine knot. The latter comes from the saying, "they are as tough as pine knots." Each of these names refers to the birds' ability to withstand extremely cold temperatures. Even at night, these pint-size birds do not seek protection from the frigid waters of the Arctic and North Atlantic, they simply sleep, bobbing along the waves.

During the day, they feed almost exclusively on minute marine crustaceans, which they can catch during short underwater excursions. Each of their dives lasts, on average, thirty–three seconds but may go up to sixty–eight seconds. In the Arctic they may also feed on small fish caught in freshwater pools during the warmer months. In turn, they are eaten by a wide variety of predators, such as Arctic Foxes, Gyrfalcons, Glaucous Gulls, White Whales, and Inuit. Although Dovekies lay only one egg per pair in the crevice of a rock cliff, with absolutely no nesting material, they are probably the most numerous bird in the eastern Arctic. Literally millions of Dovekies converge there each year for the breeding season. The Dovekie is an extremely important species, for if their numbers drop, so will those of numerous other species. Unfortunately, Dovekies are very susceptible to oil spills, and it is estimated that hundreds of thousands are killed because of them each year. Storms, too, often claim the lives of Dovekies by blowing them inland where they die from injuries or starve to death.

Reports of stranded Dovekies, like the one discovered in an icy ditch in front of Louise Mosher's home in Cow Bay, are not uncommon. Her children found the bird and brought it to her to help. She examined the tiny bird and then fed it chopped salmon as a preparatory measure for its release. In most cases, a little food or a gentle hand back into the water once the surf has calmed down, is all the help these birds need. If the bird is injured though, you may want to call the Department of Natural Resources or a sympathetic veterinarian.

Locally, healthy Dovekies are common in January along our rocky coastlines and may be seen anywhere, both outside and inside the confines of Halifax Harbour.

Snow Buntings

Snow Buntings, or "Snowbirds" as some people call them, typically choose to frequent the most exposed habitats during the winter months. Their favourite haunts include dykelands, open fields, sand dunes, and barrens. In such places they happily feed on grass and weed seeds. The cold doesn't seem to bother them much, in fact, they are frequently reported taking baths in the snow, a stunt which is deliberately avoided by most of our winter birds and has been likened to the Point Pleasant Park Polar Bear Swim. But Snow Buntings are perhaps the hardiest songbird on the continent. Some of these individuals begin their nesting in the high Arctic as early as March. Not surprisingly, they are careful to line their nest with lots of feathers. Of course, not wanting to lose any of their own protection, they collect the feathers of other birds.

After breeding, like most birds, Snow Buntings fly south for a nice warm vacation. But unlike much of our bird world, their idea of warm is Nova Scotia winters. Here, they spend their days wandering over open areas; by night they are one of the very few species that will burrow under the snow to sleep. In typical winters, a large snow storm will occasionally cause small flocks of Snow Buntings to show up at people's feeders in search of food.

No other songbird has as much white in its plumage as Snow Buntings, but they also have a lot of buffy brown on the top of their heads, backs, and tails. The full extent of their whiteness is best seen in flight, when their wings appear nearly pure white with black tips. At first glance, Snow Buntings often look like large whitish sparrows as they forage on the ground, but unlike sparrows, which move about by hopping, Snow Buntings have a stately walk. In winter, flocks of

Snow Buntings can be sighted at Lawrencetown, where they feed on grasses of the tidal flats, especially when other places are encased in ice. Large flocks of Snow Buntings are also seen regularly at Prospect, Conrads Beach, and the parking lot of Rainbow Haven Beach. Mixed in with the Snow Buntings at these locations are usually a few Horned Larks and Lapland Longspurs.

The Dark Cloud with a Silver Lining

February Delights

February is often considered our most consistent month for cold and snow. Birders can take advantage of this snow cover as an opportunity to track down the "heart attack bird." February is also the best time of year to see our most colourful saltwater duck, the Harlequin, or to search for the rare Eurasian Tufted Duck. Be sure not to miss out on the spectacular aerial display of courting Ravens. This month also provides the opportunity to learn more about Common Loons, Newfoundland Robins, and the "Butcher Bird."

February may be described as the dark cloud with a silver lining, alluding to the fact that it appears to be the worst month for birds. By mid-February, the rigours of winter have taken a heavy toll on many species of birds and have encouraged others to search out more hospitable conditions. As a result, bird numbers in the

Metro area during February are at their lowest point of the year. Interestingly though, just as winter appears to be at its worst, the silver lining emerges—nature chooses to show us the first signs of spring.

Take Cheer—Spring Is Here!

Before I became seriously involved in birding, I often heard that returning flocks of robins marked the beginning of spring. As my knowledge of birds grew, I learned that here in Nova Scotia, it was commonplace to see robins in the winter. I also began to notice that long before our breeding robins returned, many other signs of spring could be seen in the bird world. In fact, one of the best benefits of being a birder is having the awareness of spring as early as February.

February? Yes, cold, dark, miserable February carries some of the earliest signals of spring. As you sit reading this chapter in sub-zero temperatures, you may be thinking, "Good grief, it has finally happened, his brain has frozen from one too many winter birding trips!" That point is debatable, but I still say that "spring has sprung," in fact it sprang nearly a month ago. You may ask, if spring is here, why must one push themselves through a metre of snow and chip away ice to fill up the bird feeders at –10°C temperatures? Where are the flowers, the leaves, the singing birds? Well, I concede that flowers and leaves are a little scarce right now, but that is only because they are in hiding. As for the birds, you just have to know when and where to listen for them.

For the truly dedicated, tonight, after midnight, jump in your car, drive to the middle of nowhere, find a bunch of large trees, then turn off your car and listen. If you are persistent and you visit enough locations, after a few hours of listening to your bones cracking in the cold, you may just be lucky enough (providing you do not die of hypothermia), to hear the first sounds of spring. Perhaps you will hear the deep masculine voice of the male Great Horned Owl echoing through the forest as he pours out his heart in song. In fact, this "singing" has been going on since the beginning of January, and by now many Great Horneds have discovered the best way to stay warm on a cold winter's night. A few "eager beavers" have even finished the mating process and are busy sitting on eggs. What better definition of spring than a time of love, a time of new life, a time of birds singing and mating. Now, don't get me wrong, I am not saying that winter is over, I am just saying that as a birder, you come to appreciate that the winter and spring seasons have a much greater overlap than non–birders realize.

For instance, now that February is here, you don't have to practically freeze to death in the wilderness to hear bird songs. You can do it in the comfort of your own home by opening all your windows and listening. Chances are good that with a little invested time you will hear the aptly named Song Sparrow. In a typical year, as early as the first week of February you can briefly hear, if you listen carefully, the short, quiet song of the Song Sparrow. This abbreviated version of its song is most often heard about an hour after sunrise or during the warmest part of the day. As the days lengthen, the Song Sparrow sings more frequently and its song grows longer and louder. By month's end, they can usually be heard daily in full song.

Song Sparrows are our most common sparrow in the province and can be found in just about any outdoor environment. While out birding or just out for a stroll around your neighbourhood, watch and listen for the Song Sparrow. You will be amazed how this tiny bird will pick up your spirits and inspire thoughts of spring in the middle of what most people consider winter.

City Birding

....

The Heart Attack Bird

Birding is a hobby that can be easily combined with a variety of other outdoor activities, but it can, at times, take over. One of my favourite examples occurred when a group of us had set out to study mammal tracks. While walking a woodland trail, we came across what at first appeared to be a pile of feathers, but upon closer inspection proved to be fur from a red squirrel. A quick survey of the area for evidence of the perpetrator revealed no other tracks, except those of a white-tailed deer. However, the idea of a mutant meat-eating deer roaming the back woods of Nova Scotia seemed unlikely, so we searched for other clues. We soon located more fur close by, and in between the two locations, the droppings of a large bird, indicating the true predator was likely a hawk or an owl.

Pressing on, we tried to focus on the task at hand, identifying mammal tracks. While most mammals can be easily identified by clear tracks, the identity of birds can rarely be determined from their tracks. As luck would have it, we stumbled upon the tracks of one of the few families of birds that can be identified by their footprints, the Grouse family. The habitat we were in suggested the tracks belonged to a Ruffed Grouse, and this was soon verified by the discovery of the distinctive droppings of the Ruffed Grouse, which are curved and yellow in colour, resembling curved versions of the yellow catkins produced by white birch trees in the fall, or, with a little imagination, miniature bananas.

Although Ruffed Grouse may be seen any time of year, February is often the easiest month to see these birds because it is often our most reliable month for persistent snow cover, which provides the best contrast for seeing the Ruffed Grouse's tracks and droppings. For best results, visit the woods after a fresh blanket of snow has fallen. Good places to see Ruffed Grouse trails are wet deciduous woodlands like the ones found at Martin Lake in Dartmouth, Jack Lake Trail in Bedford, and to a lesser extent, Hemlock Ravine in Halifax. For an added treat, wait until there is a thick layer of soft snow in the woods. Studies have shown that about one-half of the Ruffed Grouse burrow underneath the snow to sleep.

One winter's day, after a snow storm the previous day, I was following the trail of a Ruffed Grouse and nearly died of a heart attack when the bird suddenly exploded up from underneath the snow's surface! The grouse had waited until I had almost stepped on the spot where he was hidden. His sudden exit shocked me as my face was sprayed with snow. You, too, can go in the woods and have this "fun" experience! You don't have to wait until winter to be scared by a Ruffed Grouse. Even during the summer months, Ruffed Grouse will often wait until the last minute before bolting off the ground with whirring wings. This is done purposely to startle would-be predators but often catches the woodland walker by surprise.

The Spruce Grouse uses a different defence. Instead of bolting at the last minute, they just stay put. To say that they freeze on the spot would be inaccurate, as most of the time when they are disturbed, instead of stiffening, they relax and wait until the problem goes away. I have tried this approach with my own problems, but I have not had much success with it, yet! In truth, this technique does not always work for the Spruce Grouse either. Around urban areas, Spruce Grouse are often captured by household pets, so they quickly disappear from areas that have been developed. As new subdivisions are built, Spruce Grouse retreat further into the wilderness. For this reason, though several sites always exist, it is

34

FEBRUARY

difficult to pinpoint exact locations near Metro
where Spruce Grouse can be seen, as those
locations change almost annually.

The best way to find Spruce Grouse is to learn
what their habitat looks like. Spruce Grouse
frequent wet, coniferous woodlands, with lots of
sphagnum (moss) growing on the ground. During
the summer months, they eat a variety of foods
and thus wander through a greater number of
habitats. In the winter, they feed exclusively on
fir, spruce, and jack pine needles and are found
where large or medium-size specimens of these
trees grow in numbers.

Their tracks look almost identical to the
Ruffed Grouse footprints, but their droppings are
different—straight, about 2 cm (0.8 in.) long, and
green in colour. They are sweet smelling as well
because they are composed of partially digested
evergreen needles, which do not break down
easily. In order to digest them at all, the gastroin-
testinal tract of the Spruce Grouse increases its
size in the winter.

Some people call the Spruce Grouse "fool
hen," in reference to the fact that they can be easily captured or killed. Others consider the Spruce
Grouse a dumb bird because of its tameness. I
prefer to think of them as friendly, and one
should not take advantage of their trusting
nature. I have spent hours with families of Spruce
Grouse, who after a short while accepted me as
an odd looking member of the family.

American Robins

In the past, the American Robin was primarily a
forest bird, but it has adapted so well to the
changes made by humans to the North American
landscape that it now breeds in all parts of the
continent, except the more northern tips of
Alaska and Quebec. In the fall, robins head south,
but most winter much further north than is

BIRDING IN METRO HALIFAX

generally recognized. Each year during the first and second week of February, a great number of people, especially in the Metro area, begin to get excited or concerned when suddenly small, medium, and large flocks of robins start to show up in or near the city. However, these are not our "summer robins" returning from the south to herald the coming of spring. Rather, these birds are our regular "winter robins." Each year, some of the robins that nest north of Nova Scotia elect to overwinter in the province.

Robins are the largest member of the Thrush family in North America and are surprisingly hardy. In winter, they thrive on berry-producing trees and bushes. The amount of berries available in any given year partly influences the number of robins that stay in winter, so their numbers vary from year to year. Generally, anywhere from a few hundred to several thousand robins spend each winter in Nova Scotia. Winter robins are usually seen more often in the country, as they prefer rural areas and coastal barrens, where food is more readily available. However, heavy snows in the first half of February force many robins closer to urban centres, making them more noticeable.

Occasionally, many new robins pour into the province from the north at the same time. These newcomers are Newfoundland Robins, which can be distinguished from our regular winter robins by their slightly larger size, darker red breasts, and most importantly by their dark gray heads and backs.

Robins will not come to seed feeders but can be enticed to your back yard by an offering of fruit or berries. Generally, raisins and apples are their favourite fruits, especially if the apples are overripe, rotten, or chopped into berry-size pieces. Robins will also eat bread and raw hamburger, but neither of these items are recommended for them. The best and easiest way to attract robins and other bird species to your yard on a regular basis is to plant brightly coloured fruit that lasts into the winter, such as high bush cranberry, elderberry, multiflora rose, apple, and mountain ash, which are some of their favourites. Robins and many other species, such as Bohemian Waxwings, Cedar Waxwings, Pine Grosbeaks, Yellow Breasted Chats, and Northern Mockingbirds, are attracted to Metro berry bushes as well.

Eurasian Tufted Ducks

The Eurasian Tufted Duck is very similar in appearance and actions to our North American Ring Necked Duck. Males of both species are, on average, 43 cm (17 in.) long, have purplish heads, dark chests, and black and grayish-white sides. The Tufted Duck lacks the Ring Necked's white vertical crescent on its side, and sports a tuft of feathers off the back of its head. Like the Ring Necked, it prefers fresh water but will use salt-water habitats if necessary. In Europe, the Tufted Duck is the most numerous species in its genus (a group of birds marked by common characteristics). Outside the breeding season, Tufted Ducks often gather in large flocks, which sometimes consist of literally thousands of individuals.

The first duck of this species was recorded in North America as early as 1911, on an island in Alaskan waters. For the past thirty or more years, Tufted Ducks have been seen regularly along the Alaskan coast and points southward. These regular strays on the west coast are believed to be wanderers from Siberia. Occasionally, Tufted Ducks also appear on the east coast of North America, and it is thought that these are Icelandic individuals.

In 1971, an invasion of Tufted Ducks was recorded on the eastern seaboard from the North West Territories to New York. In total, fourteen were counted. This led noted ornithologist P. A. Buckley to predict that Tufted Ducks would someday breed on our continent. Another fact that supports Buckley's theory is the observation by British birders of the birds' willingness to breed with other species of ducks. In captivity they will breed with numerous types of ducks and have been observed interbreeding with at least four species in the wild. In some cases, fertile offspring were produced. This sort of breeding behaviour increases their chances of becoming established in North America. The first time a Tufted Duck was identified in Nova Scotia was in January 1991, in Dartmouth by Fulton Lavender, Jim Taylor, and Ken McKenna. Since then, one or two Tufted Ducks have been seen each winter.

Of the Tufted Ducks that have been sighted, the majority were females and immature males, both of which look surprisingly similar to female Scaups. Because of this similarity, February is perhaps the best winter month to identify a Tufted Duck as both females and immatures are clearly showing a tuft, while earlier in the winter, their tufts can be hard to see. Places in the Metro area where Tufted Ducks have been seen in recent years are at the mouth of the Sackville River, Sullivans Pond, First Lake, Lake Thomas, Lake Fletcher, Bisset Lake, and where the Shubenacadie Canal empties into the Halifax Harbour.

Distinguishing between Ravens and Crows

Ravens and crows are the most intelligent birds in the world; they are also among the most persecuted—crows because a number of their habits interfere with human goals, and ravens mainly because they resemble crows. Crows are highly adaptive, so they continue to thrive despite human persecution. Ravens, on the other hand, have declined dramatically in number. The Common Raven in the United States has disappeared from the majority of the eastern and central states, and in Canada, they are found mostly in rural areas, where they have less contact with humans. Inside cities, large crows are often mistaken for ravens, but be assured that in city environments there are few places where one might see ravens. Such a spot is the Maritime Life Building on Dutch Village Road, where an active raven's nest can be found in some years.

Here are some tips for distinguishing ravens from crows. First, you will never see a flock of ravens in the city as ravens are primarily solitary birds except during the mating season, when the birds pair up. When sitting, ravens show a shaggy mass of feathers jutting out from their throat. An even easier way to identify them is by their wedge-shaped tails and long wings in flight. Be sure not to confuse ravens' tails with the very rounded tails of many crows. Perhaps the easiest way to separate the two is by listening to their calls. Although crows can make a variety of sounds, most are just variations of their typical "caw–caw." Ravens have two common calls, a deep "gronk–gronk" and a sharp "wok." During courtship rituals, ravens also produce a call that sounds remarkably like a bouncing ping–pong ball. None of these sounds resemble those made by crows.

Further Afield

....

Ravens

While Song Sparrows are still warming up their vocal cords, Ravens have begun their courting and nest building procedure, a rather drawn-out event that precedes laying their eggs. The pinnacle of their courtship is the courtship flight, a truly amazing aerial event that can be observed during February and March. It begins with shadow flying, when two birds fly in close formation to one another, matching each other's movements with exact precision. Ravens execute this in–flight synchronization perfectly. Their aerial manoeuvres include such stunts as power diving like a Peregrine Falcon and touch soaring—soaring side by side, with the male's wing tips lightly brushing the female's. However, the real show-stopper begins with one bird flying directly over top of the other. Next, the bottom bird flips upside down and grabs onto the talons of the one above. The interlocking birds then tumble downward through the sky. After two or more summersaults, the birds break the connection and again soar upwards, sometimes to repeat the whole process again. Although Common Ravens may be seen doing their courtship flights over the city, it is best to look for them outside the city limits, especially near farmlands.

Sheep farms are an especially good place to watch for raven breeding activity. Over the years, I have heard several stories of ravens stealing sheeps' wool to line their nests, but by far the most interesting story I heard came from Carl and Kathie Blades. Fourteen sheep are part of a small farm they run in Elderbank. The first year, the Northern Ravens visited their farm just to collect strands of wool left behind by the sheep as they brushed against the barb–wire fences. The soft wool not only made excellent nest lining on which to cradle their eggs, but no doubt provided extra warmth for incubating.

Knowing a good thing when they saw it, the ravens returned the following year to take advantage of this luxury. However, instead of the inconvenience of gathering up the small pieces of wool strung along the fences, they went straight to the source—the sheep. Imagine the surprise of a sheep when a raven landed on its back and

started pulling out its wool! The Blades reported
that the ravens would fill their beaks to capacity,
fly off, and return as quickly as possible for more
nesting material. At one point they looked out to
see five huge ravens on top of one little sheep.
They became such a nuisance to the sheep that
Mr. Blades stayed home from church one Sunday
just to chase away ravens, so the sheep could get
some peace. Fortunately, after about ten days, the
ravens figured they had stolen enough wool to
meet their needs and things went back to normal.
I imagine this is just one of the many fascinating
birding events that occurs while living on a farm.

The Butcher Bird

The Northern Shrike is a small, robin–size bird
of prey, gray in colour with black wings, a black
tail, and a black mask. Fierce by nature, Northern
Shrikes will often attack birds larger than themselves when hunting. However, its usual prey
consists of insects, mice, lemmings, and
sparrow–size songbirds. In winter, Northern
Shrikes will come to feeders to eat suet and
hamburger or to search for songbirds. They are,
however, irregular winter visitors to Nova Scotia,
and in any given winter their numbers may range
from rare to fairly common.

Surprisingly, the Northern Shrike itself is a
songbird, making them the only ones in North
America that are also birds of prey. Shrikes are
unusual in another sense. Unlike most owls and
hawks, which kill only to satisfy immediate food
requirements, shrikes will often kill more prey
than they can eat at one time and store the
surplus impaled on long thorns or along barbed-
wire fences. This habit has earned the Northern
Shrike the nickname "Butcher Bird."

In flight, Northern Shrikes can reach speeds
of up to 72 km/hr (45 mi./hr) and can be recognized at a distance by their undulating flight and

by their habit of flying in below an exposed perch and then suddenly swerving upward to land on top of it. Such perches help to mark their winter territory and provide excellent spots from which to hunt. Northern Shrikes use these perches to quietly scan the surrounding countryside for prey within striking distance.

The persistence of these birds is demonstrated in an instance related to me by Don Keith. One winter, near Main Street in Dartmouth, he sighted a Northern Shrike chasing a House Sparrow. In an effort to ditch the shrike, the sparrow repeatedly weaved his way in and out of a large hedge. Smaller than a hawk, the shrike was able to follow the sparrow into the thickest parts of the hedge. After a number of unsuccessful attempts to out-manoeuvre the shrike, the sparrow was overtaken and captured. Another advantage a shrike has over a hawk is that virtually all birds can instinctively and instantly recognize a hawk and respond accordingly; whereas songbirds must learn through experience that a shrike is a deadly companion.

A second species of shrike, the Loggerhead Shrike, is rarely identified here. This species looks very similar to the Northern Shrike, so it may often be overlooked. A typical example is the Loggerhead Shrike that probably spent an entire winter just outside Halifax city limits, in Brookside. The bird might have gone undetected had it not crashed into a window of Don Shiner's house. Mr. Shiner took the bird inside and was able to carefully examine it. He noted that the bird had an all-black bill, unlike the Northern's bill, which is mostly black but has a small beige patch at the base of the lower mandible. This field mark, in conjunction with the fact that each side of the bird's black mask was joined by a thin black line running over top of the bill, confirmed that this bird was indeed a Loggerhead Shrike. Like many birds that collide with windows, after about twenty minutes of warmth, this shrike was ready to fly away.

The bird was released, and despite the large number of birders we have in the greater Metro area, it was never seen again. Shrikes are most readily found in open and semi-open rural areas, but they do venture into cities and towns if food supplies are scarce. Metro localities where shrikes are seen regularly include places such as the Chebucto Head Road, Hartlen Point, Seaforth, and the Prospect Road.

Harlequin Ducks

Harlequins are our most colourful species of sea duck. These beautiful birds are found on the east and west coasts of North America. In the west, non–birders refer to this bird as the Painted Duck, while easterners have nicknamed pairs of these birds "Lords and Ladies," in honour of their appearance. Although they are considered rare in Nova Scotia, a few are generally seen each winter. In recent years, the Tribune Head sewer outlet has become the most reliable place in Halifax County to see these ducks. A good tip to remember when visiting this location is that the smaller size of the Harlequins can aid in detecting these birds amongst the mixed flocks of Surf and White Winged Scoters that are normally present there during February. In winter, Harlequins stay in saltwater areas where they can ride the incoming waves to the rocks and quickly tear loose periwinkles, limpets, or barnacles before the waves recede. Another good winter location to observe Harlequins in the Metro area is the section of water that can be seen at the end of Indian Point Road in Prospect.

In summer, they frequent the equally turbulent fast-flowing waters of mountain streams. There, they find food by learning to walk underwater on the bottom of the stream. This adaptation allows them to feed on caddis fly larvae, nymphs of mayflies, and other insects inaccessible to most birds.

Ian Goudie of the Canadian Wildlife Service has written a paper on the breeding status of the Harlequin Duck in eastern North America. He estimated that our east coast population is currently made up of less than one thousand birds. The bulk of our eastern breeding population is concentrated in Labrador, but there and elsewhere in the region, Harlequin numbers appear to be declining.

Winter Loons

One of the most popular species of birds in the province, the Common Loon, spends the winter months feeding along our coastal waters. Common Loons eat a variety of saltwater fish, including flounder, rock cod, herring, and sea trout. These fish are pursued, caught, and swallowed underwater, so from a bird behaviourist's vantage point, which is usually the shore, the loon's feeding behaviour is often difficult to observe. What can be seen, is that it dives with a forward lurch and is out of sight for an average of less than three minutes before it resurfaces. Whether the bird was successful in finding food during its descent usually remains a mystery.

This is not *always* the case. Once, while watching eight Common Loons diving for food at the mouth of the Lawrencetown River, one of the birds suddenly surfaced with something in its beak, which it squeezed a few times then swallowed. My curiosity was instantly aroused. Luckily, the bird repeated the performance, and I was able to see that it was a crab in its bill. I soon discovered that at least one or two of the other loons present were also feeding in this manner. I was excited because, although I have watched birds for many years, I had yet to see this feeding

F
E
B
R
U
A
R
Y

behaviour by Common Loons. Later a quick consultation with a few bird books confirmed that crab is part of the normal diet of Common Loons. It was only two weeks later, while leading a birding trip for the Halifax Field Naturalists that I again saw a Common Loon feasting on crab, this time in Sambro Harbour. Since this eye-opening experience, I have seen Common Loons catch crab at many coastal locations.

The First Month of Migration

....

Spring Is in the Air

March is an exciting month for birders as it offers them their first look at the spring birds, while beckoning them to enjoy some of our winged winter wonders before they fly away. With each passing day, it becomes more evident that although winter still has some fight left in it, its icy grip on the Metro area is loosening. Believe it or not, by March 1, spring migration has begun and the migratory "push" north is on; songbirds have already begun their long trek from South America. While most of those tropical migrants will not reach us until May, some are now entering the province. Of course, these are not songbirds but various species of sea ducks. This waterfowl migration will continue to intensify throughout March, marking the beginning of spring migrations. Locally, these migrators are plentiful on our coastal waters.

M
A
R
C
H

On land, Bald Eagles are on the move, as well as two species of owls. Near the end of March, the Metro area receives its first small land bird migrants. Of course, the ever-popular American Robin will be amongst the leaders but are sometimes preceded by other small land bird species. Another interesting species to watch for is the Killdeer, which breeds in Nova Scotia and is usually the first member of the Plover family to return in spring. Although migrating Killdeers have been recorded as early as the beginning of March, the first spring Killdeers are generally sighted around March 23. March migration may also provide you with the chance to see your first Timber Doodle.

In March, many species begin to undergo subtle plumage changes that are, in essence, the outward reflections of heightened testosterone levels. Other species, such as the Ringed Necked Pheasants, will begin actively wooing females, and in some years, White Winged Crossbills will already have young ones.

In February, we heard the first songsters of the spring. The mighty Great Horned Owl boomed out his mating call at night, while the tiny Song Sparrow sang quietly by day. By March, the Song Sparrow's solo performance turns into a chorus of bird songs as other species join in to vocalize their appreciation of spring. Back yards everywhere suddenly become concert halls for singing goldfinches, trilling juncos, and drumming woodpeckers. As expected, these new performers are most vocal on sunny days.

Since we receive our first signs of spring in early February, and spring migration continues until about June 7, one could argue that in reality, we enjoy over four months of spring in Nova Scotia. All of my out-of-province friends are envious that Nova Scotians enjoy such a long spring, so envious in fact, that after I tell them about it they never write back! Oh well, I'm off to buy some sun-tan lotion before it is sold out. Happy spring birding!

City Birding

....

Crossbills

On March 15, 1992, in Bedford, I encountered my first baby birds of the year. Along the Jack Lake Trail, amongst the pines, I came across a family of White Winged Crossbills. The three young birds were already out of the nest but were still being fed by the adults. White Winged Crossbills can build their nests as early as January and February, and when they do, they are our earliest songbird to produce young. In most years, the European Starling, a non–native, is our first songbird to breed. As early as March, some Starlings have already chosen nest sites and begun laying eggs. Their prolific breeding (up to three nests per year), their aggressive behaviour, their general lack of natural enemies, and the fact that they adapt well to man–made surroundings, make the European Starling one of the most abundant birds in North America.

White Winged Crossbills breed across Canada, from coast to coast, with eastern Canada accounting for the largest portion of its range. In North American terms, it is primarily a northern species as its breeding range extends just far enough south to include some of the northern border regions of the United States. White Wingeds belong to the Finch family and like most members of this family, they are prone to erratic wanderings. These wanderings are usually triggered by the abundance of natural food supplies and may cover vast distances. This nomadic lifestyle means that in some years they are common or even abundant in the Metro region, in other years, hardly any are spotted.

When large numbers of birds arrive suddenly in an area, their arrival is termed an invasion. Such invasions take place most often in winter and may affect areas as far south as Arkansas and Virginia. In Nova Scotia, our largest recorded invasion occurred in 1963, when many thousands of White Winged Crossbills were sighted. Other invasion years were 1985, with more than 2,000 individuals counted; 1988, with more than 1,000 birds; and in 1989, when they were reported as abundant in most areas of the province. The winter of 1991 was also a fairly good year for seeing White Winged Crossbills with over 400 sighted in Metro. Though White Winged Crossbills may breed during any month, there are two distinct breeding periods in Nova Scotia. The first nesting period is from January to April, the second and probably the more popular one runs from July to September.

White Winged Crossbills can be found in mixed or coniferous woodlands but show a strong preference for evergreen trees. They are especially fond of spruce cones, which they can open with their bills that have evolved into perfect devices to extract the seeds from tightly closed coniferous cones. The only other birds in North America with crossed bills are the Red Crossbills, and they, too, breed in Nova Scotia. Although both species are reddish coloured birds with crossed bills, the White Wingeds have two white wing bars on their wings, while the Red Crossbills have completely dark wings.

Red and White Winged Crossbills are year-round residents in Canada and can be found in each province. In Nova Scotia, the White Winged Crossbill is more common, but the Red Crossbill is more familiar. The reason for this apparent contradiction is that Red Crossbills more frequently show up in people's back yards and/or at feeders. March is when their appearance in back yards is most common. Although it is a fairly predictable event calendar-wise, only a handful of people get to enjoy Red Crossbills visiting their property in a given year.

As their name implies, all crossbills can be distinguished from other bird species by the crossed tips of their bills. Young crossbills are born with uncrossed bills, which are still not crossed when they leave the nest seventeen days later. However, within one to three weeks afterwards, their bills grow enough to be noticeably crossed at the tips.

While both types of crossbills feed on any coniferous tree, White Winged Crossbills show a preference for spruce cones; Red Crossbills prefer pines. The latter feed mostly on native pines but are also attracted to some ornamental varieties at this time of year. Mugho pine is the species that most often attracts these interesting birds. When feeding in trees, Red Crossbills often move about like tiny parrots using their bills and feet to climb along and over branches. Unlike parrots, they are extremely quiet when feeding and often the only signs of their presence is the quiet cracking of pine cones and a wide circle of discarded seed wings and cone scales on the ground below.

Plumage Changes

Observant birders will notice during March that many of our winter birds start to obtain a brighter plumage. Some species, such as the Evening Grosbeak and European Starling, are even changing the colour of their bills. During most of the year, the Evening Grosbeak's large bill is a pale yellow colour. However, in late March and early April, the grosbeak's bill changes to a beautiful lime green, a sight worth watching for. The change in the starling's bill is somehow less spectacular, despite the fact that it completely changes from black to yellow. Also watch for subtle changes in House Sparrows, Pine Siskins, White Throated Sparrows, Blue Jays, and other back yard species.

One of my favourite plumage changes of the year takes place near the end of the month. During the last week of March, one can see Black Headed Gulls starting to acquire their all-black heads. These tiny gulls are absolutely stunning at this time of year as the red of their bills, legs, and feet also grows brighter. In addition, their white undersides become tinted with pink. I can still recall the first time I saw one of these birds in breeding plumage. I caught sight of the bird's black head at a distance and moved in for a better look. When I moved closer, I discovered that his black head was actually dark brown in colour. This is true for all Black Headed Gulls but not true for all gulls with black heads. At least twenty species of birds undergo noticeable plumage changes during March in the Metro area. See how many you can discover.

Migration At Feeders

People with feeders should keep their eyes open for Fox Sparrows, as they generally start to show up in Nova Scotia in late March. These migratory sparrows become even more prevalent in April. Refer to April's "The Super Sparrow" for more details.

Feeders in March are also good places to see some of our first small land birds to return to Nova Scotia in the spring. These migrants are male Red Winged Blackbirds, Common Grackles, and Mourning Doves. If you are lucky, you might even attract a Saw Whet Owl to your feeder. In some years, Red Winged Blackbirds and Common Grackles arrive even before our spring robins. Migration specialists have noted that the northward movement of the American Robin follows an average daytime temperature of approximately 2.2°C (35°F). The migration of the first Common Grackles and Red Wingeds on the other hand, is less temperature dependent.

"R–i–n–g! R–i–n–g!"
It's the Telephone Bird

March is the time to listen for the unusual melody of Dark Eyed Juncos as they begin their spring singing. To hear their song, take a trip to either Hemlock Ravine Park or Point Pleasant Park on a warm, sunny day. Many people who have strolled through these parks at this time of year have come back wondering, "what was that bird that sounded like a ringing telephone?" Few realized that the mystery culprit was the Dark Eyed Junco. Most field guides describe the Dark Eyed Junco's sound as a high-pitched, musical trill. A trill is a series of identical notes so closely spaced that they appear to the human ear to be connected as one continuous and repetitive sound. The exact pitch of the trill varies amongst individuals, and some of these birds sound remarkably similar to the ring of a push-button telephone, but don't be fooled!

Bald Eagle

While some of us find all birds interesting, even those who have little or no interest in our avian friends are usually impressed by certain species. One such bird is the Bald Eagle. Who would not be impressed by a bird that stands over 1 m (3 ft.) high, has a huge beak, eight massive talons, and a wing span of nearly 2.5 m (8 ft.)? Adding to the bird's magnificent appearance is its appealing plumage, which consists of a dark chocolate body that contrasts boldly with its strikingly white head and tail.

Nova Scotians are extremely lucky to live in one of the top eagle hot spots in North America, providing exceptionally good birding opportunities. Bald Eagles breed throughout the province with the greatest number of nests occurring on Cape Breton Island. However, outside the breeding season, Bald Eagles appear in concentrated numbers along the Shubenacadie River near Stewiacke and around the farmlands of Kings County. January and February are the best two months to enjoy this natural phenomena.

Eagle migration starts in early February but is more evident in March, as eagles stage a mass exodus from their winter feeding grounds. By mid-March, most adult Bald Eagles are paired up and in the vicinity of their proposed nesting sites. Bald Eagles generally return to the same nest site each year, providing they were not unduly disturbed in the previous breeding season. In preparation for egg laying, which begins mid-April, new material is added to the nest throughout the month of March. During this month, adult Bald Eagles are frequently seen flying over the Bedford Basin with nesting material in their talons. Most often the items are grass, seaweed, or small sticks, but once I saw an eagle with a branch that was over 2 m (6 ft.) long. Through my binoculars I could see that this bird was heading to its nest, located in a large white pine between Hemlock Ravine and the Bicentennial Highway. Although Bald Eagles breed throughout the province, this is the only pair that currently breeds within Halifax city limits. I know of two other eagle nests in the Metro area. One is located on Grand Lake and the other at the Head of St. Margarets Bay.

The Department of Natural Resources keeps records on all the eagle nests in the province, and these are also the only local nests that they are aware of. If you know of other eagle nests, they would like to hear from you. However, one word of caution. Osprey nests are just as large as eagle nests and often the two get confused. A nest which has been used for several years by either species can weigh more than 2 tonnes. Ospreys are also sometimes misidentified as eagles, so be sure to take a good look!

Wood Ducks

Wood Ducks are by far the most colourful breeding duck in the province. Although they are most numerous in Nova Scotia during the summer months, a few are present during other times of the year. Most of the summer breeders generally arrive between mid-March and the second week of April. It has been noted that mated pairs usually show up to nest in the same tree cavity or nest box each year, or at least that was thought to be the case. Through the banding of Wood Ducks, it was discovered that the same female does show up each year to the same cavity or one in close proximity, but the male is usually a different bird. From this information it was ascertained that the female must lead the males to the nest tree. The unusual habit of nesting and perching in trees is how the Wood Duck received its name.

Males first acquire their breeding plumage in January and shortly thereafter start to go through quite an elaborate series of displays to win a female. However, it is the female that makes the choice. This mate-choosing process can lead to interesting birding opportunities. In Lower Sackville, Catherine Tanner and Dennis Theman were putting out corn to attract ducks to their property. One year, during the last week of March, a very shy female Wood Duck arrived to feed with the Black Ducks. On April 11, she was joined by two male Wood Ducks, each of which was vying for her attention. By the next day, she was parading around with five full-plumaged adult male Wood Ducks trailing behind her. After that, all six birds disappeared for a few days; she returned on April 16 with her new mate. One would presume that he was one of the original five contenders. Regardless, the pair continued to visit the feeder together until about the end of April. This is consistent with Wood Duck behaviour as once a female has selected her appropriate mate, she sticks close to him. On the water, the female is usually seen swimming alongside the drake, occasionally caressing his feathers with her bill. During this courtship time, the hen will chase away any other females that come near.

After the pair bonding, the nest site is chosen but no nesting materials are carried into the tree cavity. The birds rely on natural chips of wood on the cavity bottom for the foundation of the nest. The inner cup of the nest is a lining of feathers, which the female pulls from her own breast. Next she will lay anywhere from eight to fifteen cream-coloured eggs, which are slightly smaller than a chicken's egg. Interestingly, some Wood Ducks' nests have been found to contain between twenty–five and fifty eggs. The extra eggs come from other females that sneak into the cavity to lay their own eggs. This process is called egg dumping, or intraspecific brood parasitism. Regardless of how many eggs are in the nest, incubation is not done until the female has com-pleted her egg laying. This way, all eggs will hatch at the same time, about thirty days later.

The young ducks spend their first twenty–four hours in the nest, after which they climb up to the entrance and jump out. Studies show that young Wood Ducks are capable of climbing as high as 2.4 m (8 ft.) to a cavity entrance. To aid them in this endeavour, the young birds are born with extremely sharp toe nails and a sharp nail at the tip of the bill, which is later shed. These are features that other species of ducks never develop. The young ducklings learn to feed themselves almost instantly by imitating the female and by tasting just about anything that moves. Although they eat a variety of aquatic insects at first, even-tually their diet will become about 90 per cent vegetable matter.

Breeding Wood Ducks are rare in our part of Halifax County, but they do breed on Drain Lake, near Sackville. The recent widening of

Highway 101 may change that though. On the positive side, in recent years there have been many people in the Metro area erecting Wood Duck boxes, an effort that may lead to increased numbers of these attractive ducks. Currently, Wood Duck boxes have been erected at places such as the Frog Pond, West Lawrencetown Marsh, and Sullivans Pond. An excellent place to view a male Wood Duck in Metro in March is Sullivans Pond.

Further Afield

....

Waterfowl Migration

One of the most inspirational birding events of the year is the migration of Canada Geese, which starts in early March. The sudden arrival of thousands of new Canada Geese along our Atlantic Coast is a sure sign that the spring waterfowl migration has begun. Anywhere in Metro, one can look up and see flocks of these easily recognizable birds passing above the city. If you want to be sure to see these birds, keep in mind that many of the best places for viewing Canada Geese lie along the Eastern Shore. In March, it is possible to see as many as ten thousand Canada Geese at one time at the West Chezzetcook Marsh. These geese may be seen from Dyke Road or Shore Drive. If the tide is on the rise, Shore Drive can be a spectacular location, as some of the geese can be very close to the road.

Trumpeting flocks of Canada Geese can also be observed from the Seaforth Causeway, Rainbow Haven Beach, Conrads Beach, and Martinique. These locations are best near dusk or dawn as wave after wave of Canada Geese sweep in off the ocean waters. Just as one flock drifts out of sight, another often swings onto the horizon. At times it is possible to see three or more flocks staggered across a sun-painted sky, creating a mystical setting. One March morning I was so overcome by the beauty of these birds that I laid in the snow to watch these massive birds stream overhead on an ancient pathway to their northern breeding grounds. It is hard to describe how or why the northward migration of Canada Geese affects the human soul, but it truly stirs the spirit; you do not want to miss it.

By mid-month, migrating Canada Geese are joined by other spring waterfowl. At coastal locations, look for migrating Red Throated Loons, Great Cormorants, Horned and Red Necked Grebes, Common Eiders, Common Goldeneyes, and Buffleheads. The Red Necked Grebes and the Red Throated Loons are especially worth looking for as their drab winter plumage has been replaced by their spring colours. Other ducks that migrate in late March and early April are Greater Scaups, White Winged Scoters, Oldsquaws, Northern Pintails, Green Winged Teals, Hooded and Common Mergansers.

Great Cormorant

Great Cormorants, like many other waterfowl, migrate along our coasts in March. At this time, they are often mistaken at a distance for Canadian Geese, as both species fly in "V" formations. They can be distinguished in four ways: Great Cormorants are noticeably smaller than Canada Geese; they are mostly black in colour; they do not hold the "V" formation as well because individuals are constantly shifting their position in the flock; and the most important difference is that Great Cormorants fly silently, unlike Canadian Geese, which are usually heard long before they are seen.

By March, most Great Cormorants have obtained their breeding plumage. Although they remain mostly black in colour, they develop a large white oval patch on their sides. This is called a flank patch and is quite conspicuous when the bird flies. Another white patch borders their pale yellow chin pouch. Great Cormorants can be found in the Metro area throughout the winter but start to head north in mid-March.

In early April, the smaller Double Crested Cormorant arrives to take the place of the Great Cormorants. These are the cormorants with which most people are familiar. Cormorants make up one of the most ancient bird families. If fact, our cormorants today are almost identical to their distant ancestors. Evidence of how little these birds have changed over the past ten thousand years is found in their plumage. Cormorants are the only water birds in the world that do not have waterproof feathers. As a result, cormorants can often be seen in the process of drying themselves. Watch for these large black birds standing near water with outstretched wings. In the water, cormorants often swim with their bodies completely submerged, only their heads and necks remain above the surface of the water. This unique method of swimming makes it easy for anybody to identify a cormorant even at a great distance. Each summer thousands of people slow down or stop to take pictures of birds that have built their nests right on the pylons running parallel to the Pictou Causeway. Few realize that the birds are Double Crested Cormorants and are a common sight in Halifax Harbour and surrounding waters during the summer months.

Saw Whet Owl

The Saw Whet has several common names, but its official name, the Northern Saw Whet Owl, is the longest name of any owl in Eastern North America. Strange fate for a bird whose maximum length of 20 cm (8 in.), makes it the smallest owl on this side of the continent. Its scientific name is

Aegolius acadicus. "*Aegolius*" is Latin for a kind of owl, but more interesting, at least from a Nova Scotian point of view, is "*acadicus,*" which is Greek for "of Acadia" or "of Nova Scotia," the place where this tiny owl was first discovered.

Saw Whet Owls can still be found in Nova Scotia, in any month of the year. However, March and April are the two best months for "discovering" Saw Whets for two reasons. First, although some Saw Whets winter in the province, an extensive banding program by Acadia University on Bon Portage Island has proven that many leave the province in October and return again in the spring between March 8 and April 19.

Evidence of this spring migration is also seen at bird feeders, when, each year a lucky few have the opportunity to see a Saw Whet Owl at their feeders during March. The Saw Whets usually visit the feeders in search of mice that are attracted by split seed. Although on cloudy days they may be seen during the middle of the day, they are more often seen very early in the morning or very late in the afternoon. However, the best time to watch for them is in the evenings, by leaving an outdoor light on. The Saw Whet may be a little put off by the light at first but will soon learn to accept it. Normally, Saw Whets will visit a given feeder anywhere from a day to fourteen days, depending on weather conditions and available food supply.

The second reason March and April are the best times to find Saw Whets is that this is the period males begin searching for mates, and to attract mates they sing. Throughout Eastern North America, their song is heard from March to May and is seldom heard after May. In the greater Metro area, Saw Whets may be heard singing in March but are most frequently heard during the second half of April and the first week of May. In recent years, the most reliable place to find a singing Saw Whet has been at Hardwood

Lands. However, Saw Whets can be found any-where natural hardwood stands are present. Their song is an evenly spaced, single note that is whistled repeatedly at the same pitch for three or four minutes at a time. The consistency of the song causes people to wonder if it is man-made. It is not, then, surprising to learn that when Jeannine Shirley first heard the sound of a male Saw Whet in the Bayside woods, she thought it was being electronically produced. The Saw Whets common name comes not from its song but from its call, a nasal call that sounds like a saw being whetted or sharpened.

At 18 cm to 20 cm (7 in. to 8 in.), the tiny, brown-coloured adult Saw Whet Owl is often initially mistaken for a youngster of one of the larger owl species. Unknown to many is the fact that most baby owls are white, and they do not grow their darker plumage until they are almost ready to leave the nest, when they are either the same size or larger than the parents.

Saw Whets are Nova Scotia's third most com-mon species of owl in the summer, but by winter, the majority of our birds have headed south for warmer locals. Depending on the weather, Saw Whets begin to return again to the province in mid- or late March. Be sure to take advantage of any opportunities you have to see a Saw Whet, as these owls are unbelievably cute, partly because their wide-eyed expression resembles the inno-cence on the faces of puppies or young children.

Woodcock

Woodcock are unusual members of the Sandpiper family. Unlike most sandpipers, which are associ-ated with mud flats, coastlines, and beaches, the Woodcock prefers wet thickets, moist woodlands, and bushy swamps. Most Woodcock return to Nova Scotia, on average, by March 21. In early spring, (March and April), the nasal "beep" call of the male Woodcock, which sounds almost identical to the call of the Common Nighthawk, can often be heard in the evenings coming from open or semi–open areas. Male Woodcock come to such areas to perform elaborate courtship flights to attract females. In these flights, the male leaps from the ground, rises in widening circles to about 91 m (300 ft.), hovers momentarily, then descends like a falling leaf, while giving a series of liquid "chips." The nasal "beep" call, however, is given only when the bird is on the ground, a good clue to the identity of the caller. Nighthawks, for example, only give their call while in flight.

Woodcock most often begin their courtship performances at dusk or at dawn during March and April. The display lasts between thirty to sixty minutes and can be viewed as either an impressive site or a humorous one. A long time ago, the Woodcock picked up the name "Timber Doodle," given by non–birders who encountered it in the forest. A "doodle" is a foolish person—a perfect name for a bird that looks like it should be on the shore but repeatedly flies from the ground toward the sky in such an erratic fashion that it never really gets anywhere.

I was always impressed by the Woodcock's nuptial dance, until I saw the most peculiar Woodcock in my life. I was walking along the Waterline Road in Bedford in the middle of the afternoon, when I suddenly heard a Woodcock during his courtship flight. I hurried down a short 25 m (82 ft.) path to the right of the main trail and there he was, dancing in the sky. As I watched him, he landed on the ground only a couple of metres away and marched up to my shoes and inspected them closely, apparently unaware that I was attached to them.

The next day I told others of this crazy Woodcock that was doing his dance in the daytime, in the middle of June, well after its regular breeding season was over. Later that day, I and a couple of birding friends went back to see if we could find the bird. Sure enough, he was there. Again, he paid no attention to us; he was too busy going about his business. We laughed, thinking how ridiculous it was that a Woodcock would be trying to attract a mate at this time of year. Furthermore, this poor individual was not doing the courtship flight properly. We concluded that he was an obviously inexperienced male.

A couple of days later I took more friends to see this nutty Woodcock. There he was, flying in circles, flipping and flopping, occasionally doing something that resembled the real courtship manoeuvres. We were enjoying a hearty laugh as we watched the bird land about 6 m (20 ft.) from us. We waited quietly with grins on our faces for the next takeoff. Then we noticed the reason for his delay—a female had stepped out of the bushes and was moving towards him. Just before they went off together, I was sure that Woodcock smirked at me; if I didn't know better, I would swear he was thinking, "He who laughs last, laughs loudest!"

The favourite food of the Woodcock is earthworms. Studies show that earthworms make up at least 75 per cent of the Woodcock's diet and that the Woodcock may eat more than its weight in earthworms in a single day. In March, they are sometimes seen poking about in people's yards, near the foundation of a home where heat from the building has softened the ground. In April, many Woodcock are found in wet alder thickets, where earthworms are abundant. (A good thing to remember if you need bait for fishing!) After April, Woodcock become a very difficult bird to see, due to their secretive nature and their fast getaway flights when discovered. Although in April, Woodcock are so busy actively pursuing a mate, they are easy to find. Two of the best places to observe mating Woodcock are in the alder bushes lining the road and parking lots at Crystal

Crescent Beach, and the alder bushes along the old railway bed at West Lawrencetown Marsh, or in those along the road to Conrads Beach.

Red Throated Loons

Many people are aware of and have come to love the Common Loon, but few know that a second species can be seen in the Metro area. This second species, the Red Throated Loon, is smaller than the Common Loon and is named after the colour of its throat. Red Throated Loons can be seen in the Metro area twice a year—once as they head north to the Arctic breeding grounds and again in the fall as they work their way south. In the spring, migrants move at a much faster pace than they do in the fall. As a result, the viewing period for these birds is noticeably shorter in the spring. On the plus side, spring Red Throats are clearly showing their full colours, making them easier to identify. Concentrations of Red Throats begin to appear about mid-March, and most are gone by mid-April. Spring Red Throats are often seen at Seaforth, Cow Bay, and Hartlen Point but may be seen at any exposed location along our coast.

Pheasants

Although Ring Necked Pheasants are year-round residents in Nova Scotia, they become more noticeable in late March as male pheasants gain their spring plumage and start their age-old quest for a female. At this time, males will do just about anything to attract the attention of a female pheasant. During mating rituals, males appear to be concentrating so intensely that they often fail to notice people or approaching cars. On more than one occasion, I have had to stop my vehicle in order to avoid hitting a pheasant that was "dancing" in the middle of the road. I have even had a male pheasant jump out of a ditch and chase my car, perhaps pursuing his own reflection in my hub-cap. Fights between males intensify in April as they firmly establish their breeding territory.

One April, Pat Bonang of Seabright watched in fascination and sometimes with concern as two Ring Necked Pheasants fought vigorously in her back yard. She viewed the battle between the two birds for an hour and a half before she had to leave. Upon her return, it was obvious that the battle was over territory. The two birds had divided the property in half, with one male controlling all land in the back of the house, while the other controlled all the land in the front. Although the battle appeared at times to be quite vicious, as both birds took running leaps at each other with outstretched talons, neither bird sustained any noticeable injuries. Even in the most violent of territory disputes amongst birds, injuries are rare.

Common Eiders

Common Eiders are strictly saltwater birds, preferring rocky coastlines with plenty of shoals and reefs. The winter season for Common Eiders runs roughly from late December to late February. During this time, Common Eiders are fairly stationary and occur in flocks ranging in size from thirty birds to a thousand individuals, but most flocks consist of fifty to three hundred birds. Although eiders can be seen in Metro during any month of the year, the most exciting time to view them is during their northward migration. This migration starts slowly in late February, builds in March, and peaks in April. From mid-March to mid-April, huge rafts of birds—from 100 to 10,000—may be seen. Popular places to view these rafts are Hartlen Point, Tribune Head, Portuguese Cove, Chebucto Head, and Sandy Cove.

In March and April, these rafts are scanned

carefully by birders in hopes of spotting the occasional King Eider. Such efforts usually lead to the discovery of one or two each spring. At a distance, the orange bill shield of the King Eider is difficult to see, as is the blue on its head. The black on the back of an adult male King is easy to spot if the bird is side-on or back-on to the observer. However, when flocks of eiders are swimming head-on, experts watch for a bird that has a slight buffy cast over its white chest. That individual is usually the King Eider. This is a little-known identification trick, as the colouring is shown but not mentioned in the standard field guides.

Later in the summer, Common Eiders can be seen frequenting places such as Chebucto Head and Conrads Beach. At such locations watch for eider crèches, a group of thirty to forty birds composed mostly of young eiders. Each crèche is only attended by a few females that not only look out for their own young, but for all of the other young eiders present. After a short period, they are relieved by other females who have been busy feeding in deeper waters. This interesting "babysitting" behaviour is very unusual amongst birds but appears to work successfully for the Common Eider.

Short Eared Owl

Although Short Eared Owls are less common than Barreds—the most common owl in the province—they are more frequently seen for two reasons. Short Eareds, unlike Barred Owls, frequently hunt during the daylight hours—although they do prefer early mornings and late afternoons, partially because of greater rodent activity. A second reason these owls are more easily spotted than their woodland cousin is that they hunt in open areas such as grassy meadows, dykelands, and sand dunes.

Short Eared Owls may be seen during any of

the winter months, but March is when most Short Eareds are sighted in Halifax County; an observer may see a Short Eared Owl flying over the golf course at Hartlen Point, sitting on the abandoned buildings on Devils Island, or cruising low over the grasslands at the end of Dyke Road. They may also be seen hunting over the dunes at Conrads Beach or Rainbow Haven Beach. In short, they favour any location that has a high population of meadow voles (a mouselike animal), their favourite food. Short Eareds are more common in years when meadow vole populations are high.

Remember, dawn and dusk are the best times to be at these locations. The ears, properly called ear tufts, of the Short Eared Owl are difficult to see, but these owls are easily identified. In flight, they have long wings that show large, light, buffy wing patches. Even in poor light they can be identified by their bouncy, floppy, mothlike manner of flying.

Purple Sandpiper

Imagine waves crashing against an exposed rocky shoreline in the middle of the winter, when these surf-pounded rocks are by far the harshest habitat in the province. It is difficult to believe that any land bird would want to spend its winters there; however, the tiny Purple Sandpiper calls it home. They eat and sleep in this rough coastal environment. Like miniature mountain goats, these birds scurry sure-footedly over wet, slippery rocks, pausing to find food in the cracks and crevices. They will also sort through piles of kelp washed up onto the rocks, but their preferred method of feeding is to dash between the crashing waves to snatch up marine insects as they are washed ashore.

Purple Sandpipers breed in the Arctic and winter along the Atlantic coast. In winter, these sandpipers have the distinction of living farther north than any other shorebird. The back and wings of these starling–size birds are dark gray and in the right light show a purple iridescence. Like starlings, Purple Sandpipers always travel in flocks. In the Metro area, an average-sized flock would contain from a dozen to fifty birds. Unlike starlings, these sandpipers are gentle, friendly birds which will allow the observer to walk within a metre of them. Up close, one can also identify them by their dull yellow legs.

On a calm, sunny, winter's day, it can be fun clambering over the large rocks like the ones at Sandy Cove or Crystal Crescent Beach, searching for Purple Sandpipers. High tide or nearly high tide are the best times to go, as at low tide Purples often fly out over the water to reach freshly exposed rocky ledges. Purples may be seen during any of the winter months, but for some unknown reason, I have always had the best luck in March. If you prefer to walk close to the water, there is a trail that runs to the right of the Chebucto Head parking lot and overlooks the shoreline below, where, each winter, Purple Sandpipers live among the wind, the waves, and the rocks.

April Showers Bring Birds and Flowers

....

Mysteries Of Migration

The migration of birds is a subject that has fascinated humans for years. Old birding literature is filled with accounts of bird migration. Some statements, such as, "Swallows spend the winter buried in mud at the bottom of ponds," now seem quite ridiculous, but they were once undisputed as facts.

Today, although many of the mysteries of migration remain, we have begun to unravel some of its secrets. For instance, it has been discovered that during spring migration, land birds generally choose to travel along the interior routes of the continent when heading north because areas farther inland tend to warm up faster than coastal areas; as a result, insects emerge sooner, providing a source of food for the migrants.

It has long been known that one of the main reasons birds migrate north is to find enough space to raise a family, since breeding takes up more space than regular living. What we have come to better understand over the years is just how important the individual timing is of each migrating bird. In other words, those individuals that arrive on the breeding grounds too early, risk death by starvation; those who arrive too late find that all the best breeding territories and mates are taken. When it comes to bird reproduction, timing is everything.

Much of what happens with our migrating birds in March is still evident in April. In this sense, the first half of April is very similar to the last part of March. In another way, it is very different because even during the first week of April, it is evident that seasonal changes are taking place. This evidence builds daily, escalating to the point where days become brighter and nights become warmer.

In April we have an average rainfall of 110.1 mm, which plays a very important part in hastening the onset of spring. Generally, in years that the rains come late in April, we have a later spring, and when they come early, so does spring—and the birds. Of course, other factors affect the timing of spring but our precipitation level is one of the most significant. Rain helps to warm and soften the ground, making it easier for new growth and insects to emerge; it supplies much-needed moisture; and the turbulent winds often associated with rain systems can carry migrating birds along with them, especially if the storm comes from the south. When these spring storms do occur, they bring us a greater than normal number of colourful species. In the Metro area, one can expect to see any or all of the following species: Indigo Buntings, Blue Grosbeaks, Rose Breasted Grosbeaks, Scarlet Tanagers, and Northern Orioles. They may also carry with them one or two southern rarities. In the recent past, species that have been sighted after spring storms include southern birds such as the Purple Gallinule, Hooded Warbler, Worm Eating Warbler, Summer Tanager, Laughing Gull, Franklin's Gull, and Vermilion Flycatcher.

In April, spring migration can be observed at feeders, coastal locations, freshwater lakes, marshes, and in woodlands. At feeders, watch for the returning of the Song Sparrows and Mourning Doves. This is the best time of year to distinguish easily between the male Mourning Dove and the female by a wash of pink over his chest. Even before April, there is a good chance you may have seen a Song Sparrow in your back yard, but if not, there is still time to attract one, since Song Sparrow numbers peak in early April. Early April is also your last chance to hear the sweet, musical song of the American Tree Sparrow. Their song is not a loud one, so the listener must be nearby to hear it. Tree Sparrows begin to sing in late March. If you are lucky enough to have these delightful sparrows at your feeders, open the window a crack and listen for their song when they are in view. Outside the city limits, Tree Sparrows can be found feeding in roadside alder bushes like the ones lining much of Marine Drive. During the second half of April, feeder-watchers should prepare for returning Purple Finches, White Throated Sparrows, Dark Eyed Juncos, and Pine Siskins. You may even see a Fox Sparrow or a Rose Breasted Grosbeak. The rarer Blue Grosbeak or an Indigo Bunting are other species to watch for.

Both inside and outside city limits, the migration of hawks is noticeable. The species to look for are Merlins, Sharp Shinned Hawks, Broad Winged Hawks, Northern Harriers, Ospreys, and the American Kestrel. However, the greatest number of American Kestrels will be seen from the middle to the end of April.

Rusty Blackbirds return to our area between late March and the middle of April and may be observed in wet woodlands. A dirt road that starts at the corner of Kearney Lake and Hammonds Plains Roads leads to a patch of woods where these secretive birds may be found. This wooded road is known locally as the water line road as under it run the pipelines that carry the Halifax water supply from Pockwock Lake.

In April, most woodlands are good places to see the return of Northern Flickers, Ruby Crowned and Golden Crowned Kinglets, Hermit Thrushes, Sharp Shinned Hawks, Merlins, Yellow Rumped Warblers, Palm Warblers, and Winter Wrens. A particularly good place to see Winter Wrens is the Mount Uniacke roadside Picnic Park. At this location, one may see up to a dozen Winter Wrens during the third or fourth week of April, which is absolutely remarkable, considering they are almost impossible to see during the summer due to their secretive nature. At this park in April, it is possible to walk right up to newly arrived singing Winter Wrens.

The mature hardwoods in the Timberlea area have always been the best place in the Metro area to find nesting Broad Winged Hawks. Broad Wingeds are one of our more obscure breeding hawks that return to our area in late April. This is also a good time and place to see the Yellow Bellied Sapsucker. Sapsuckers live in woodlands that are dominated by large aspens and birch. They can be most easily tracked by their loud distinctive drumming, heard in the early mornings.

In early April, at freshwater lakes in Metro, the first Tree Swallows, Ospreys, and Belted Kingfishers may be seen, as well as returning Ring Necked Ducks. Rocky Lake on the Rocky Lake Road is a favourite spot of spring Ring Necked Ducks and is a good place to see them. Drain Lake is the most reliable Metro lake in April to find Wood Ducks and Soras.

The first part of April is a good time to visit coastal marshes like the West Lawrencetown

Marsh and the West Chezzetcook Marsh to see migrating Northern Harriers, Green Winged Teals, Northern Pintails, American Wigeons, breeding Red Winged Blackbirds, and American Bitterns. During April and May, the occasional Bonaparte's or Black Headed Gull may also be sighted at the West Chezzetcook Marsh.

Later in April, the West Lawrencetown Marsh is a good place to see returning Blue Winged Teals and breeding Common Snipes. The American Woodcock can be found in the alder thickets lining the roadway tracks that lead into the marsh and in the alders along the road going to nearby Conrads Beach. Conrads is also an excellent spot in April to see Willets, Savannah Sparrows, Piping Plovers, and Belted Kingfishers. In recent Aprils, one or two of the rarely seen Snow Geese have been sighted at Conrads and at West Chezzetcook. Along Nova Scotia coastlines watch for migrating Common Mergansers, Northern Gannets, Double Crested Cormorants, Black Scoters, Killdeers, and Great Blue Herons.

Bird Day

The idea of a Bird Day originated in Oil City, Pennsylvania. The purpose of the day was to set aside some time to teach school children the importance of protecting birds. Over the years, many schools have created programs and exercises to commemorate this event. In some areas, Bird Day is celebrated on April 3, the birth date of John Burrows. In others areas, April 26 has been chosen, the day John Jones Audubon was born, for whom the National Audubon Society was named. Like Audubon, Burrows was a naturalist and a writer who spent his whole life teaching people about birds and nature. Bird Day is an important tradition that would be nice to see more widely celebrated in the Metro area; it is a an event we all can take part in and benefit from.

City Birding

....

The Super Sparrow

Fox Sparrows, like most ordinary sparrows, are ground feeders and spend a great deal of their time either on or very near the ground. However, when it comes to scratching, Fox Sparrows are premier scratchers as they just love to kick about in fallen leaves. Their exacting technique is very interesting to watch. Unlike a chicken or a Ring Necked Pheasant, both of which scratch alternately with one foot, then the other, the Fox Sparrow scratches with both feet at once. To accomplish this, it hops forward then slides back. The resulting movement draws the interest of many observers as it is very rhythmical and appears almost as if the Fox Sparrow is participating in some sort of line dance. However, the Fox Sparrow's true talent is not its dancing but its singing, which consists of rich whistling notes. To add to its intriguing nature, instead of singing from an exposed perch like most birds, it sings from a hidden location.

Not only does this bird have style and talent, it is also a "hunk" as far as sparrows go. In actual measurements it is only 4 cm to 6 cm (1.6 in. to 2.4 in.) larger than other Nova Scotia sparrows, but those few centimetres make it appear much larger than its cousins. Like all sparrows, it is brown—not just an ordinary brown but a rich rufous brown like a fox's coat. Watch for Fox Sparrows near the end of March and in the first half of April.

Canadian Lakes Loon Survey

The Canadian Lakes Loon Survey is organized by the Long Point Bird Observatory in Ontario. The project uses volunteers across the country to gather information on breeding Common Loons. First started in 1981, the purpose of the project continues to be helping to improve dwindling loon populations. Locally, the project is spearheaded by the Canadian Wildlife Service and focuses on Nova Scotia's loon population. The survey's aim is to establish how many loons there are in the province and to pinpoint exactly where they are breeding—which lakes are used by loons and which lakes are not. Such information can help us to better determine exactly how many Common Loons there are in Nova Scotia. The survey can also help to monitor local populations and to discover how much of the loons' breeding success and habitat is affected by human and industrial disturbances, mercury poisoning, and acid rain.

Assisting with the survey are the Nova Scotia Department of the Environment Youth Conservation Corps, personnel from the Canadian Parks Service, and the Department of Natural Resources. Many members of the general public who have cottages or live near areas with breeding loons are also helping out. However, it is clear that with the large number of lakes in Nova Scotia, many more volunteers are needed, even in the Metro area.

The survey begins each year in April and continues until October. Although it is sometimes referred to as the Nova Scotia Loon Survey, it is in full cooperation with the Canadian Lakes Loon Survey. If you would be interested in participating in the survey or know of anyone who would be, you can contact the Canadian Wildlife Service at the Bedford Institute of Oceanography, P.O. Box 1006, Dartmouth, Nova Scotia, B2Y 4A2, or call (902) 426-3430.

Here is your chance to help one of our most beloved Nova Scotia birds. It is sad to think that one day the enchanting call of the Common Loon could be just a memory in this part of the country. Let's prevent that from happening.

Purple Finches

Purple Finches breed and overwinter in all ten Canadian provinces. However, like every member of the Finch family, they are very erratic travellers, so the number of birds present in any given year varies greatly, especially during the winter months. In the Metro area, Purple Finches are generally more common in the summer during the breeding season. Unlike most species, which show a preference for breeding in either the city or the country, Purple Finches are equally happy to nest in urban or rural areas. In Nova Scotia, the presence of coniferous trees, especially spruce, appears to be their primary concern when it comes time to nest. Purple Finches in the northeastern states, on the other hand, appear to be less fussy and will just as quickly choose any of the other evergreen trees for building their nests. In the west, they are even less particular and will use both softwoods and hardwoods.

Although the occasional Purple Finch can be heard softly singing its warbling song in February, most of these birds reach their peak volume in April and May. Egg laying usually begins in late May. The four or five greenish blue eggs are incubated by the female for only two weeks. After this, both the male and the female feed the young. The nestlings of most bird species are fed insects because they are high in protein and easy to digest. Young Purple Finches, however, are generally fed seeds regurgitated by their parents. Fourteen days after birth, the young birds are ready to leave the nest and join the adults on feeding excursions. During this period they continue to eat seeds but also start to eat insects and a lot of berries.

Male Purple Finches are not actually purple; they have more of a raspberry coloration. The females are brown and resemble sparrows. At feeders, the female can be identified by her eating preferences. Unlike sparrows which prefer millet, Purple Finches choose to feed on sunflower seeds or Niger seed. For the first year, the young males look just like the adult female. The first sign of their reddish coloration generally appears on the back, just above the tail, in the area called the rump patch, and in the throat area.

At this time, they are occasionally mistaken for House Finches. Male House Finches can vary in colour from brick red to raspberry colour to orange, but unlike the male Purple Finch, they have heavy brown streaks on their sides and belly. As of 1996 House Finches are still fairly rare in Nova Scotia, but that could change quite quickly in the next couple of years.

Ospreys

Ospreys spend their winters in South America, Mexico, and southern portions of the United States. Their northward migration in spring begins in February and continues until the end of May. The first Ospreys arrive in Nova Scotia each year near April 5; they are widespread by May. When migrating, Ospreys closely follow coastlines, rivers, and other major waterways. In Canada, Ospreys breed in all ten provinces and both territories. Their large stick nests, sometimes weighing more than a tonne, are often built on power poles and other prominent locations. These nests are often mistaken for eagle nests because of their large size, and Ospreys are sometimes mistaken for Bald Eagles as they are near the size of an eagle. It is estimated that there are more than 250 active Osprey nests in Nova Scotia. Osprey nests are also fairly common in the Metro area. They may be seen at many locations on power poles. However, if you do not know of any particular sites, I will quickly mention three. In Dartmouth, a power pole nest can be easily observed at the end of Portland Estates

Boulevard. Power pole Osprey nests may also be viewed from Exit 5 of Highway 103 in Tantallon or along the Kearney Lake Trail.

Ospreys mate for life, and if they are successful in raising young at a particular nest site, they will return to that same nest the following year. As a result of this behaviour, some nests have been recorded as used for up to twenty years. Each year, the nest grows larger as new material is added to fix any damage that occurred during the winter months. Nest repairs begin as soon as both birds arrive at the nest. Their three eggs are added a few weeks later. The eggs are incubated for twenty–eight to thirty–three days solely by the female. During this period, the female does not hunt but is fed frequently by the male. Once the young hatch, both parents search for food. The extremely hearty appetite of the young, who are almost always hungry, means that the average Osprey feeds almost exclusively on fish, a habit which has earned it the commonly used name "Fish Hawk."

Ospreys are especially adapted to catching fish. Their keen eyes can spot fish up to 61 m (200 ft.) away, although most of their hunting is done from 9 m to 30 m (30 ft. to 100 ft.) above the surface of the water. Upon spotting a fish, an Osprey will either instantly dive feet-first into the water or hover near the water's surface and then dive. When diving, the Osprey sometimes becomes almost completely submerged. Its long legs and claws help it to reach deeper still. Once it grabs onto the fish, its outer toe is pushed backwards and locks into the fish. This reversible outer toe is not found on other hawks. The bottom of the Osprey's toes also have sharp protrusions called spicules, which help to keep the fish from slipping. Once the Osprey catches his prey, he shakes loose any excess water and repositions the fish in his talons. Fish are always carried head-first, to reduce wind resistance. Small fish are carried by one foot while larger fish are carried by two. Ospreys usually return to a favourite feeding post to eat the fish or to the nest during breeding season. These birds consume their food slowly, taking time to enjoy their meal, a process which is usually drawn out over several hours.

Ospreys are common in the Metro area; however, many of the lakes they nest along no longer hold enough fish to feed their young. As a result, many can be seen making frequent trips between their breeding lakes and the salt water to search for fish. They have even developed the habit of visiting the small ponds in the Public Gardens to catch the goldfish there. It is an impressive sight when one of these large birds drops into such a small body of water. Park officials do not mind Ospreys catching the goldfish. In fact, they are happy about it as there are now far too many of them in those ponds. Goldfish live for a long time and are voracious eaters, so they can grow to be quite large. Watch an Osprey at this park and you will be impressed not only by its size but by the size of the goldfish it is catching.

Crow's Nest

Throughout April, crows can be observed collecting materials for nest building. They gather strips of wood fibres and rootlets to line the main frame of the nest, usually composed of large sticks. Next, the crows gather grasses, fur, hair, moss, or anything of relative softness to build a soft inner cup in which to cradle their eggs.

April is an excellent time to look for crows' nests because the trees in which they are built are leafless. Once you start looking, you will probably be amazed by how many you will see; there appears to be one on every block. The many crow nests in the south end of Halifax and other parts of Metro stand as ample testimony that crows are as abundant in the city as in the country. In fact, some believe that there are now more crows in the city than in the countryside. Crows are intelligent birds and learn quickly how to adapt and how to obtain what they want.

A good example of this bird's intelligence was once observed by Linda Payzant. A Herring Gull had found something interesting and took it to the roof of a building to inspect it. As he began to eat the tasty morsel, a crow walked up behind him and pulled his tail. The gull turned around to see an innocent-faced crow taking a few steps backwards. Once the gull reverted his attention to the food, the crow came forward and pulled his tail again. When this performance was repeated a third time, the larger gull whirled around and lunged at the impudent crow. The crow responded by flying over the top of the gull, grabbing its meal, and flying away. I can imagine this crow laughing to himself as he disappeared into the maze of the city.

Further Afield

....

American Kestrels

The American Kestrel's rufous body, blue wings, and striking facial pattern makes it the most colourful falcon in Nova Scotia. Its tiny size— smaller than a pigeon—also adds to its appeal. Falcons are the fastest members of the Raptor family, which includes all the various species of hawks, eagles, kites, and vultures. Their long pointed wings allow them to produce great bursts of speed in order to overtake their prey and capture it. Kestrels have been clocked at speeds as fast as 65 km/hr (40 mi./hr). Unlike the rest of the Falcon family, which specializes in feeding on other birds, the American Kestrel will eat birds but it prefers to feed on insects. One of the Kestrel's all-time favourites is grasshoppers. For this reason look for Kestrels around grassy fields and dry meadows like those at Oakfield Provincial Park and along Route 224. The birds can be seen sitting very erect on overhead wires or other perches, looking for prey or hovering above an open area. The majority of Kestrels return to the Metro area in April and breed here in relatively small numbers compared to the rest of the province. However they will use nest boxes, so they could be encouraged to breed in greater numbers.

Common Mergansers

The Common Merganser is the largest member of the Merganser family and the largest duck to breed on inland waters. Although loons are larger, they are not considered a type of duck. Like the Wood Duck, the Common Merganser lays its eggs in tree cavities but will also use a hole in a bank or cavity amongst boulders. The female merganser lays from seven to fifteen eggs. In the summer, look for Common Mergansers along the Mill Lake Road in the Crook's Brook area and any places where eels are common, as they are a favourite food. Merganser families may be found along woodland stretches of large rivers, such as the Sackville River, where it's exciting but not unusual to see a female Common Merganser with as many as a dozen young ones bobbing along behind her.

American Bitterns

A summer resident that often goes unnoticed is the American Bittern, the song of which is heard mostly in the spring; it starts in April and is quite loud and unusual. Some have described it as sounding like an old broken water pump. This distinctive call can be heard from quite a distance on a still night; however, locating the bird can be rather difficult as they are masters of disguise. American Bitterns live almost exclusively in cattail marshes, where their protective brown-streaked plumage provides excellent camouflage for this 60 cm to 80 cm (23 in. to 31 in.) high bird. To add to this camouflaging effect, American Bitterns will often point their long bills skyward and compress their bodies laterally so they better imitate a cattail. They will go as far as to sway in unison with the cattails when they are blown by the wind. The cattail stands at West Lawrencetown Marsh and Lawrencetown Lake are two good places where American Bitterns can be found.

Golden Eagle

Compared to the Bald Eagle, the Golden Eagle is very rare in Nova Scotia, and contrary to popular belief, it is smaller in size, not larger. The favourite habitats of the Golden Eagle are moun-tains and hilly regions as far removed from humans as possible. Adult Golden Eagles are nearly all dark brown and get their name from the golden wash of feathers on the back of their heads and necks. Young Bald Eagles are also mostly dark brown, but with closer observation, they show irregular blotches of white on the underside of their wings or body when in flight. Many of the birds reported as Golden Eagles prove to be young Bald Eagles, so be careful. More Golden Eagles have been sighted in Nova Scotia in April than any other month, so keep those eyes open. Fall is another good time to watch for Golden Eagles.

Glossy Ibises

Especially during migration periods, before you leave the house to go birding, it is helpful to sit down and establish which birds you are likely to encounter on the trip. Seasoned birders often automatically recall which birds they may see at a particular time of year from past experiences. Personal notes are also helpful in recognizing annual bird cycles. If you are new to birding, books can often provide information as to when a type of bird is likely to pass through or arrive in your general area.

For instance, during one Easter weekend, while I was birding along the Eastern Shore, I kept my eyes open for a Glossy Ibis, as most Glossy's are seen in Nova Scotia during the months of April and May. Although I didn't see any, shortly after I arrived home I received a phone call regarding a Glossy Ibis that a birder had seen the same day at Black Point Park in Queensland. Two days later, another Glossy Ibis was found by a birder at West Chezzetcook Marsh. In the days that followed, more were sighted at Lawrencetown Lake and six other locations in the province. Although the Glossy Ibis is considered rare in Nova Scotia, this en masse arrival is typical of their species. It is interesting to note that during the same time the Glossy Ibises were present, over one hundred arrived in Maine, their northernmost nesting area.

Although a Glossy Ibis appears all dark at a distance, up close or in good light they are a glossy purplish maroon with some iridescent pinks and greens thrown in. This heronlike bird can be identified by its long downward curving bill.

Swallows

Swallows are found in all parts of the world, except the polar regions and New Zealand. Worldwide, seventy–nine species of swallows are known to exist. For many people, the true sign of spring is when the swallows return to their region. In some areas, the returning of the swallows have generated so much interest that they have gained international attention. Such is the case with the famous swallows of Capistrano, where hundreds of Cliff Swallows gather each year to nest on the walls on the San Juan Capistrano Mission in southern California.

Of the six species of swallows found in eastern North America, five migrate to Nova Scotia to breed: Bank, Barn, Cliff, Tree Swallows, and the Purple Martin. Tree Swallows are the first to migrate northward and generally arrive in the province during the first half of April. Unlike most songbirds, which migrate at night, swallows are day migrators and feed primarily on the flying insects that they gather in flight with their wide, gaping mouths. Swallows eat all types of flying insects, including mosquitoes, blackflies, and some bees and wasps. They are also known to skim insects such as the water boatmen from the surface of the water and grasshoppers from the tops of grasses.

Occasionally, unexpected spring storms will catch Tree Swallows off guard. Late snows can be devastating, with hundreds of swallows dying from cold or starvation. Tree Swallows have been known to survive short durations of cold weather by feeding on bayberries or the seeds of bulrushes and sedges. Temperature has long been recognized as an important factor in swallow migration. Researchers have demonstrated that the northward movement of Barn Swallows closely followed an average daily temperature of 9°C (48°F). In years with cool springs, Tree Swallow migration can be delayed for weeks.

When they do arrive, Tree Swallows are the most widespread swallow in the Metro area. They can be seen on just about any local body of water. Barn Swallows, too, are fairly common and can be seen at a variety of locations, but if you do not know of any sites, try Hartlen Point, where they breed on the golf course. Bank Swallows are harder to find, but small colonies can be seen at

Conrads Beach, Todds Island, and West Chezzetcook Marsh. Cliff Swallows are the hardest of our local breeders to find, but they do breed each year at Three Fathom Harbour and the Halifax International Airport. The fifth swallow species, the Purple Martin, is occasionally seen migrating through the Metro region, but it has never lived here, and I predict they will never breed in the Metro area.

Swallows can travel quite a distance while feeding each day, so it is not surprising to see large flocks made up of different species, feeding over a body of water. For example, on Lake Micmac in Dartmouth, I have often seen Tree, Barn, and Bank Swallows skimming together over the surface of the water. I do not know of a location in the immediate vicinity where I could find a Barn or Bank Swallow nest.

Large flocks of swallows should also be checked for rare species. A rare species that has been sighted in the Metro area more than once is the Northern Rough Winged Swallow. When one of these swallows is seen, it is most frequently found feeding with Bank Swallows, but they have also been observed travelling with migrating flocks of Tree Swallows.

Eastern Phoebes

Most species of flycatchers wait until May to return to Nova Scotia, but the Eastern Phoebe typically returns during the first half of April. If the weather is cold at this time, they may be seen along the shorelines feeding on flies hatching in the piles of seaweeds. If the weather is a little warmer, they are more likely hunting over a slow-moving stream. It is unusual to see an Eastern Phoebe in city back yards, but it can happen, as Joanne Creelman of Dartmouth can attest. Amazingly, one April a phoebe visited her back yard and cheerfully sang its "fee–bee" song, wagged its tail, and gave its distinctive sharp "chip" note. In short, it did all the things a phoebe should do when a bird-watcher is trying it identify it. Rarely is a bird obliging enough to put on such a perfect performance. Spring and fall migrations are the best times for Metro birders to see an Eastern Phoebe as few nest in the Metro area, but they have been found nesting on the Mersey Paper Road. Eastern Phoebe's are most famous for their habit of building their nests on the underside of small wooden bridges. During the summer months, look for these quiet birds in such locations.

Spring in all Its Splendour

A Mixed Blessing

Although I have grown to love all the seasons,
spring is my favourite. I especially love May,
when the season is at its zenith—life is bursting
forth everywhere. Not only is it a great month to
hear and see birds, it is an excellent time for
nature lovers to find and identify wild flowers,
fossils, animals, amphibians, reptiles, trees, bushes, fish, insects, and many other forms of wildlife
with which we share the planet.

As I see the plants and animals around me
come alive, I feel as if I, too, am awaking from
slumber. As the sun shines and birds sing, I can
feel new life rushing through my veins. It may be
just the kaleidoscope of sights, sounds, and smells
that heightens my senses. On the other hand, my
mind and body may be acknowledging, on a sub-
conscious level, the tie that binds all living things,
in which case the natural response is a feeling of

excitement and peace that comes from feeling like part of a greater force.

To find out for yourself just how inspiring spring can be, get up early some May morning and get away from the noise of the city. Go someplace where you are alone with nature. Whether you sit or walk, be sure to listen to the sounds around you—the wind, the water, and the birds. Smell the fragrances of new life as they float gently through the air. As you quietly survey the surroundings, you will become more aware of the living things all around you; you may begin to see new things that will evoke a sense of wonder or joy. It may begin as a tiny spark inside but the sensation will grow in time. The discovery that somehow nature can trigger something wonderful inside of us is what the early-morning expedition is about.

A word of caution: Nova Scotia has been "blessed" with about a dozen species of mosquitoes and about three hundred species of blackflies. There are times in the woods when I feel like Pig Pen, that character from the Charlie Brown comic. Instead of dirt swirling around, though, I am surrounded by blackflies and mosquitoes. I'm sure those blood-sucking varmints come from miles around to try to drain me of my life force. Over the years I have tried all kinds of things to keep them at bay: sprays, lotions, light-coloured clothing, vitamins, garlic pills, natural repellents, mind over matter, and plant juices. I have tried them all. Of the sprays and lotions, Muskol, with its 100 per cent deet formula, works the best by far and lasts the longest. Unfortunately, I have also seen it melt plastic, so I now use it only if I have to.

I have found that a clear-mesh bug jacket is perfect protection from the largest to the smallest insects. These jackets also come with a hood, which I use when I do not need to see perfectly, as the mesh does affect visibility slightly. With the hood up, I can still see the birds, and it presents no interference when I am looking through my binoculars. However, when I am walking, I find it a little harder to detect the fleeting motions of birds or animals. So when birding, I often wear a hat soaked liberally with insect repellent.

For my face and hands, I use a light spray. I have found that Off Skintastic is a good middle-of-the-road choice. It does not work for long, but it isn't harsh on my skin. I prefer pumps over lotions and oils only because it is possible to keep your palms and finger tips free of insect repellent so that you can touch things without staining them or eat a snack without the tasty addition of repellent. Even if the bugs do not bother you much, my advice is to bring along some insect repellent, just in case. Even a few biting insects can quickly ruin a beautiful day. I have found spots where the bugs were so thick they would fly into my nose and mouth when I breathed. For those skeptics, grab some shorts and a t–shirt, and I will be glad to take you there!

City Birding

....

Migration at Feeders

In May, there are still a lot of birds to watch for at feeders. One of the most widespread species will be the colourful White Throated Sparrow, along with the Chipping Sparrow. While the White Throated is most prevalent in back yards and woodlands with a lot of broadleaf trees and bush-es, the Chipping Sparrow prefers open areas with scattered evergreens. For this reason, Chipping Sparrows frequently nest in people's yards as this is a perfect place to find an evergreen tree sur-rounded by grass. If you were not lucky enough to see an Indigo Bunting or a Blue Grosbeak in April, your chances of attracting one of these rarities are even greater in May. This is also true for the Rose Breasted Grosbeak.

Female and immature Rose Breasted Grosbeaks with their brown streaked plumage may look similar to large sparrows, but their massive grosbeak bills quickly give them away. Male Rose Breasteds are even more stunning, with a striking black-and-white pattern that is combined with a bright rose–red triangle patch on their upper chest. This triangular patch is widest at the top of the chest and tapers down to a trailing point, vaguely resembling a bleeding heart.

Some believe that sighting a Rose Breasted will bring the observer good luck. It is thought that the person who observes one of these birds can expect someone to be sympathetic to their problems and perhaps even offer a helping hand. Lucky or not, Rose Breasted Grosbeaks are always a thrill to observe. Like Evening Grosbeaks, Rose Breasteds love sunflower seeds but do not travel in large flocks like their cousins. In most cases, they show up at feeders by themselves or occasionally with a mate. In the Metro area, they may be seen throughout the summer months but most frequently visit feeders in April and May, during spring migration.

One of my favourite accounts of a Rose Breasted Grosbeak at a feeder comes from Azor Vienneau. At his house at Lewis Lake, he designed a feeder with a series of wooden bars. The purpose of the feeder was to keep the larger birds out and allow the smaller birds, like the chickadees, a chance to get some food. When the feeder was completed, he placed it in the centre of his picture window and the chickadees quickly took advantage. The feeder successfully kept away the larger birds, until one day a very determined male Rose Breasted Grosbeak managed to squeeze himself through the bars by bracing his feet against a tiny ledge and pushing. Once inside, the grosbeak ate contentedly. However, when he was ready to leave, he no longer fit into the opening he had come through! Fortunately, a sympathetic hand was nearby and the bird was released through the door that was used to fill the feeder. The bird darted away but the story does not end here. The bird continued to feed for a week and a half, squeezing into the feeder and getting released by Mr. Vienneau, who was so moved by the experience that he wrote a poem about it.

> *... And when it was time for the Grosbeak to leave,*
> *a graceful departure it couldn't achieve.*
> *The bars were too tight for a stomach so full,*
> *and nothing would work, neither a push or a pull.*
> *I had to go out and open the door,*
> *and out he came, like a jet with a roar.*
> *I watched him fly off like a shot through the trees,*
> *I'd seen the last of that Grosbeak, I believed.*
> *But in two or three hours he came back to feed,*
> *back in the box to devour the seed.*
> *For a week-and-a-half, he came back for more,*
> *and each time he finished, I opened the door.*
> *He gave such delight to me and my wife,*
> *bringing excitement and change to our life....*

Who knows, perhaps these birds are good luck charms. Other unusual feeder birds in May are White Crowned Sparrow, Brown Thrasher, Scarlet Tanager, and the Northern Oriole.

May is also the time to expect Ruby Throated Hummingbirds. Many people do not realize that they are a common species in the Metro area. In most years, they return to feeders around May 12 but can be seen as early as May 1.

Back yard birders may also notice in May that the normally noisy Blue Jay suddenly becomes quiet and secretive. The reason for this abrupt change of character is that they have started nesting. Enjoy the silence; it will not last long!

Spring Warblers

For many, the best part of spring migration is the
return of the warblers. Warblers spend most of
the year in the tropical and/or subtropical regions
of Central and South America. In spring, like
many species, they migrate northward to find
adequate space for breeding. Of course, not all of
the more than one hundred species of warblers
found in South America move into the temperate
regions of North America to breed. Among those
that do, twenty–two species of warblers come as
far north as the Halifax/Dartmouth region.
Warblers are tiny insect-eating birds. Many
species are greenish in colour with bright yellow
somewhere on their plumage. At least one species
of warbler is present in just about every type of
habitat found within our provincial boundaries.

Woodland areas are especially good places to
look and listen for warblers. In fact, most of the
birds singing in the woods in May and June are
some type of warbler. The males do the singing
to attract females and to declare their territory.
Warblers will use their song to defend their
breeding area from other males of the same
species and will actively chase them away if necessary. However, other species of male warblers are
usually left alone, as long as they are not directly
competing for the same natural resources. In
most cases, the different species of warblers can
coexist in the same area, despite the fact that they
are all insect-eating birds, as they have each
developed specialized feeding methods and tastes.
The majority of warblers arrive in Nova Scotia in
May. Two species, Palm and Yellow Rumped
Warblers, are first seen in late April.

Certainly the return of the warblers in May is
one of the highlights of the spring migration,
especially at those spots where more than a dozen
warblers can be seen and/or heard at one time.
Fortunately, the Metro area has plenty of good

spots to watch and listen to warblers. Some of the most accessible locations are the Frog Pond and Fleming Park, Shubie Park, Blue Mountain Drive Trail, the Public Gardens (in early May), and Hartlen Point. There are also numerous woodland trails where a variety of warblers may be encountered. To locate the greatest number of warblers, go early in the morning, when they do most of their singing. Shortly after dawn is the best time, but if this is too early, try to get out by 9:00 A.M. After 10:00 A.M. the warblers sing less, and after 11:00 A.M. things get really quiet.

The Public Gardens is strictly a transient warbler location—any of the twenty–two species of warblers may be seen there in May, but after May, when migration is over, very few warblers will be present. In fact, once summer arrives, about the only warbler species you are likely to see at the Public Gardens is the Yellow Warbler, the most common one inside Halifax city limits. The female is the only all-yellow warbler found in typical urban settings. The male is completely yellow as well, except for some light reddish streaks over the front of his chest and belly. Yellow Warblers can be distinguished from other yellow birds, like the American Goldfinch, by their short, thin bill—the trademark of all North American warblers, except the Yellow Breasted Chat. Yellow Warblers are so common in the city that if you take a careful walk around your neighbourhood, you will probably see one.

All of the above mentioned locations, with the exception of the Public Gardens, have both transient and breeding warbler populations. The Frog Pond and Fleming Park (also called The Dingle), are linked through connecting pathways. This is an excellent location to view our common warblers. In the deciduous sections, Yellow Warblers, Black and White Warblers, and American Redstarts are regulars. Watch the pond side bushes for the Common Yellowthroat. In the evergreens,

Northern Parulas, Yellow Rumped, Black Throated Green, and Magnolia Warblers can be found. There is also a possibility of Nashville and Tennessee Warblers in the park, but these are more common in younger deciduous woods, such as those at Shubie Park, one of the best spots to see the Chestnut Sided Warbler as well. Chestnut Sided Warblers build their nests in young broadleaf trees and greet the passerby with a pleasant "please, please, please to meet cha."

The Blue Mountain Drive Trail (also called the Kearney Lake Trail), is a good place for some of the rarer warblers. A relatively short walk in the trail will take you to a power line. Along the power line or in the adjacent clear cuts is the place to look for one or two pairs of Mourning Warblers, and lots of Palm Warblers. Just past the power line on the main trail, you will come to a hill of large hardwoods, pause there to see the Ovenbird and beautiful Black Throated Blue Warbler. As you walk the trail, watch for mature evergreen trees, the home of Bay Breasted and Blackburnian Warblers. The Blackburnian Warbler is a "must see" bird as the intensity of the flaming orange of the head and throat just cannot be portrayed by a picture. Another evergreen inhabiting bird species that lives along the trail is the Cape May Warbler, which favours a mixture of young fir and spruce trees.

The Northern Waterthrush is a species that can be encountered on this trail but nearby is an even better location to see this bird and another species, the Canada Warbler. From the Kearney Lake Trail, drive along to Kearney Lake Road to the Hammonds Plains Road and turn left. Within a mile you will see a big blue milk carton on the right-hand side of the road, the Farmer's Dairy sign. It marks the entrance of the road leading to their factory. On the left side of this road there is a noticeable section of swampy woodland and dark tangles, a favourite habitat of both the

Northern Waterthrush and the Canada Warbler. A few metres farther is a dirt road, which is a great place to walk if you wish to increase your chances of seeing these two species and other warblers as well.

About the only warbler that one can not find breeding inside the city limits is the Blackpoll Warbler. Blackpolls, with their black cap and white cheek look similar to Black Capped Chickadees. Their preferred habitat is low-lying coniferous areas, such as black spruce bogs, so look for these at such locations.

At Hartlen Point, Blackpolls breed in small numbers, as do the hard-to-find Wilson's Warblers that love to frequent swampy low-lying areas with mixed patches of alder, birch, or willow. Of course, most of our common species of warblers can also be found breeding at Hartlen Point. Nearly every birder has favourite locations to look for warblers; the ones mentioned above are good spots to become familiar with each of Metro's twenty–two breeding species.

Yellow Shafted Flickers

The Northern Flicker is a species of woodpecker that has two distinct colour forms. At one time, it was believed they were two separate species, the Red Shafted Flicker and the Yellow Shafted Flicker. The latter is the subspecies of the Northern Flicker that is found in the Metro area and most of eastern North America. Flickers are generally found here only in the summer as they feed primarily on insects. They sometimes visit people's yards to catch ants, their favourite insects. They catch them by digging directly on top of or beside an anthill. It is fascinating to see these birds in action, and to see how they withstand the counterattack of the ants, which is still a mystery. Another truly amazing aspect about these birds is that they are the only ones in the world to have feathers with yellow shafts. Most other species of birds have clear or white shafted feathers, which is why the name, Yellow Shafted Flicker, suits. If you spot a flicker on the ground, check the location after it leaves. You are likely to find ants, and if you are lucky, one of their unique feathers.

Yellow Shafted Flickers breed around Metro from April to September. In spring and summer, its call is one of the loudest in the woods. In fact, it is often mistaken for a Pileated Woodpecker. To distinguish the two, remember that the Pileated's call starts slow and speeds up, while the flicker's song starts and stays fast. If you are not able to tell which species is calling, just follow the sound, and you will probably see the bird. This is especially true if it is a Yellow Shafted, as flickers often call repeatedly for quite a long time.

Sex-crazed Robins

Heather Proudfoot of Dartmouth is just one of a number of people who have had a problem with American Robins fluttering up against their windows at this time of year. Although it may appear that the robins are trying to get in out of the cool weather, the real drive behind this odd phenomenon is sex.

Each year, a small percentage of American Robins experience an overactive sex drive. This exaggerated hormonal heightening can occur in male or female robins, but it is more frequently observed in males partly because they do most of the defending of the pair's breeding territory surrounding the nest. Robins, like most birds, set up a defensive zone to help guarantee that there will be enough food available to feed themselves and their young when they hatch. This means keeping other robins.

The male's role is also to keep other male robins away from his mate. It is common to see them chasing away other male robins and fairly common to see the female robins chasing their own female kind. Occasionally, an individual will become overzealous and chase anything in sight, including his own reflection.

Upon seeing another male robin in his territory, the first thing a male does is sing, thus indicating his claim. In most cases, this is all that is necessary to get rid of an intruder. However, if singing does not work, he will fly towards the invader and scold him. This often leads to a short chase, resulting in the trespasser leaving the territory of the defending male. If the encroacher still does not leave, the same actions are repeated a number of times, but if he stands his ground, that part of the territory can become his.

In defending territories, intimidation techniques are usually sufficient. Occasionally though, some robins will physically attack other robins. They become so blinded by their aggression that they will spend two or three hours a day fighting with their own reflections in windows and car mirrors. After a couple of weeks this behaviour usually disappears. This could be the result of their sexual aggression subsiding, or perhaps they finally realize they are wrestling with themselves. The Dark Eyed Junco is another species that frequently exhibits this type of overactive behaviour. If you have problems with a robin or any other species fluttering up against your windows, you can stop it by placing something on the outside of the window that will break up the reflection. Specialty stores sell items called Bird Savers for this purpose.

Spring Migration

While rainy weather can hasten migration in April, it can slow it down in May. A typical example occurred in the spring of 1993. In my personal notes I wrote, "Spring migration continues to be slowed down by damp, cool weather.

However, there was a noticeable change which took place in both birds and weather between May 7 and 8. On the seventh, I made a stop at two birding locations in Bedford, and found only two species of warblers. The following day at the same locations, I rapidly encountered eight species of warblers." Later, I learned that on the same date, other birders in Halifax, Hants, and Lunenburg Counties also recognized a noticeable surge in the number of warbler species present.

Bug Lovers Beware!

If you love bugs and enjoy having them around your property, do not feed the birds this summer! Recent studies have shown that yards which have active feeders in them, almost always have fewer insects than those without. Strangely enough, instead of feeders discouraging the birds from eating your favourite insects, they actually encourage them.

Here's how the phenomenon works. Feeder birds usually have four to eight young. Those young must grow quickly enough to leave the nest within two to four weeks. To facilitate this rapid growth rate, the nestlings as a group must consume hundreds of insects per day. Finding enough food for themselves and for their young is a time-consuming process, which scientists estimate takes about 90 per cent of the adult bird's waking hours. To conserve time, the parents will travel only as far as necessary to find food. A feeder is a great time-saving device for the adults, as it is a place where they can quickly access an abundant source of seeds for self consumption. To further conserve time, the parents will often collect insects for their young in the general area of the feeder instead of burning time and energy to fly elsewhere. In short, feeders decrease the number of insects on your property by encouraging birds to frequent your vicinity.

Northern Orioles

Northern Orioles are medium-size, bright orange
birds, famous for their unusual pensile nests.
Orioles generally return to Nova Scotia each
May. Males arrive about two weeks before the
females and set up remarkably small territories.
Once paired, the couple keep in constant visual
or auditory contact, but the nest-building is
done wholly by the female. She may fix up her
nest from the previous year to reuse it or may
tear it or other nests apart to gain material for a
new one. The long woven sack of a nest is sus-
pended like a pendulum, typically high up in a
tall tree with drooping branches. The eggs are
incubated for about two weeks. After hatching,
the young birds are quite noisy in the nest. They
grow quickly and are ready to leave their abode
twelve to fourteen days later. It is at this time
that the female leaves the young birds to roam
widely, while undergoing a moult of her
feathers. During this period, the conspicuous
fledglings are cared for by the male for about
two weeks. The young birds are then ready to
leave the male and fend for themselves. They
start to drift southward while beginning their
moult. The male will remain on the territory
until he finishes his moult, and then he, too, will
head south.

Orioles feed on a variety of insects but are
especially fond of tent caterpillars and potato
beetles. They are also attracted to cherries,
grapes, oranges, and sugar water. Diane
Henriksen of Bedford was faithfully putting out
orange halves for years, in hopes of seeing a
Northern Oriole. "It is just part of my feeder
routine," she says. "Before I carry out my bucket
of seed, I just automatically slice in half one apple
and one orange to to take outside." When asked
why she has stuck with it for so long, she replied
that the robins like to nibble on the fruit, and of

course, there is always the chance that a Northern Oriole may show up some day. Indeed, one May a Northern Oriole not only showed up, it picked an orange half almost completely clean. Persistence does pay!

In Sackville, Don and Lois Codling had an unusual Northern Oriole appear briefly in their apple tree one spring. Orioles are often associated with fruit trees as they enjoy eating the fruit and extracting nectar from their blossoms, plus their favourite food, tent caterpillars, is often found in such trees. What made this bird different was that instead of being orange and black it was bright yellow and black. This abnormal colour occurs only rarely in Northern Orioles and is believed to be the result of a lack of red pigment in the feathers. Even a chestnut-coloured oriole was seen one spring in Metro by Christine Aikenhead at her home in Williams Lake. In this case, though, the bird was a normal-coloured male Orchard Oriole, which are rarely seen in the Metro area. Most sightings of Orchard Orioles in the province occur in the spring.

Scarlet Tanagers

Scarlet Tanagers are brightly coloured birds that spend most of the year in tropical habitats from Mexico to Brazil. In the summer, they travel northward to breed and can be found nesting in Nova Scotia in small numbers. The best time to watch for these birds is during their spring migration in April and May. The unbelievable colour of the male Scarlet Tanager in spring has made this bird one of my all-time favourite species. The flaming scarlet red plumage of the male is so brilliant that it is unsurpassed by any other North American bird. In fact, this bird's red feathers are so dazzling that they appear to be glowing. To add to the impressive effect, the Scarlet has jet black wings that contrast in such a way as to emphasize its red plumage. The intensity of the Scarlet Tanager's colour is not matched by even the brightest Cardinal, which looks dull in comparison. I am not alone in this viewpoint.

When Peter Kerswell saw his first Scarlet Tanager in Tantallon, he commented that this bird was brighter and more beautiful than any of the magnificent birds he observed in the jungles of Africa. Until you see one of these birds yourself, it is difficult to imagine how breathtaking they can be. Even the best photographs in the finest books do not do justice to this bird's colouring.

Despite its bright colours, it is amazing how hard it can be sometimes to spot a male tanager, but one look at this bird can make the effort worthwhile. Scarlet Tanagers are most often heard before they are seen, so listen for the song and watch for a slow-moving bird high up in the tree tops. A Scarlet Tanager sounds like a robin singing with a sore throat, so take notice of the "Rs" in its song. The Scarlet Tanager also gives a diagnostic "chip–burr" call.

Like its cousin, the Summer Tanager, Scarlet Tanagers are attracted to oak and other tall decid-uous trees, where they forage in the upper canopy for a variety of insects, including the occasional bee. In the South, locals often refer to tanagers as the "bee–bird" because of their fondness for bees, wasps, and hornets. Scarlet and Summer Tanagers are highly skilled at catching wasps in the air and will even raid hives in search of the tasty insects. Although rarer, a few Summer Tanagers may also be seen in the spring in Metro. The males are entirely rose red in colour and have large pale bills. Females have the same pale bill but have a greenish-yellow plumage, which is slightly darker above than below. Both sexes are 18 cm to 19 cm (7 in. to 7.5 in.) long and are usually spotted in the upper canopy of forest and the tops of tall trees. The song of the male sounds very similar to that of the robin but is slightly faster paced.

Most spring sightings of both species occur at feeders. Although they will eat seeds, their favourite hand-outs are fruit. Oranges work well but bananas are best.

Further Afield

....

Piping Plovers

With the arrival of April, Metro's white sand beaches have become home to the rare and endangered Piping Plover. Nesting begins about mid-May. Each summer, volunteers from across the Maritimes work hard to prevent the extinction of the Piping Plover, a bird that is listed as endangered in both Canada and the United States. Each spring and summer, hundreds of Piping Plover eggs are destroyed accidentally by people visiting maritime beaches, and the Metro area is no exception.

Fortunately, this is a species that each of us can easily help in a variety of ways. First of all, become aware of what a Piping Plover looks like. Adults are the colour of dry white sand and blend in well with this beach habitat, so well in fact that they are difficult to see, especially when they are standing still, and sometimes even when they are running. With binoculars, you will see that Piping Plovers have a black band across the forehead and a second black band across the breast. In some birds, this breast band is incomplete. These plovers have yellowish–orange legs and a bill of the same colour with a black tip. To the unaided eye, their plumage provides excellent camouflage in this sandy habitat. Even experienced birders have a hard time spotting them.

The very similar looking Semipalmated Plover is often mistaken for a Piping Plover by the inexperienced. Sanderlings and other sandpipers, too, are often thought to be Piping Plovers when they are seen on white sand beaches. You can avoid making these mistakes by remembering that unless you are having a very difficult time seeing the bird, it is probably *not* a Piping Plover. Also remember that Piping Plovers are rare.

Once you know what adult Piping Plovers look like, you can help protect them by not disturbing the birds. When parents are off the nest, the eggs can easily chill, overheat, or fall prey to predators. Keeping skittish parents away from the nest—their natural defence is to leave the nest to distract predators away from it—is one of the ways that beach goers unknowingly contribute to the decline of Piping Plovers.

You can also avoid stepping on the Piping Plover's nest, which is more difficult than it first sounds. The Piping Plover's nest can be any one of the hundreds of tiny depressions found on the soft white sand of a beach. To make things worse, their eggs are almost invisible against the sand. Generally, most Piping Plovers make their nest along the top third of the beach in order to avoid flooding. So when walking or sunbathing, avoid the top of the beach. Softly whistled notes or birds pretending injury may warn you of nest locations. Instead of looking for the nest, respond by carefully walking to then along the water's edge to avoid crushing the well-camouflaged eggs and leaving a trail for nighttime predators.

Garbage left lying on the beach will attract predators of the Piping Plover, such as gulls and crows. Rats, skunks, raccoons, and foxes are nighttime scavengers that will also be encouraged to spend more time on a beach if they find edible litter, so try not to leave behind any debris. You may even want to contribute to the Piping Plover's longevity by picking up any trash you spot on the beach.

Fortunately, Piping Plovers use only a small portion of the beach, so with a little care on our part, it can be relatively easy for both plovers and people to share the same beach. To foster this sort of symbiotic relationship, volunteers called Piping Plover Guardians are working on a number of beaches in the Maritimes, helping people learn about and appreciate the Piping Plover. If you want to become involved with them, write to the Halifax Field Naturalists, c/o Nova Scotia Museum, 1747 Summer Street, Halifax, Nova Scotia, B3H 3A6.

The person who initiated the project is Stephen Flemming, a biologist who is interested in birds and has done a fair amount of work with the Piping Plovers over the past few years in the Maritimes. Stephen said he first got the idea for the project in 1991. It stemmed from what had happened to the Piping Plovers the preceding year in the Maritimes and across North America. Prior to 1991, Nova Scotia had been working on Piping Plover programs for several years along with Prince Edward Island among other provinces and some states, but none of these efforts had been coordinated. It was decided in 1991 that an international survey of all known Piping Plover breeding areas would be done simultaneously to give a better idea of how many Piping Plovers existed in North America. The survey showed that there were only 5,422 left on the continent and that roughly 10 per cent were found in the Maritimes. When you look at plover population dynamics, that is a very significant portion of the population. Studies done in Massachusetts have indicated that in order to maintain the Piping Plover population in the Maritimes, we need each pair to produce a mini-mum of 0.9 chicks, almost one chick per pair.

The objective of the Piping Plover Guardianship Program is not only to reach that reproduction goal but to reach a point at which we can see that each pair is producing at least one and a half chicks. Researchers feel this sort of accom-plishment would lead to a rapid increase in the

Piping Plover population. Locally, the program is making a difference, but it needs more help, and most importantly, the cooperation of the general public.

Keep in mind that most of our Piping Plovers arrive by mid-April, although a few appear as early as late March, and nesting begins about mid-May. The plovers lay four cream–coloured eggs flecked with small brown and black spots, allowing them to blend in perfectly with the background sand. If the first nest fails, the plover will try again but will lay only two or three eggs, in which case there may still be nests present on the beach as late as June or July.

Young pipers can run within hours after hatching, but if they are forced to run too much they will burn more energy than they can consume and will die. This is common amongst two-week-old chicks, for example, when they are chased by unleashed dogs whose owners are completely unaware that their pet is doing any harm.

Beaches known to be important to Piping Plovers locally are Conrads, Martinique, Rainbow Haven, Clam Harbour, Stoney, and sometimes Lawrencetown. So please, be particularly cautious when visiting these beaches. Many of them will have signs, helping people to avoid stepping on specific nests. If you visit a beach and see Piping Plovers but no nest warning signs, please call the Halifax Field Naturalists, the Canadian Wildlife Service, or the Department of Natural Resources.

Bay Breasted Warblers

Twenty-two species of warblers breed in Nova Scotia; however, some, like the Bay Breasted Warbler, are seen only occasionally during the summer months. Unlike most warblers, which have enjoyable songs, the Bay Breasted's song consists of several thin, high-pitched notes. Since many warblers are first located and identified by their sounds, the Bay Breasted's rather drab song means it often goes undetected by birders. Bay Breasted Warblers also have a tendency to avoid settled areas, choosing instead to frequent the tree tops of coniferous forests. They are most common on Cape Breton Island but occur throughout the province, including the Eastern Shore. Two reliable places to look for these birds are in the woodlands of East Chezzetcook and those in Goodwood where they breed in small numbers; they breed at other locations in the greater Metro area but are difficult to detect.

Kings of the Forest

Most people have heard the song of the Ruby Crowned Kinglet, as it is one of the loudest vocalisations rendered in Nova Scotia woods. However, only a few non–birders have actually seen the mighty songster; despite his volume, the Ruby Crowned Kinglet is not much bigger than a hummingbird at only 10 cm to 11 cm (3.9 in. to 4.3 in.) in length and weighing between 4.5 g and 7.5 g (less than 1 oz.). You can recognize Ruby Crowns by watching for a small, greenish-coloured bird with a bold, white eye ring. A further clue to its identity will be its extremely active nature. Trying to identify this tiny songster by its ruby-coloured crown can be difficult as the bird's rapid movements make it tricky to keep it within your binocular's limited field of view. The best time to look for the ruby-coloured crown is when the bird is singing from a stationary perch or when the bird is excited or upset, resulting in feathers of the crown to being fully raised and extended.

For a real challenge, try finding a Ruby Crowned Kinglet's nest. They breed in coniferous or mixed forests. Their nest is constructed mostly of mosses and lichen and hangs like a pendulum from the branches of a tree. The nest is usually built close to the tree trunk and can range in height from 0.5 m to 33 m (2 ft. to 108 ft.) above the ground. The inside cavity of the nest is usually large enough to completely conceal the incubating female and to provide enough room for five to nine baby birds. Ruby Crowneds lay an average of eight eggs, a surprising number for such a small bird. Nest construction generally begins near May 1, and the last egg is laid in the nest by May 24. Ruby Crowned Kinglets head south again in the fall, with the peak of their migration occurring during the first two weeks of October.

However, a second species of kinglet, the Golden Crowned, can be found in Nova Scotia year-round. Like their cousin the Ruby Crowned, they are very active birds, often seen hovering at the tips of tree branches, gathering insects. The Golden Crowned is also especially fond of plant lice and benefits many trees by eating the eggs of bark beetles. Golden Crowned Kinglets are fonder of pure evergreen habitats than the Ruby Crowneds. Although their nests are very similar on the outside, the Golden Crowneds usually line their nest with feathers of other birds. Robie Tufts, the leading bird authority in Nova Scotia for many years, found that the feathers of Ruffed Grouse were used most often. Tufts also reported that while the female was incubating, the male was often seen nearby, quietly muttering to himself. The female would join him about every fifteen minutes to be fed, at which time his voice would perk up considerably.

As a child, before I had a good pair of binoculars, I was often frustrated by futile attempts to see which birds were making those high-pitched noises in the tops of evergreens. It seemed that no matter how long I spent staring into those tree tops, I could not clearly see those birds. Like most people, whether they realize it or not, I usually heard these mysterious birds on just about every woodland walk I took as these birds are common in our coniferous woodlands. Eventually, I learned to recognize those high-pitched sounds as the Golden Crowned Kinglet. Now their tiny tree-top twitterings make my winter days warmer and my summer days brighter.

Egrets and Herons

Egrets are typically thought of as white, heronlike birds found in the southern states; however, they can also be seen in the Metro area. April and May are two of the best months for seeing egrets and other species of southern herons. For example, more Great Egrets have been sighted in Metro in

April than any other month. Many of the sightings of Snowy Egrets and Glossy Ibis have also occurred in April with an even greater number of these birds seen in May. May is also the choice time for spotting Cattle Egrets, Little Blue Herons, Tricolored Herons, Green Herons, and Black Crowned Night Herons.

Besides these native herons of North America, another species that is worth looking for is the Little Egret. They are widely distributed natives of the Old World. Little Egrets spend their winters in South Africa and migrate to Europe between mid-March and late May. European sources report it is common for this species to wander extensively off course during migration. So it is not surprising that this species was discovered in Nova Scotia in 1989. In fact, it is probable that this species was present in Metro long before then; however, the Little Egret is so similar in appearance to the Snowy Egret, that it can be easily overlooked. It is only during their spring breeding plumage that the two species can be distinguished, and even then, they appear very similar. Both the Snowy and the Little Egret are small, pure white herons with black bills, dark legs, and yellow feet. A closer inspection will reveal that the Little Egret in breeding plumage has two long white plumes extending from the back of its head, while the Snowy sports several shorter head plumes. One may also notice that the area on the Snowy Egret's face between the eye and the base of the bill is bright yellow, while the same area on the Little Egret is greenish blue or orange. Another subtle difference between the two is that the Snowy Egret always shows at least a little yellow extending from the feet onto the back of the legs.

Since that first sighting of a Little Egret near Halifax in 1989, they have been spotted in Nova Scotia every spring. Watch for these birds when birding on the Eastern Shore or along the coast towards Crystal Crescent Beach. Little Egrets are truly fascinating birds to watch. I still vividly remember my first sighting. It was a cold, dark, rainy Sunday, but despite the miserable weather, the beauty and grace of this bird lifted my spirits. I especially enjoyed the stratagem the bird employed to catch minnows. He would stir up the bottom of the pond with his feet, causing the minnows to move from their hiding places into the open water, where he could snatch them up. It is said that Snowy Egrets employ the same technique.

The Main Breeding Season

....

Home Sweet Home

The spring migration grinds to a halt in early
June. By mid-June even the newest arrivals have
begun nesting procedures. In fact, more birds
begin to build their nests in June than any other
month. This is the main reason many of the birds
that first arrived in April and May are more easily
observed in June. They have established their
individual territories and are vocalising their
chosen locations.

This is a good time to learn your bird sounds
if you haven't done so already. Many birders
start to learn, or in most cases reacquaint themselves, with the songs of various species as early
as March. The goal is to become familiar with
the way each bird sounds in order to recognize
them quickly when they return in the spring.
This is done by listening to taped recordings of
birds. There are several good tapes that help a

person learn bird songs. On these educational tapes, the name of the species proceeds the singing bird. If you have a good auditory memory, these tapes are all you need to begin to learn bird vocalisations. If not, you can also purchase tapes with instructional information on how to learn bird sounds. Not only do these teach you how to distinguish similar sounding birds, but they group them together on the tapes so that you can hear the differences for yourself. It takes a little effort to learn bird sounds, but it will open a new world of possibilities.

Many of those new to birding are not aware that the term "bird-watching" is now almost archaic. Sure, birders still enjoy watching birds, but the term "bird-watcher" came from an era in which most people first identified birds by sight. Nowadays, most birders first recognize birds by sound. The latter method makes bird detection and identification much easier as you almost always hear a bird before you see it. In fact, birders may only see about a quarter of the birds they hear. A person who knows their bird sounds sees a greater variety of birds than those who don't. When out birding, they save time by selecting from the sounds which of the birds present they would like to see—the ears, not the eyes, are the birder's most valuable sense.

An easy way to start identifying bird sounds is to begin with the birds you hear near your home. Most of the songs will be those of common species, but they are also the birds that you hear most often when you are out birding. By learning the most common sounds, you are better able to identify the less common ones of rarer species. As well, common birds are good to practise on because most are fairly approachable, so you can hear them again and again.

As with other aspects of birding, keeping notes on the sounds you hear and identify will greatly increase your ability to learn and remember bird songs. Most people begin with identifying by sight the birds they are hearing. Next, they describe on paper the way the song sounds to them. This is important as each species' song sounds different to different people, so describe the song in whatever manner will help you remember it. Do not be discouraged if the next time the bird sounds different to you. For example, Dark Eyed Juncos have a very musical, bell–like trill, but they can also use a dryer trill. The important thing to remember is the similarities not the differences. One of our most varied songsters is the American Redstart. The Redstart regularly uses seven or eight different song patterns, but birders have learned to identify the American Redstart's songs by focusing on the quality of its voice, not just the patterns. The Redstart's squeaky voice is the similarity that gives it away no matter how many different song patterns it uses.

Learning bird sounds can help you to see a greater variety of birds or just help you to have some fun. Imagine how impressed your family and friends will be when you take a quick glance at a tiny bird singing high up in a tree and say, "Looks like a Yellow Rumped Warbler to me!" With a second glance you can add, "Yep, I can see the yellow rump." They may not believe you at first, but if they double-check the identification with binoculars and a field guide, they will be singing a different tune. At this point, you can choose to enlighten them or leave them basking in the awe of your greatness!

Whether or not you choose to learn bird sounds in June, there are still plenty of birds to see. In fact, there are so many reliable birds around that zealous birders often choose June to conduct their "big day," a twenty-four-hour period in which a group or groups of birders try to find as many species of birds as possible. This is often done to help a charity or just for fun. These big day events can easily turn up over a hundred species on a June day. The current challenge is to see if a 150 species can be seen in twenty-four hours. Many believe it should be possible.

City Birding

....

Summer Shorebirds

Six species of shorebirds breed in the Metro area, four of which can be seen easily in June, the fifth with a little patience. The only species that is difficult to find is the American Woodcock. (See March's "Woodcock" to fully understand why.)

Our most widespread sandpiper in the Metro area is the Spotted Sandpiper. They may be seen walking along the shores of any of our Metro lakes and streams. Their peculiar habit of teetering on rocks as if they are about to fall into the water separates these birds from all others. Its flight is distinctive as well. Instead of typical up-and-down flaps, they fly with the wings curved downward, using rapid, shallow, vibrating beats.

Another city shorebird is the Killdeer. In the country, Killdeers nest in rocky farm fields. Inside our city limits, they are most common in industrial parks, where they can find the stony fields to which they have become accustom. In Ontario, breeding Killdeers are so hard-pressed to find rocky areas that they lay their eggs on highway shoulders. In the States, some Killdeers have been found nesting on the gravel rooftops of buildings. The presence of numerous small stones is essential for Killdeer nests as their speckled eggs need to be camouflaged against a stony background. Killdeers are members of the Plover family and can be easily identified by the two wide, dark bands crossing the white chest. Each year, a few people mistake them for Piping Plovers. Be assured that the latter are found only on white sandy beaches. (Conrads Beach has become the only local beach that has breeding Piping Plovers every summer; however, they may be seen on any of our white sandy beaches in June.)

Conrads Beach is also a great place to see the Willet. These active shorebirds can be recognized by the wide, white wing stripe that is readily seen in flight. These birds are our most common coastal shorebirds in June. They build their nests on dry hummocks in any of the salt marshes along our coast. The Common Snipe chooses freshwater or brackish marshes in which to breed. Although they may be observed probing the muddy areas of these marshes, they are more frequently seen calling loudly from a perch or doing their courtship flight above the marsh. A good place to look for these birds is the West Lawrencetown Marsh, a traditional breeding site of the Common Snipe. After the Woodcock, the Common Snipe is our most difficult summer shorebird to locate.

Birdnappers

Starlings and robins may nest anywhere from one to five times during the breeding season. In the Metro area, both species normally nest up to three times in the summer months. By mid–June the first crop of starlings and robins have hatched and are out of the nest as are the young of a few other species. As a result, this is the time of year when people often find baby birds or have young ones brought to them.

If you happen upon a baby bird, check first to see if it is mobile (i.e., able to run or fly). If the bird is immobile, the nest has to be close, though, it may be well concealed. Look carefully for the nest and place the young bird back in it. Handling the bird will not cause the parents to abandon their young because of human scent. This is a common misconception that is often passed on to keep children from handling or touching baby birds. The truth is that most birds have almost no sense of smell; however, if too much time is spent at the nest site, the parents may abandon it.

If the young bird is mobile, move away from the area as quickly as possible; it is common for the young of many birds to leave the nest before they can fly. Parent birds are often nearby gathering food and usually will not return to feed the young when a person is present. Cats or dogs can prevent the parents from returning. You can help by keeping the area clear and watching the baby bird from a distance. If after an hour or so, no parent bird returns, the young bird may be lost, but this rarely happens. In most cases, they are actually "birdnapped" by well-meaning individuals.

Remember, the chance of survival is extremely low for a baby bird raised outside its natural environment. The first difficulty to arise is providing the young bird with a nutritionally balanced diet. Parents may feed their young up to three hundred different species of insects, which are high in protein. Human care–givers, unless they are exceptional, just can not match that type of service; however, protein-rich foods, such as hard-boiled egg yolk and fresh ground beef, can be used as temporary replacements. Unfeathered chicks need to be fed once every half-hour during the daylight hours; once an hour if they are feathered. If you are not prepared to take on this responsibility, leave the bird where it is as you are unlikely to find any organization or an individual who is able to do it for you.

City Birds

My favourite definition of a weed is simply "a normal plant or flower that is growing where it is not wanted." In Nebraska, corn-growers are plagued by a plant they consider the scourge of the earth. This killer weed grows faster and taller than the corn, depriving it of its much-needed sunshine. In the east, we call this "weed" the sunflower and marvel at how the heads of the flowers turn hourly to always directly face the sun.

We also have "weeds" in the world of birds. These undesirables may have some bad habits, but they are not bad birds; they are just species growing in a place where they are not wanted. Some of these are birds that were introduced purposely by humans into new areas of the world. Since these species had no natural enemies at the new locations to help keep their population under control, they quickly spread. The European Starlings, or "sky rats" as they are often called, are a typical example, but like them or not, they are here to stay! We must learn how to live with these birds by adapting our lifestyles to accommodate other creatures, as other animals must do. In the case of the starlings, many people use birdhouses and feeders that do not allow starlings to dominate. In the summertime, starlings are welcome to use many people's lawns; their narrow, pointed bills are excellent tools to extract lawn-damaging insects, such as cinch bugs and cutworms.

Pigeons, too, will take over feeders and yards if permitted. Avoiding cheap mixes and keeping your bird feed in feeders that don't allow them access are the keys to preventing this problem. Pigeons are not welcome at my feeders, but a visit to a city park would not be the same without them, where feeding the pigeons is fun for children of all ages. Watching the antics of courting pigeons is always enjoyable. In May or June, the Public Gardens is a great place to see males trying to impress the females by puffing out their neck feathers and strutting around with their tails dragging, fan-shaped, on the ground. Watch for wing clapping as well. Researchers have found that sexually active pigeons make a clapping sound with their wings in flight. These happy claps can be easily heard and seen. Books such as *The Stokes Nature Guides to Bird Behaviour* are excellent volumes if you would like to better understand the actions of pigeons and other birds.

Pigeons are not stupid birds, as many once thought. If that were the case, they would not be able to survive in such large numbers in a predominantly man–made environment. I once live-trapped a pigeon at my feeders when I lived in Dartmouth. I drove to Halifax and released it in the Public Gardens. (Don't tell anyone!) In order to recognize the bird if it came back, I placed a small dot of blue paint in one corner of its tail. Two weeks passed and there was no sign of him, so I drove back to the Public Gardens. There he was, happily feeding only a few feet from where I had released him. A dumb bird? I think not. If someone placed me in a garden paradise, I wouldn't be anxious to leave either!

Another species that has adjusted well to the Metro way of life is the English Sparrow, also called the House Sparrow. One summer day I was catching a quick meal at the McDonald's in Bedford. I was happily munching on my Big Mac, when I noticed that the House Sparrows had learned a cute trick. They would hop up onto the hood of a car and then move right up to the windshield and peer in. If you ignored them, like I did at first, they would give the occasional chirp to draw your attention. They then would give you the best sad puppy–dog expression they could muster. Each time I glanced their way, I noticed one or two birds eyeing my burger, while others watched my every move. Their little eyes followed each piece of food from my hand to my mouth. Finally, I folded under the pressure and threw them a few french fries. After talking to others, I learned that the House Sparrows at the Chickenburger, another Bedford restaurant, have learned to prompt people with the same manoeuvres.

At the Burger King in Halifax, I am told that if you park your car to eat, almost instantly, Ring Billed Gulls arrive out of nowhere to stand patiently nearby, waiting for a hand-out. The McDonald's on Main Street in Dartmouth was famous in the early eighties as the most reliable place in the province to find Ring Billed Gulls. They have adjusted so well to city life that they have become the most common "seagull" in Metro parking lots. These faster and more agile relatives of the Herring Gull have replaced the larger and more awkward gulls at such locations.

Of course, the master adapter is the American Crow. As if it were a game of chess, crows have countered the actions of humankind for centuries and will probably continue to do so. Growing up, my father would tell us children of an experience he had as a teenager one summer while visiting relatives on Cape Sable Island. He had set out near dawn to look for a cow that had gone missing the night before. The early morning fog had enveloped the island in a thick blanket, transforming once-familiar objects into mysterious shapes. The ghostlike veil also made it difficult to see very far in any one direction. He began his task by checking the fence line. As he was searching, he thought he heard someone nearby say, "Hello Walter." He was quite surprised as he had believed he was all alone in the field. Looking around, he expected to see the person who had spoken, but he could see no one. Deciding that it must have been just the wind and his imagination, he continued on. After a few steps, he heard again a strange sounding voice saying, "Hello Walter." He stopped dead in his tracks and took a good long look around. There was definitely no person present. In fact, the only other living creature visible through the swirling fog was a big black crow peering at him from the nearby fence. Having grown up hearing numerous maritime ghost stories, he wasted no time getting back to the house. Once safely inside, he related his story to his cousin. She laughed and told him that a local man had a pet crow, which he had taught to talk. That man's name was Walter.

Although crows do not have tongues evolved for speech, there are several stories of crows learning to speak. In the Metro area, Andrea MacIvor had an interesting experience with a flock of crows that came to her Portuguese Cove property. One morning, she was busy filling her bird feeders when she heard someone say, "Hello," but the voice came from above. She looked up, and to her delight, there was an American Crow looking at her, saying hello. She immediately rushed into the house to get her mother, Irma Warrington. They both marvelled at the soft, gentle "hello" of the bird, so unlike the harsh cawing most often associated with these birds. Ms. MacIvor spent five years saying hello to the crows in her area, but this was the first time that one had greeted her in this manner. Such stories make it easy to believe that even our most common birds have a lot to offer.

A Chance Encounter

Flickers, like most woodpeckers, are generally considered a solitary species, but that does not mean they forget to look out for their own kind. Rich Peckham of Bedford found out first-hand just how strong a bond can exist between solitary species. One day he was birding in Admirals Rock Park in Bedford, when he spotted a Sharp Shinned Hawk chasing a Northern Flicker. Sharp Shinned Hawks are one of the very few birds of prey that are skilled at hunting birds in the woods. Their round-tip wings allow them to chase birds through the thickest underbrush. This particular Sharp Shinned was in the process of bearing down on the Flicker, getting closer and closer, until he was merely centimetres from his victim. He extended his scalpel–like talons, but just as he was about to strike, the Flicker made an unexpected last-minute manoeuvre and escaped. Within seconds the hawk was once again hot on its heels. The Flicker cried out in alarm and suddenly a few other Northern Flickers appeared, and then a few more.

Soon the Sharp Shinned found himself outnumbered and broke off the pursuit. The Sharpie landed in a nearby tree to plan his next move. He realized that the Flickers were joining him there and not just one or two; he was surrounded by several Flickers. He reacted quickly by diving towards one of them. The Flicker fled deeper into the woods, but a terrible shrieking sound indicated that the Sharpie, with his lightning speed, had struck. Once again, the Sharp Shinned came into sight, but his talons were empty.

By then the woods were literally alive with angry Flickers! The Sharpie and the Flickers eyed one another, and the chase resumed. This time it was the Sharp Shinned out in front with an angry mob on his tail. With a powerful burst of speed, the Sharpie disappeared into the distant greenery. The quick exit brought the dramatic event to a close, but for the lone birder on the scene, it will last a lifetime.

Within a few minutes of the Sharp Shinned's departure, the woods reverted to a deceptive calm. The only signs of the action-packed event were a few Flickers, and they too faded quickly into the background. But somewhere out there, a predator will strike again. So, the next time you are in the woods and all you see is a bunch of trees, remember those trees are home to hundreds of individuals, and at any moment you may catch a quick glimpse into their lives. But only if you are looking.

Chimney Swifts

In recent years, many people have learned about the large numbers of Chimney Swifts that gather in the Annapolis Valley during migration. However, very few people are aware that Chimney Swifts breed in Metro. In the eighties, an old chimney on Windmill Road in Dartmouth housed a large colony of them. Unfortunately, in the mid-eighties, the chimney was torn down during their breeding season, killing virtually all the birds present. Since then, only one or two families of Chimney Swifts can be seen each summer flying over the north end of Dartmouth. Where these particular swifts nest is currently unknown.

In Halifax, small numbers of Chimney Swifts nest in the old chimneys of Kings College. Listen for their distinctive, rapid, twittering call and then look up to see these tiny birds passing overhead. Two or three can often be seen flying in a half-circular formation, one behind the other. They have a slender cigar-shaped body and two relatively long curved wings. They fly in a very unusual way. First, they rapidly beat or vibrate one wing several times, and then they do the same with the second wing. Their flight is unlike any other bird I have seen. In reality, it is an optical illusion. In the thirties, researchers used slow-motion photography to prove that Chimney Swifts do beat both wings in unison. Since they always beat one wing harder than the other, it appears as if the wings are beating alternately. A series of rapid, shallow wing beats is then followed by a short glide.

In July, the young ones start to join the parents in the air. I have discovered that the young can be recognized from their parents by size and colour. In flight, their wings are just slightly shorter and they appear more of a gray brown compared to the grayer plumage of the adults.

Except when incubating eggs or sleeping, swifts spend all their time on the wing. In fact, it is believed they spend more time flying than any other land bird in the world.

Further Afield

....

Sharp Tailed Sparrows

Due to the wide variety of birds that migrate through Nova Scotia, both our spring and fall migrations are rather drawn-out procedures in, which take place over a period of months. Migrating birds can be seen from March to June. Typically, the end of spring migration is marked by the arrival of the Sharp Tailed Sparrow, the last of the breeding species to return to Nova Scotia. Sharp Tailed Sparrows are generally reported in most areas of the province by the end of the first week in June. These small sparrows live in salt marshes and are often detected by their unusual song, part of which resembles a short blast of air escaping from a tire. Places like Conrads Beach are perfect spots to hear and get to know this peculiar sparrow.

Pearl Island

Pearl Island (called Green Island on some maps) is a tiny speck of land at the mouth of St. Margarets Bay. On our provincial maps, often only a lighthouse is shown with the name Pearl Island appearing beside it. The Natural History Map of Nova Scotia lists the island as a wildlife management area. An extra notation indicates that the island is a locally important breeding area for Atlantic Puffins, Leach's Storm Petrels, Razorbills, and Black Guillemots.

Unfortunately, all of these species have suffered serious declines in their breeding populations, caused mostly by the predation of Great Black Backed Gulls and Herring Gulls. Historically humans, rats, feral cats, and gulls contributed to the decline of seabird colonies. Today, the gulls are the largest force behind seabird destruction. In the last few decades, gull numbers have grown astronomically; experts everywhere agree that gulls now represent a serious threat, which, if left unchecked, will mean that certain bird species will be lost forever. In Nova Scotia, we see the damage gulls can do. In the past, the province had several islands where Atlantic Puffins bred. By 1971, a Canadian Wildlife survey revealed that only the Bird Islands and our local Pearl Island had breeding Atlantic Puffins. In the summer of 1995 a pair of puffins were sighted on two islands off southwest Nova Scotia. It is believed they were attempting to nest, but no one knows whether they were successful.

In June 1992, four persons interested in the preservation of Atlantic Puffins spent ten days on Pearl Island. The volunteers were Peter Dooley and Trip Denice of the National Audubon Society, Krista Amey, a university student who did work with the terns near Brier Island, and myself. The purpose of our visit was to collect data on the bird life found on and around the island. Twenty–nine species of birds were seen, either on or near Pearl Island, and thirteen species were recorded as breeding. The most numerous were the gulls. The greatest number of Great Black Backed and Herring Gulls counted at one time ranged between 300 and 400 adults, but the number of gull nests with eggs indicated that there were at least 570 adults present. Furthermore, if all 453 freshly built gull nests were being used, as many as 906 gulls may have been present.

Pearl Island was once home to 10,000 Leach's Storm Petrels, but over the years gulls have reduced this number to 445 pairs, a reduction of over 95 per cent. We found thirty–seven adult petrels that had been killed by gulls. Six of the Common Eider nests discovered had also been destroyed by gulls. Six pairs of Common Terns and fifty pairs of Arctic Terns had nests at three locations; however, heavy predation of the eggs and chicks by the gulls, means that few, if any, terns will reach adulthood. One hundred two Atlantic Puffins were sighted, with an unknown number of nests. The remains of three eggs and six adults taken by gulls was also observed. Current observations and past data suggest as well, that few, if any, young puffins will survive. Other birds found breeding on the island were a pair of Razorbills, a pair of ravens, and an unde-termined number of Black Guillemots and Savannah and Song Sparrows.

If you have a boat, this is a great area to visit to see Puffins and other seabirds, but please remember it is unnecessary and illegal to come within a half–mile of Pearl Island or to land on it.

Pileated Woodpeckers

One of Metro's most striking birds is the Pileated Woodpecker, whose name refers to the red crest or "pileum" on its head. The Pileated is a crow–size woodpecker with a stout, chisel–like bill used for pecking and drumming, and a long spearlike tongue used in probing for wood–boring insects. A stiff tail and specially adapted feet, with two toes gripping forward and two backwards, brace the Pileated Woodpecker for climbing.

Pileated Woodpeckers are uncommon in Nova Scotia and appear to be declining in numbers because they rely on large, old–growth trees for their survival. Although their decline probably started as soon as the first European settlers began removing the virgin forests, their numbers have recently taken a sharper drop with the current forestry trend of shorter cutting cycles, which do not allow many of the trees to gain a wide enough diameter to benefit the Pileated. Though Pileated Woodpeckers may be found anywhere in the province where large coniferous or deciduous stands exist, in Nova Scotia they show a marked preference for hardwood stands.

The Ivory Billed Woodpecker was once the largest woodpecker in North America. It, too, relied on mature hardwood forests for its survival, but the desire for timber and our poor forestry practices led to the complete destruction of this beautiful Woodpecker in North America. Now the Pileated Woodpecker is the largest wood-pecker in North America, and unless forestry practices change, it too will be driven out.

In Metro, the woodlands surrounding Fall River have far more Pileated Woodpeckers than any other outlying communities. Inside city lim-its, the best place to see Pileated Woodpeckers is the Blue Mountain Drive Trail. Outside the city limits, besides Fall River, Pileateds are often reported at Lake Echo, Mount Uniacke, Goodwood, and Enfield. Nearby Oakfield Park is an excellent place to view these magnificent birds. The Pileated is one of the few birds that, no mat-ter how often you see one, you are still impressed by its appearance. Its size alone is shocking if you are accustomed to seeing only the Downy and Hairy Woodpeckers. The Mount Uniacke Estate park boasts possibly as many as six pairs of these giants on the property.

Although Pileated Woodpeckers can be seen in any month, June is perhaps one of the best times to go looking, when young Pileateds are either out of the nest or are about to leave it. Either way, these noisy young will often lead you straight to the whole family. One of my most memorable birding experiences was a family of Pileated Woodpeckers I encountered after I entered the woods to check out a suspiciously interesting sound. There, right in front of me, were six Pileated Woodpeckers, two adults and four young ones, all feeding on the bottom 0.3 m (4 ft.) of a large tree trunk.

A Birding Challenge

John James Audubon was an artist, an author, an explorer, and probably the most famous natural-ist of North America. His book *The Birds of North America*, published in 1827, brought him worldwide fame and the honour of having the National Audubon Society named after him in 1905. Audubon was responsible for describing and naming many species of North American birds, one of which he named the Traill's Flycatcher, in appreciation for the help that Dr. Thomas Traill gave him regarding his then soon-to-be-published book. This name stuck until 1973, when the American Ornithologists Union changed it due to relatively new information unearthed by various researchers.

One of these researchers, R. C. Stein, discov-ered that the Traill's Flycatcher was in reality two very distinct species although remarkably alike. These two "new" species received the common names Alder Flycatcher and Willow Flycatcher. In honour of Thomas Traill, the Willow Flycatcher's scientific name was chosen as *Empidonax traillii*.

How these two species could be taken as one for so long is understandable as even today it is difficult to tell the two apart. The most recent publication available to birders on the identifica-tion of Alder and Willow Flycatchers is a book titled *Advanced Birding*. This book contains exten-sive comparative information on these two species but also states, "on present knowledge, Willow and Alder Flycatchers cannot be separat-ed by sight alone, not even in the hand." Despite the fact that these two species look virtually identical, they can be separated from each other in three ways.

The first and most easily noted difference is their songs. The Alder Flycatcher's song at first does sound very similar to the Willow's, but as you become more familiar with it, you begin to pick up subtle differences between the two. The main thing to listen for is where the emphasis is placed. The Willow Flycatcher places the accent on the first syllable and the second syllable appears to drop slightly in pitch, while the Alder Flycatcher emphasizes the second syllable.

The second method is less reliable than the first as it is based on habitat. As their name implies, the Alder prefers to nest in alders, and the Willow in willows. The problem arises when you find a mixture of alder and willow trees growing together.

The third way to separate the two is by looking at their nests. Willow Flycatchers generally build their nests at greater heights, and most importantly, they place a lot of cottony material in their nests, while Alders do not. This method is the one that is least likely to be misinterpreted and would be the preferred method of most birders if it were not for the fact that these nests are difficult to find.

Other than these differences, Alder and Willows are much alike; there is even little behavioural difference. For example, both have identical food preferences. Not surprisingly, both often feed on flies. What is surprising is the variety of other foods they eat. Approximately 41 per cent of their diet is composed of bees and wasps. They also eat at least sixty–five species of beetles and a number of non–flying insects, such as spiders and millipedes. They even regularly consume elderberries and blackberries.

Probably the biggest difference between Alders and Willows from a Nova Scotian perspective is that Alder Flycatchers are common in the province, Willows are not. Until 1990, only three sightings of Willow Flycatchers had occurred in the province—one breeding pair and two singing males. However, recent events indicate that Willow Flycatchers may be more common here than realized. Noted Nova Scotian birder, Sherman Williams, found not one but *three* singing males in a stretch of woods near Avonport, suggesting that perhaps Willow Flycatchers are more common in Halifax County as well. After all, Alder Flycatchers are one of the more common species outside city limits. They also occur inside city limits where alder bushes are present. To prove or disprove the presence of Willow Flycatchers in the greater Metro area could be an interesting birding challenge for the right person.

Goatsuckers

June is a good time to look for Goatsuckers, a family of birds so named because it was at one time widely thought that these plain-coloured, swallowlike birds, with wide gaping mouths would steal milk from farm animals left in the field at night. The most common member of the Goatsucker family to occur in Metro is the Common Nighthawk, the other and much rarer is the Whip Poor Will.

Common Nighthawks normally feed at night, but once their young hatch, they also feed during daylight hours. A good place to observe Common Nighthawks during the day in June and July is Oakfield Park. See why these birds are so interesting to watch under "The Unnoticed Nighthawk" in September. Unlike the Nighthawk, which can be active during the day or night, the Whip Poor Will is strictly a citizen of the night. Both birds feed on moths, mosquitoes, beetles, and other night-time flying insects, with the Nighthawks preferring to feed high in the sky and the Whip Poor Wills near the ground.

The Whip Poor Will is so named for its call, a fairly loud, rapidly reiterated whistled "whip–poor–will." The bird usually begins calling within an hour after dusk, calling becomes less frequent during the middle part of the night, then peaks again an hour or so before dawn. Their calls are usually about one to two seconds in length, with an average of ten to fifty repetitions at one time. One exceptional case was a Whip Poor Will that was recorded calling its name 1,088 times, nonstop. Whip Poor Wills are typically found in open areas near deciduous forests with lots of leaf litter. The eggs of the Whip Poor Will are laid on top of the leaf litter and incubated throughout the day by the female whose leaflike plumage pattern camouflages her and her eggs from even the most sharp-eyed observers.

Whip Poor Wills are rare in the province and are declining. During a warm quiet night in June with a brightly lit moon is the most likely time you will find one if you go looking. Unfortunately, many of the places in the Metro area that did have Whip Poor Wills have been developed, or the Whip Poor Wills have disappeared. In recent years, the only reliable area for these birds has been the woodlands along Long Pond on Herring Cove road. At times, a Whip Poor Will may be seen at this location flying by the streetlight at the end of Dale Avenue.

The Whip Poor Will's whistled song is an exciting sound on a still summer's night. If you are lucky enough to hear one, try shining a light in the direction of the call. You will be amazed when you see the two bright ruby-red eyes that will be looking back at you. Of course, be careful not to harass the bird—one look is enough. Many people are happy just to hear the bird that is associated with warm summer evenings of the deep South.

The Quiet Month?

....

Head for the Coast for the Most

July can appear to be one of the quiet months for birds, but this appearance is misleading. True, the woods are considerably quieter than they were in May and June, but it is not because there are fewer birds present. They are still there, but most of them are so busy trying to find food for their young that they have less time for singing. To get an idea of how busy some of these species are, we can look at what researchers have discovered about the Yellow Warbler. During a typical summer's day, a pair of Yellow Warblers will make about 300 visits to their nest to feed their four offspring. Imagine if they had eight young as the Black Capped Chickadees do!

While the woods are seemingly quiet, the Nova Scotia coastline is not. July is an excellent month for exploring the seashore to search for shorebirds. In July, about a dozen interesting

J·U·L·Y·

species of shorebirds can be encountered, including Nova Scotia's largest shorebird, the Whimbrel. Beat the heat of the city while exploring coastal locations such as Conrads Beach, Smelly Cove, West Lawrencetown Marsh, West Chezzetcook Marsh, and Martinique Beach.

If you do spend time in the city, July is the opportune time to enjoy the its most talented songbird, the Northern Mockingbird. Unlike other species endemic to urban areas, (i.e., pigeons, crows, starlings), this species is well liked and beneficial.

Back yard birders are likely to see one of their favourite species, the goldfinch, disappear in late July, but another equally popular species, the Ruby Throated Hummingbird, may arrive to fill the void. July is the time for all bird lovers to learn the right way to deal with baby birds.

City Birding

Flightless Birds Spotted in Nova Scotia

Each July, the Nova Scotia Museum, the Department of Natural Resources, and Nature Centres across the province are inundated with phone calls about baby birds found on the ground. These flightless birds are common and are in fact part of the normal development of many species. This apparent problem originates with spring nest construction, when it is important that the nest is small enough to allow the mother to properly cover the eggs when incubating and protect the naked or partially feathered chicks after hatching. As the chicks grow more feathers and develop, they are able to better regulate their own body temperature and brooding is not as necessary.

Once the young are fully feathered, the nest is no longer needed and is usually abandoned as it can draw undue attention to the young birds. For the next couple of days to a week, the young birds are still cared for by the parents, but they live on the move, learning to strengthen their flight muscles and gaining knowledge of their environment. During this period, the parent birds lead the chicks to likely feeding or resting places and leave them alone for longer lengths of time to help them develop independence. It is during this time that they are often spotted and "rescued" by people because the baby birds appear to be abandoned. In fact, adult birds are excellent parents and never abandon their young; they willingly risk their own lives to save their offspring.

Shortly after a young bird is taken, the parents will protest. If it is released while the parents are present, they will gladly take it back but will usually wait until any humans are gone. Upon seeing a baby bird, you can best help by keeping cats and dogs out of the area and watching the bird from a distance. If the parents do not attend to the youngster within an hour or two, the bird may be lost and may need help; unfortunately, there are no organizations that take care of baby birds. Fully feathered baby birds should be fed at least once an hour during a sixteen-hour daylight period. Although they need to be fed frequently, they don't eat much at one sitting. The parents of most young songbirds feed them insects, but the type of insects vary greatly from species to species. An excellent substitute is hard-boiled egg yolk, as it is high in protein. The egg yolk should be moistened slightly with milk or water and fed from the end of a toothpick. The baby bird will probably have to be force-fed by prying the beak open and placing the food in its throat. Usually two to three ant-size pieces are plenty. Be sure not to give the youngster any liquid; at this point in their lives they get all the moisture they need from their food. Within days after they learn to fly and start to feed themselves, they are ready to be released into the wild. From this point, instinct and trial and error will teach them what to eat and what not to eat.

Northern Mockingbirds

By July, most species of songbirds are pretty much done singing, but the Northern Mockingbird continues to sing throughout the day and sometimes the night. In fact, one year, north end Halifax residents were literally serenaded day and night by a talented songster. I thought perhaps locals would have considered this bird an annoyance, but when I spoke to them, I found otherwise. Nancy McNair thoroughly enjoyed the songs and made an excellent recording of the performance. She reported that the singing lasted nearly all night, stopping only between 2:00 A.M. and 4:00 A.M. However, another nearby resident, Gail MacLean, said the singing started in her neighbourhood about 3:00 A.M., so perhaps he changed locations.

Unlike some endurance singers, this "musician" is a joy to listen to as he is constantly adding new material to his repertoire. He is able to produce an endless supply of music using the songs of others combined in new ways to create long strings of melodious tunes. The sounds are truly amazing as he is able to perfectly imitate the other songbirds and even vocally blend in sounds of inanimate objects, such as bells and car horns. No human performer can outdo him; he is able to run through as many as twenty different songs in a minute, earning him the name Northern Mockingbird. In fact, they have been recorded repeating the songs of more than 150 bird species. Scott Merry discovered a pair of mockingbirds in Seaview Park in Halifax after hearing what appeared to be an American Robin, a Song Sparrow, and a Blue Jay all singing from the same bush.

Gail MacLean watched a mockingbird for over a week and noticed that it used two feeding techniques. It either sat on top of a post and darted to the ground to capture any moving insects it spotted, or it would run along the ground in short steps, much like a robin, searching for insects. Unlike the robin, he sporadically flicked open his wings as he hunted, revealing large white wing patches. Scientists believe that these conspicuous patches cause the insects to flush from their hiding places, making it easier for the mockingbird to find them.

In summer, about a dozen Northern Mockingbirds usually nest in the Halifax/Dartmouth area. Good, reliable places to observe the mockingbird in Metro include: Fort Needham Park, Birch Cove Park, Seaview Park, and the Fairview Cemetery. It was at the latter one summer that a mockingbird helped me to unduly impress British birder Neil Williams. Wanting a picture of a mockingbird, he asked me where one would likely build its nest. I pointed to a nearby bush with closely knit thorn-covered branches as the type of location a mockingbird would choose. No sooner were the words out of my mouth than a Northern Mockingbird suddenly appeared and flew to that very bush. Looking closer, we saw that the bird had settled onto a well-concealed nest. Needless to say, I was instantly promoted to legendary status!

Raptor Rehabilitation

The Department of Natural Resources and the Nova Scotia Bird Society have Raptor Rehabilitation Programs designed to assist hawks and owls in two ways: first to care for injured birds of prey until they are ready to be released back into the wild, and second to raise baby raptors that have lost their parents. Like the injured birds, they too are released into the appropriate natural habitat once they are ready to fend for themselves. In the early nineties, Natural Resources added a new dimension to their Raptor Rehab program. Specialized tags were developed and attached to a leg of each bird that was released. These tags are very similar to the aluminum bands used by the Canada Wildlife Service and the United States Fish and Game to identify individual birds, which do not interfere in any way with the bird's daily activities; they provide valuable information, such as the life spans and ranges of the birds tagged. Natural Resources began banding released birds in the spring of 1991. Their first feedback came in July 1992, after James Kinnear noticed a dead bird on Bayers Road in Halifax had a silver band on its leg. The number in the band, "A–1," indicated that this was the first bird banded in the program with an "A" size band, the size used for small hawks. Natural Resources data revealed that the bird was banded on August 6, 1991, as a young Merlin and released near St. Margarets Bay. The fact that the Merlin had made it through its first winter was a good sign—on average only 10 per cent to 30 per cent of young hawks do. Owls have also been outfitted with these bands.

The bands contain an identification number, the initials "NSLF," and the words Halifax, Canada. If you should find a bird wearing one of these bands, note the date and place where you found the bird and its apparent cause of death or injury. If the bird is dead, remove the band and send it to the nearest detachment of Natural Resources; if the bird is still alive, write down the band information and contact the department. Locally, their head office is in Waverly and they can be reached at (902) 861–2560. They also have a detachment at Lewis Lake, phone (902) 876–2308. There is also a twenty-four-hour Zenith number for wildlife emergencies: 1–800–565–2224.

Evening Grosbeaks

Since 1938, Evening Grosbeaks have been regular winter visitors to Nova Scotia. In the late fifties, small numbers of them started to spend their summers in Nova Scotia, but even today less than 10 per cent of the Evening Grosbeaks seen in winter are present in summer. However, the number of breeding pairs continue to increase—a relatively large flock of Evening Grosbeaks was reported on July 13, 1992. The flock consisted of thirty to forty birds and was sighted by Tom Adams in Labelle, Queens County. Evening Grosbeaks are not as common in the Metro area in summer as they are in other parts of the province, but they are found in our area every year in increasing numbers. Soon flocks of thirty to forty birds in summer will be commonplace.

American Goldfinches

The American Goldfinch has long been nick-named the wild canary because of its bright yellow colour and rather long musical song. At feeders, goldfinches prefer to open the seeds while remaining on the perch, rather than taking the seed away to be opened. This allows us to observe goldfinches for more than just a few minutes at a time. Its habit of staying put, combined with its bright colour and song, make it a favourite among feeder watchers.

In the last few weeks of July and the first few weeks of August, goldfinches will disappear from many feeders. This is natural since August is when most goldfinches start to nest. The American Goldfinch is the last of our summer breeders to build a nest. This unusual behaviour is part of the goldfinch's special adaptation to its environment. Most birds will build a nest early in the spring, so when their young hatch, there will be plenty of insects available to feed them. This is true of even seed-eating birds. The goldfinch nestlings, however, are able to digest seeds for food, so their hatchings are usually timed to coincide with thistle plants and other composite flowers are going to seed. Only those lucky enough to have some open habitat near their property that has both thistle plants and young deciduous saplings are likely to enjoy the goldfinch's presence throughout the summer.

Hummingbirds

For those of you who have missed out on Ruby Throated Hummingbirds in your garden earlier in the summer, do not give up. During mid- to late July, our hummingbird population doubles— the result of the first batch of baby hummingbirds leaving their nests. At first, the youngsters are led around by the female, who usually takes them straight to the closest food source she can find. However, the young hummers quickly become independent and start to search for their own territories. It is then that you may get lucky.

Flying Fish?

Two of the main reasons I chose my current apartment are that it provides an area conducive to bird feeding and it has a great view of the Bedford Basin. For years I have enjoyed watching and studying a great variety of birds and other wildlife from my living-room window. In summer, I am entertained by flying fish. Although I have read of their incredible abilities to leap out of the water and soar through the air, I never imagined I would see not only one but several flying by a third-storey apartment window! These fish must be extremely powerful; they jump like this all summer, and most of them are carrying a 1.8 kg (4 lb.) Osprey on their backs.

Further Afield

....

Goodbye Summer, Hello Fall!

In July, many people are just starting to enjoy summer, so most are surprised, even dismayed, to hear that the first fall migrants have arrived in the Metro area. Each year, about July 5, shorebirds begin to trickle in from their breeding grounds in the high Arctic. Short Billed Dowitchers are usually the first species to be seen in numbers. Flocks of these birds suddenly appearing on stretches of mud flats are a sure sign that fall migration has begun.

Each passing week brings a greater number and variety of shorebirds. By mid-August, there are so many around that even non–birders start to notice them. For seasoned birders, these large numbers are exciting, but for those new to birding or new to shorebirds, trying to separate and identify thousands of birds can be mind-boggling and frustrating. That is not the way birding is supposed to be, so here is a suggestion. Instead of waiting until August to look at shorebirds, start in July when there are fewer species to sort through.

You can begin by becoming familiar with Short Billed Dowitchers as they will be the most numerous species on the mud flats in early July. Within a week or two the Dowitchers will be joined by small flocks of other shorebirds. The most likely species you will encounter are Black Bellied Plovers, Semipalmated Plovers, Lesser Yellowlegs, Ruddy Turnstones, Semipalmated Sandpipers, and Least Sandpipers. Before going out into the field, you may also want to look up these species in your field guide in order to determine their distinguishing features. Learning how to identify some of the shorebirds in July and some in August may prevent bird overload and make the whole birding experience much more enjoyable. Some of the best places to look for shorebirds in July are Smelly Cove, Seaforth Causeway, West Chezzetcook Marsh, and Conrads Beach.

Early Arrivals

In some years, large numbers of shorebirds arrive in Metro earlier than they should, but this does not mean that winter is fast approaching. Instead, it is an indicator of what has happened in the past couple of months in the most northern regions of the country. There are two theories as to why shorebirds migrate early. The most popular one suggests that they come early because the Arctic spring or summer was warmer and/or dryer than usual, allowing the nesting sandpipers and plovers to start families earlier, thus leave earlier. Good weather could also mean that more food was available to feed nestlings and thus they were able to develop more quickly. The second theory is also weather based: Perhaps persistent cool weather caused nesting species to lose their first and second clutch of eggs. (Although most species will make a second attempt after losing their first clutch, very few will make a third attempt after a second failure.) Thus with little hope of breeding and perhaps of food, the shorebirds start their southward descent.

As more information is gathered and exchanged between Nova Scotia and the Arctic regions, maybe the true explanation will be reached. It is most likely that a much more complex chain of events determines the timing of shorebird migration, events that vary from year to year and can be affected by natural occurrences and human actions. Therefore, what has been found to cause an early migration in one year may not be the cause of an early migration another year. Hopefully time, research, and collaboration will unravel a few more of the mysteries of migration.

Whimbrels

A vast variety of shorebirds migrate through the Metro area each year on their way to their southern wintering grounds, beginning as early as July for some species. Although many of Nova Scotia's shorebirds share similarities, one species that stands out from the crowd is the Whimbrel. At an average length of 45 cm (18 in.), the Whimbrel is Nova Scotia's largest shorebird. What accounts for a good portion of its length and adds immensely to its spectacular appearance is its downward curved bill. The Whimbrel's bill ranges in length from 7.5 cm to 10 cm (3 in. to 4 in.), depending on its sex and age.

This long, decurved bill is fully extended during flight, making it easier to identify this species, even at a great distance. With its bill and neck extended and its long legs trailing behind, this is an interesting bird to observe in flight. To compliment its visual display, Whimbrels normally produce an unusual sounding series of long, rolling, tremolo notes that have a tendency to catch one's attention, especially if there is more than one bird present. Flocks fly in long irregular lines or like Canada Geese, in a "V" formation.

Whimbrels are coastal species, best found along headlands that have good-size sections of cranberries or crowberries. Whimbrels love these berries and will spend many hours feeding on them each day. Two good places to look for Whimbrels in the Metro area are the cranberry patches at Hartlen Point and Martinique Beach. They may also be seen in large salt marshes, like the one adjacent to Rainbow Haven Beach, or feeding on mud flats. They seem to particularly like mud flats that are next to sandy beaches, perhaps because the mud has more sand content, allowing them to find a greater variety of food. While feeding on mud flats, the Whimbrel is an impressive sight to watch as it walks along, probing the mud at various spots to varying depths. It is truly amazing when its long bill completely disappears into the mud, is fully withdrawn, and quickly inserted again up to the bird's eyes.

In the early 1800s, three species of Curlews—the Eskimo, the Long Billed, and the Hudsonian Curlew (or Whimbrel, as it is called today)—were either common or abundant as fall migrants in Nova Scotia. By 1857, the largest of the three, the Long Billed, was considered very rare, and by 1885, it was noted that both the Long Billed and the Eskimo Curlew, thought at one time very common, were then exceedingly rare. This was a modest appraisal on the Long Billed's part as the last sighting in the province was of a lone bird at Windsor in September, fifteen years prior to the 1885 assessment. By 1903, only the Whimbrel could be found in Nova Scotia, and its numbers were declining. By 1920, it was noted by Robie Tufts, Nova Scotia's leading bird conservation officer, that Whimbrels, which once numbered in the thousands, had been reduced to a few hundred during the preceding two decades.

Without a doubt, the Whimbrel, like the other members of its family, would have been extirpated from Nova Scotia if it were not for the Migratory Bird Treaty signed between Canada and the United States in 1916. The treaty made it illegal to hunt any non-game birds that migrated between the two countries. This ended, for the most part, the mass slaughter of Curlews and other shorebirds, which occurred on an annual basis.

The treaty was enacted in hopes of preventing further species from suffering the fate of the now extinct Passenger Pigeon. Shorebirds in particular were excessively killed during their spring and fall migrations. Of all the shorebirds, the Eskimo Curlews' population suffered the most; literally hundreds of thousands were destroyed. Their numbers were so devastated that even today the

Eskimo Curlew is considered to be on the brink of extinction. Although the Metro area is still one of the four most likely places in the world to see an Eskimo Curlew, it is doubtful that one will be seen here ever again.

White Winged Crossbills

July marks the beginning of the second breeding period for White Winged Crossbills in the Metro area—the first period starts in January. If you come across nesting crossbills from July to September and would like to know more about them, see "Crossbills" in March for additional information.

The Season of Shorebirds

....

The Main Event

The main event of August, as far as most birders are concerned, is the passing of literally hundreds of thousands of shorebirds through Nova Scotia. These shorebirds have bred in the vast Arctic, and the majority are now heading to their wintering grounds in the Southern Hemisphere. When travelling south, most species of shorebirds choose a coastal route, making Nova Scotia one of the top places in Canada to enjoy this spectacular event.

Mud flats are one of the best habitats to see a variety of shorebirds. Some species are also attracted to sandy beaches or even rocky coastline if there is enough seaweed present to host nutritious insects. Luckily, Nova Scotia has no shortage of coastline. In fact, it is probably impossible to get more than an hour's drive away from the coast. As a result, interesting shorebirds may be seen in any part of the province. Metro birders are especially fortunate as one of greatest areas in the province to study shorebirds is the shoreline just outside Dartmouth which stretches from Hartlen Point to the West Chezzetcook Marsh.

Though shorebird is a term which can be applied generally to almost any species of bird likely to feed along the coastline, it more accurately refers to various families of sandpipers and plovers, and it is this particular group of birds that I am referring to when I use the term in this book. In Nova Scotia, approximately thirty common species of shorebirds can be observed in the fall; however, as many as fifty species have been recorded over the years, with new ones discovered almost annually.

Although the migrating shorebirds grab most of the attention in August, they are not the only birds on the move. Back yard birders will notice that hummingbirds are starting to disappear. City birders should look up to see a migrant that many never realize is there—the Common Nighthawk. After you see these birds for the first time, you may wonder how in the world you missed them before!

In early August be sure to set aside some time to watch the Ospreys. Your efforts will be rewarded with one of the best circus acts of the year. A visit to the Bedford Basin to see the Atlantic Puffin's closest relative, the Black Guillemot, is also a worthwhile trip.

This is an excellent time to watch ponds and coves for two species of rare herons that are often sighted in August—Green Herons and Yellow Crowned Night Herons. Keen birders should also keep tabs on the hurricane reports because even if they are almost completely wound down, they can bring us some of the most fantastic birds of the year.

City Birding

Gone Fishing

Without a doubt, the sport of birding has many appeals, some of which are difficult to define. Take for example the exciting, peaceful feeling that arises from observing the recurring events of nature that have existed for perhaps millions of years, demonstrating the power of nature; they somehow connect an observer with the natural rhythms of the planet. These events help us to better understand the natural world and to see the world on a broader plane. While some events, such as spring and fall migration, are very showy and easily observed, others are more subtle but can be equally moving, especially to the educated observer.

One such event that takes place in August in Metro is the Osprey's "Fine School of Fishing Finesse," when the adult Ospreys teach their young how to catch food for themselves. This is interesting behaviour to observe, but it is easily missed as it starts during the first half of August and lasts only a few days to a few weeks.

It begins with the parents leading their young to one of their best fishing spots and showing them how they catch fish. While the young will imitate some of the parents' techniques, they are generally quite reluctant to actually catch a fish and pester the adults for food until they are fed. The second phase of their fishing lesson begins with the parents catching the food but not giving it to the youngsters. Instead, they make sure the fish is dead, then they drop it onto the surface of the water and encourage the young to get it. The young Ospreys usually don't catch on quickly, so the parents swoop down, grab the fish, and drop it onto the water again. This action is normally repeated several times in a day, or over a couple of days, before the young try to scoop the fish off the water themselves. At first, usually the oldest chick makes the attempt, but it is soon joined by its younger siblings. The typical result is a great deal of splashing as two or three birds dive for the same fish, and then you can see their bewilderment as each one comes up "empty handed." Luckily, their accuracy quickly increases, and they are soon ready to move on to their third and final phase, catching fish under the surface of the water. Although they miss a lot of fish at first, after several tries they generally catch a meal. Interestingly, at this most difficult stage, they appear to rely more on their instincts than on their parents' help to accomplish the task.

The Unnoticed Nighthawk

Each year, hundreds, sometimes thousands, of Common Nighthawks fly over the Metro area in early to mid-August. These tern–size birds are dark brown, mottled birds, which are identified by a noticeable white band cutting vertically across long, pointed wings at approximately mid-point. They are high flying birds, so they also go unnoticed by many city dwellers.

Evidence of just how unaware most city dwellers are of the Common Nighthawk is the fact that many nest on the gravel rooftops in Halifax. On warm summer evenings in downtown Halifax, the call of the Common Nighthawk can be heard clearly, long after dark, yet most pedestrians seem to be unaware of this distinctive call, a loud nasal "beer." You would think that the word alone would catch the attention of some!

Reaching speeds of 60 km/hr (37 mi./hr), males bank sharply to produce a "burrroom" sound with their wings. This aerial manoeuvre has earned males the nickname "Booming Nighthawk." These birds feed exclusively on flying insects—moths, beetles, mosquitoes, and flying ants, to name a few. Nighthawks breed in Halifax in June and July. Most of the individuals reported in August are birds which are passing through the city on their way south. They begin their southward trek each year about July 30, with thousands winging their way over the twin cities in August.

Hummingbirds: Keep those Feeders Up!

Birds have always been interesting to humankind, but in the past only limited information was known about them. These segmented facts were often used to draw conclusions about birds, some of which later proved to be true, while others have led to popular myths that exist even today. Some bird myths have persisted for so long and are so widespread that they are often taken as fact and even pop up from time to time in writings about birds.

One such myth which resurfaces widely each year in late summer has to do with hummingbird feeders. It is a widely held misconception that if you do not take in your hummingbird feeder in late summer or early fall, it will encourage the hummingbirds to stay later than they should. Although this fallacy was disproved several years ago, thousands of people are still unaware that it is indeed a myth. Unfortunately, it's a myth that is perpetuated in several bird books, especially those more than ten years old, and has even appeared on the boxes of some hummingbird feeders.

So for the record, bird experts agree that hummingbirds will migrate south when they are supposed to, regardless of how long a humming-bird feeder is left out. In fact, research shows that the longer you leave feeders out, the better it is for the hummingbirds. Before migrating, they must double their body weight. This extra weight, stored as fat reserve, is what the hummers use as an energy source to complete their long journey. By the time they reach their South American wintering grounds all this extra fat has been used up, plus half their normal body weight—a 75 per cent reduction! Late-hanging hummingbird feeders not only help our local birds but are usually the ones to attract stray hummingbirds from the west, such as the Rufous and Black Chinned Hummingbirds.

Our only eastern North American humming-bird, the Ruby Throated, starts to leave Nova Scotia in late August, with the majority heading south during September. However, stragglers are regularly seen to the end of October, and occasionally a hummingbird is sighted after October. If you see one then, look at it carefully, as there is a greater chance it is one of the western species and not one of our delightful Ruby Throateds.

Metro's Only Free-flying Mute Swan

Where the Sackville River empties into the Bedford Basin has long been a popular spot for unusual waterfowl visitors; however, one Bedford Basin bird oddity was a bit of a mystery. An immature Mute Swan was first sighted in August 1992 by Doug Beattie. It arrived in the basin during stormy weather and spent time floating on the water and resting on the shore. At first the bird would not come to humans for food, but it eventually accepted hand-outs from local residents who had been watching out for and enjoying the bird. The question was where did he or she come from.

Mute Swans are natives of the Old World, but they were brought to North America, where they have been domesticated for use in parks, wildlife sanctuaries, and private collections. These captive swans usually have the flight feathers on their wings permanently clipped to prevent them from escaping. Occasionally, these flightless Mute

Swans do breed in captivity and produce free-flying young, which sometimes escape before their keepers crop their wings. That particular bird in the basin was a swan born that year, suggesting that this was what happened.

Exactly where this Mute Swan came from, though, was a point of much speculation. A few years previous, an immature Mute Swan was sighted in the exact same location. It was later discovered to be one of the swans born in the Public Gardens in Halifax that summer. In the summer of 1992, though, three cygnets (the official term for young swans) were hatched at the park and all three were accounted for when this young one arrived in the basin.

Those who keep swans and other waterfowl are often encouraged to place bands on the legs of their birds to aid in identification in case they do get lost. This Mute Swan did not have any. Obviously, though, the swan did belong to someone. Later that year the owner, from Harrietsfield, was found and a number of unsuccessful attempts were made to capture the swan. Although there were concerns that the swan would not find enough food to survive through the winter, it did, with help from Doug Beattie and other local bird lovers, and it is alive today. In the fall of 1995, a young male swan named Ziggy was purchased by local residents Petar and Lelia Kovacevic to keep this female swan company. The two birds get along wonderfully and it is hoped they will someday mate. The only drawback in their relationship is that he can fly and she can not.

Now, I am sure that many of you have seen swans in parks before and perhaps have admired their beauty as they glide gracefully over the water. However, until you see a swan in flight, it is difficult to fully appreciate how beautiful these birds are. Several mornings over the last few years, I have looked out over the Bedford Basin and have seen the elegant, rhythmic beat of the Mute Swan's wings. Each time, it gave me a feeling of serenity. Once it shared the sky with a Bald Eagle, which did not detract from its majesty. So if you want to experience the true grace of this bird, don't miss the opportunity to see Metro's only free-flying swan.

Passerine Migration Begins

As the middle of August approaches, Passerines join the fall migration in increasing numbers. Their numbers will continue to grow, until they peak in September. So, if you have been meaning to get out and do some birding, now is the time to do it! A greater variety of birds can be seen in Nova Scotia late in August and in September than any other time of year. It is not uncommon to see fifty species of birds in one day at this time, and some keen birders have seen over one hundred species in a twenty-four-hour period. In August, many smaller birds travel in mixed flocks.

When large numbers of birds suddenly migrate into an area, the phenomenon is called a wave. For safety, most smaller birds migrate at night. Knowing this, keen birders often go outside then to listen for migrants. If a wave of birds is passing overhead, the occasional whisperlike call note will be heard. If you hear a lot of these call notes, there is a good chance the next morning will be good for seeing birds.

Further Afield

....

Shorebirds

Of the thirty species of shorebirds, six are common summer breeders, eight others can easily be observed migrating in July, and two are primarily seen offshore on sea-birding trips. This leaves ten land species that should be watched for in August and four that are best seen in September. Of course, if you didn't get out "shorebirding" in June and July, don't fret as all thirty species can be encountered in August.

In the Metro area, there are eleven common species that can be seen at any of the places where shorebirds gather. Some of the more popular spots are: Hartlen Point, West Lawrencetown Marsh, Conrads Beach, Lawrencetown Lake, Three Fathom Harbour, Smelly Cove, Seaforth Causeway, and West Chezzetcook Marsh. The eleven easiest shorebirds to find include: Black Bellied and Semipalmated Plovers; Semi-palmated, Least, and White Rumped Sandpipers; Killdeer; Short Billed Dowitchers; Greater and Lesser Yellowlegs; Willets; and Ruddy Turnstones.

August and September are good months to look for Red Knots. Only small numbers of these birds pass through the Metro area and many of them seem to slip through in early August. Red Knots often favour stony feeding areas, such as the stretch of shoreline at Hartlen Point, which faces Devils Island. Early August until early September is the best time to watch for Hudsonian Godwit and Stilt Sandpiper. The far western end of Conrads Beach is a good location to see Hudsonians. The West Lawrencetown Marsh is an excellent place to find Stilt Sandpipers; it is also one of the best places for new birders to look for shorebirds. The big advantage of this location is that even at low tide, the shorebirds are only 1.5 m to 3 m (5 ft. to 10 ft.) away from the foot of the railroad bed you will be walking on. The train tracks have been removed at this location so it is easy to walk without staring at your feet!

Come mid-August, it is time to start searching for Solitary and Western Sandpipers, Sanderlings, and Wilson's Phalaropes. Solitary Sandpipers, as their name implies, are not normally found with other sandpipers and prefer to feed on their own. For this reason, they are often spotted in freshwater ponds and small coves where little strips or patches of mud are found. City ponds and lakes are no exception to this rule, but most Solitaries are still seen in roadside ponds and coves along the Eastern Shore. One of the best ponds to see a Solitary is the Teal Pond in Three Fathom Harbour. Although a portion of this pond can be seen from the road, it is a good idea to get out of your car and walk along the shore of the pond—as many of the best birds are often hidden from sight of the road.

Western Sandpipers are a bit of a long shot, but a few are seen each fall between mid-August and late September. Many of the sightings have taken place at Hartlen Point, so it is probably the best location to search for one.

Conrads Beach is the place to visit to look for Wilson's Phalaropes and Sanderlings. The Wilson's may be seen on the piles of kelp on the beach or more likely on the small section of sandy mud stretching back from Conrads Beach towards West Lawrencetown Marsh. The Sanderlings can be seen at the same locations, but it is more fun to watch them on the main part of Conrads, as they run in and out with the waves. As each wave recedes, they scramble to grab any bits of food washed in before the next wave crashes over them. Each of us has probably played this "wave game" at one time or another, where you walk along the beach as close as possible to the water's edge then jump back with excitement when a big wave comes rolling in. The game continues until one wave comes in faster than expected and nicks you. Watching Sanderlings brings back happy memories of this childhood game, and as a result, people tend to like them.

If by chance you have never played this game,

watching wave-chasing Sanderlings still has appeal. When running with the ebb and flow of each wave, their tiny legs move so quickly it makes them appear animated. Even hardened teenagers have commented that the movement is "cool looking." The Sanderling's running reminds me of that short little Martian from the "Bugs Bunny Show." He wore a suit of armour and had a big head and short little legs that moved just like the Sanderling's do. You may laugh, but I am not the only adult who remembers cartoon characters; others compare the Sanderling's movements to the Roadrunner's!

The period from late August to mid-September is the best time to watch for the uncommon Baird's Sandpiper. Again, Conrads is the location along the Eastern Shore that most consistently has reports of Baird's Sandpipers. Late August is also time when White Rumped Sandpipers start to become more numerous. White rumps have black legs and a bill just like the Semipalmated Sandpiper; it is often difficult for newer birders to pick out some of the slight plumage differences between the two types. So if you are in doubt, just wait until the birds in question fly. White Rumps truly have pure white rumps, while the similar Semipalmateds have a thin black strip running up the centre of their otherwise white rumps, dividing it into two smaller white patches.

Identifying shorebirds is not as difficult as it first appears. Just because they show up in large numbers does not mean you have to identify them all at once. Learn about them one species at a time, and don't worry about the rest. You will find that knowing in advance what species you are likely to see and being familiar with their appearance makes the process a lot easier.

Ruddy Turnstones

Although many shorebirds are plain-coloured, Ruddy Turnstones are rather striking in appearance, showing sharply contrasting black-and-white patterns on their heads and breasts. The belly is pure white below but the bird's back and upper parts are a rich orange chestnut mixed with some black. In flight, Ruddy Turnstones catch the eye because of the large white patches on their wings, back, and tail. Immature Ruddy Turnstones are mostly brown in colour, lacking the chestnut upper parts of the adults, but they do have bright orange legs similar in colour to the reddish orange legs of their parents.

Turnstones are so named for their habit of flipping over small stones on rocky shorelines in search of food. This unusual method of feeding allows them to take advantage of food that is inaccessible to other shorebirds. A reward for the quiet observer is hearing a chorus of clicking stones as they are flipped by a flock of these endearing birds.

Black Guillemots

The Black Guillemot is a close relative of the well-liked Atlantic Puffin. Since Black Guillemots are easier to see in Nova Scotia than the puffin and they share many of the same characteristics, it also has the potential to become a favourite species. Like the puffin, guillemots are fish-eating birds that breed on inshore islands, sometimes forming large colonies. They will also nest singularly along the shoreline on rocky cliffs, or in between the cracks of large boulders. In other places, they have adapted to using the holes in jetties. Their ability to conceal their nests at a variety of different sites has helped them to survive in larger numbers than the Atlantic Puffin.

In the Metro area, we see the most guillemots in the middle of the winter.

In the summer, Black Guillemots concentrate around their breeding colonies. The closest known colonies to the greater Metro area are located at Sambro Island, Blandford, Pearl (Green) Island, Ironbound Island, and the islands near Ship Harbour. Guillemots lay their eggs in June, and the young hatch in July. After leaving their breeding grounds, some books state that the adults generally herd their young out to sea. Locally, this is not always the case. Each August, a few Black Guillemots with their one or two young in tow, are seen feeding in shallow waters along the shorelines; most of these sightings have occurred in St. Margarets Bay. This is not surprising when one considers that the colonies at Blandford and on Pearl Island are not far away. The Bedford Basin, on the other hand, is not a place where one would expect to see these birds. Yet, in recent years, at least one family has been showing up faithfully at this location around the middle of August. The big attraction there to these birds may be the abundance of rock eels, an all-time favourite food of the Black Guillemot. They may also be occasionally seen feeding at The Dingle or along other sections of the harbour shoreline.

By mid-August, some adults have begun to moult, trading in their jet-black plumage for a silvery winter coat. Otherwise, they hold onto their most striking features—a large white wing patch and bright red legs and feet, which help to make them a species easy to recognize. Even in flight, the wing patches and red dangling feet can be easily seen. While swimming, their size—smaller than an average duck—and their pointed bills are two additional features that aid in recognizing of them.

Guillemots belong to the Alcid family, which is the only family of birds in North America that regularly uses their wings to propel themselves underwater. This method of diving is also used by the Penguin family in the Southern Hemisphere and is often referred to as underwater flying. The favourite habitat of the Black Guillemot is rocky coastlines with stony bottoms, where they will dive as deep as 50 m (165 ft.) to reach the bottom. Once on the bottom, they will flip over loose stones to find eels, crab, and other saltwater crustaceans.

Green Herons

Now, I know some of you are going to see the name "Green Heron" and think I forgot to use its new name, "Green Backed Heron." Although a few years ago the American Ornithologists Union did change the Green Heron's name, in 1994 they changed it back. So, the name is current.

Migrating Green Herons that spend the day resting and feeding account for most of our Nova Scotia sightings. As weak flyers, these birds prefer to migrate under the protective cover of darkness. The sudden appearance of the Green Heron in a pond, where it was not seen the day before, is a good example of this bird's migratory behaviour.

Due to the secretive nature of the Green Heron, they are more likely than other herons to occur in small ponds, especially if the pond has thick bushes or other cover nearby. Other good places where you may see one of these birds is along wooded streams or tree–lined marshes. Interested people should be on the lookout for this tiny heron especially during May and August, when most sightings occur.

Adult Green Herons are small, greenish blue above, have a black crown, and a chestnut–coloured neck. Immature birds are similar in appearance and can be recognized by the many dark streaks on their necks and breasts. At a distance, both adults and immatures appear dark, and in flight they have been described as resembling a crow with strongly bowed wing beats.

Yellow Crowned Night Herons

The Yellow Crowned Night Heron is one of the rarer "southern herons" that visit the province. Yellow Crowneds have been slowly expanding their range northward and can now be found in Massachusetts. During the breeding season, adults acquire usually three relatively long white head plumes. By the time the young are raised, the plumes are usually gone and the Yellow Crowned Night Herons begin to disappear from the breeding grounds. Many of the Yellow Crowneds make their way north to places such as Nova Scotia. This post-breeding dispersal may be the reason that most sightings of Yellow Crowneds in the Metro area have occurred during July, August, and September.

Yellow Crowneds may visit either freshwater habitats or saltwater environments. When feeding in fresh water, the favourite food is crayfish, though on the coast, they prefer fresh crab. The hard outer skeleton of the crab prevents most herons from making it a meal, but the Yellow Crowned's bill, which is thicker, allows it to take advantage of this tasty morsel. As the name suggests, Night Herons feed at night as a rule; however, Yellow Crowned Night Herons routinely feed during the day, much more so than their close relative, the Black Crowned Night Heron.

A place where Yellow Crowneds have been seen on more than one occasion is under the bridge at Rocky Run, a location rich in crab. However, these rare herons may show up at any location with an abundance of this delicacy. One thing to keep in mind is that more immatures than adults are spotted in the Metro area. Immature Yellow Crowned Night Herons resemble immature Black Crowneds. Both immatures are mostly brown in colour with whitish speckles on their backs. However the Yellow Crowneds' spots are much finer, and they have longer legs, which extend past their tails in flight. Adults of both species are easily distinguished. You may wish to refer to a field guide for more details.

Benefits of a Hurricane

Although no one likes the destructive forces of a hurricane, they can create interesting opportunities for nature observers. As hurricanes travel up the coastline, they will often pick up wildlife from various locales and carry them northward. As a result, the species travelling with or just in front of the hurricane may be from as far away as the Caribbean Islands, South and Central American countries, or the southern United States. As the hurricane winds down, the animal species are dropped off. The number and variety of species vary, depending upon the origin and strength of the hurricane and the course it travelled. Though many of the species affected by hurricanes are birds, various kinds of insects are also carried northward; tropical moths raise the greatest interest. Even a wide assortment of airborne pollens may be blown northward. Unusual marine creatures can also be seen in Halifax Harbour if the hurricane passes over an extensive stretch of ocean before touching down. The aftermath of hurricanes provides us with the opportunity to study and enjoy tropical and subtropical species, a luxury usually enjoyed by those who have the money and time to travel South.

Strange birds are definitely the most noticeable and pleasurable side-effects of hurricanes, although they are rather short-term. Within a day or two, most of the birds have rested enough to head back to the South; some of the stronger flyers may leave within a few hours after the hurricane has passed. Hurricanes, by nature, are highly unpredictable, and as a result, the effects any one hurricane will have on birds is difficult to predict. To more fully understand the variety of ways that hurricanes may affect our area, you just have to review the aftermath of some of the most recent hurricanes whose effects reached the Metro area.

In September 1989, Hurricane Gabriel blew no migrants our way, but it created huge 9 m (29 ft.) waves, completely changing the face of Conrads Beach by depositing hundreds of tonnes of sand, which filled in a massive tidal channel that flowed from West Lawrencetown Marsh to the open ocean. The results of that storm are still affecting the bird population at that location as the marsh and its associated habitats slowly convert to a more freshwater environment.

Those same hurricane-produced waves, washed an exhausted Red Necked Phalarope onto the Lawrencetown Beach. Luckily, Lynda Conrad was on hand to rescue the bird and provide it with alternate periods of rest and feeding until it was strong enough to be on its way. At its final release, the Phalarope paused briefly as if to thank its rescuer before it flew seaward. Again in 1995, Phalaropes were washed ashore by 6 m (20 ft.) waves produced by Hurricane Felix. In this case, though, the species were Red Phalaropes and all returned to the sea under their own steam.

In September 1989, Hurricane Hugo didn't bring any bird rarities, but it did create an interesting opportunity for birders at Hartlen Point, where two observers, Eleanor Simonyi and Fulton Lavender, caught sight of a Pomarine Jaeger as it winged its way past the point. Pomarines are the largest North American Jaeger and when not breeding, they spend their time at sea. They are virtually never seen from land in Nova Scotia.

In 1991, Hurricane Bob delivered an assortment of goodies all along the eastern seaboard. Unfortunately for birders, Bob, like most hurricanes, had petered out to a measly storm by the time it reached Nova Scotia. Even then, it would have had a profound effect on the Metro area had it not done something totally unexpected. Instead of travelling along the Atlantic coast, as is the pattern, the storm veered off-course and headed into the Bay of Fundy, where it deposited such exotic species as Royal Terns, a Sandwich Tern, and a Gull Billed Tern.

Southern Terns are a common side-effect of hurricanes. Besides the aforementioned species, a variety of other terns have been observed after a hurricane, including Sooty, Least, Caspian, Forster's Terns, and Black Skimmers. In the past, such bizarre sightings as a Greater Flamingo and White Tailed Tropicbirds were also a direct result of hurricanes that originated hundreds of kilometres south of Nova Scotia, teaching us that just about any bird species associated with coastal habitats is a possibility after a hurricane. Over the years, the various beaches, headlands, harbours, and coastal marshes in the Metro area have acted as a natural catch pit—a place that attracts or catches birds on a regular basis—and haven for many storm-blown strays, providing them with places to rest and feed before returning south.

So, the next time a hurricane hits the Metro area, even if it is downgraded to a tropical storm or southern gale, go out and do some exploring. You may be amazed by what you discover, you may create one of your most cherished memories.

S·E·P·T·E·M·B·E·R

The Peak of Fall Migration

The Perfect Time to be a Birder

September is one of the highlights of the year for Metro birders because a greater number of birds can be observed now than in any other month. Suddenly, birds can be seen anywhere—you could spot an interesting species on the way to your car, while out shopping, or just by glancing out the windows at work. Not only are numbers up, but the variety is also at an all-time high as migrants stream through the Metro region from other parts of Canada. At migration traps, such as Hartlen Point, the possibilities are almost unlimited as birds, thousands of miles off-course, join in with our regular migrants. Come September, it is a good idea to keep a pair of binoculars handy or even invest in a good pair of miniature binoculars to carry with you, so you do not miss out on any good birding opportunities.

Birders who live on the coast of the continent often consider September one of the most exciting times of year because of fall migration. Although fall migration takes place throughout North America, many species of birds will first head toward the coast and then proceed in a more southerly direction as they follow its contours. This causes a build-up of birds in the coastal flyways. Nova Scotians in particular are lucky as we are situated in the middle of the Atlantic Flyway. This means that literally hundreds of thousands of birds pour through Nova Scotia each fall. Migration through Nova Scotia begins in the first half of July with the sandpipers, plovers, and other shorebirds that spent their summer breeding in the Arctic. In September, the migration reaches its peak as hundreds of other species of birds join in on the southward push. Not surprisingly, along with our regular migrants, a good number of rarities are seen during this time of year.

Although the majority of the September migrants are not seed eaters, they are attracted to back yards with feeders by the presence of seed–eating birds, which indicate that such yards are a safe place for birds to congregate. Since most small birds migrate at night to avoid predators, when daylight comes they usually find themselves in unfamiliar surroundings. To compensate for this, they quickly join local birds and follow them around to discover where the safest places are to rest and feed. Naturally, many of these migrants are drawn to back yards with feeders through this process. Many passerines (small land birds) choose to follow Black Capped Chickadees around as they are friendly and are very good at finding food. This is such a common practice during fall migration that birders often discover other species of birds by checking through the flocks of chickadees. Over the years, I have seen more than one hundred different species travelling with these small birds. Feeding flocks of chickadees use clearly recognizable call notes to keep in constant contact with each member of the flock, making it easier for birders to find them and a variety of migrating songbirds.

September marks the peak of the passerine migration, the best of seabird migration, a chunk of the shorebird migration, the start of the waterfowl migration, and part of the southward movements of many other species, from hawks to herons to hummingbirds. So, grab your binoculars and head for the bird-filled outdoors!

City Birding

Traps Important to Back Yard Birders

Fall migrant traps is a term used to describe places where larger than normal concentrations of southbound birds show up. Some of the most widely known migrant spots in Nova Scotia are Brier Island, Bon Portage Island, Seal Island, Cape Sable Island and our local Hartlen Point. These locations are frequently visited by birders because they often produce interesting and unusual birds.

These hot spots represent not only high concentrations of birds, they are also indicators of what is happening in the rest of the province. For example, during the same time that good numbers of Northern Orioles were detected at Seal Island, Shelburne County, reports of sightings of Northern Orioles started to come in from Metro back yards. Knowing what birds are around at particular times greatly increases a person's chance of seeing and enjoying the different species.

Blue Jays: Not Just Another Pretty Face

If a list were made of the most beautiful birds in the province, the Blue Jay would certainly be included. Its brightly coloured plumage of blue-and-white combined with a crest and long tail gives this bird a striking appearance. Closer scrutiny by the observer reveals three distinct shades of blue. Its Latin name also refers to the beauty of the bird—*Cyanocitta cristata*, when translated, means "blue chattering bird with a crest."

The Blue Jay is a member of the Corvid family, which is known for highly developed brains; its members are the most intelligent birds in the world. Though a surprise to some, jays share this family with ravens, crows, and magpies, all of which are difficult to outsmart. For example, in the days before long lenses, photographers relied heavily on blinds to get closer to birds. Two people would enter the blind and one would leave. The birds, thinking that the humans were gone, would go about their natural business. However, Blue Jays and crows continued to squawk and stay aloft until every person in the blind had left, no matter how many people would stay or leave. Somehow, they knew when there was someone left in the blind. It was later discovered that Blue Jays and crows can count, an ability not normally found in other families of birds.

Pet Blue Jays have been taught to talk—a capacity that is usually found only amongst members of the Parrot family whose specialized tongues allow them to do so. The Blue Jay's tongue is not adapted for speech. It is only the bird's higher intelligence that allows it to accomplish this feat.

In the wild, favourite foods of the Blue Jay are acorns, followed closely by beech nuts. Fruit, berries, insects, and seeds also make up a large part of its diet. Blue Jays are quick to discover new sources of nutrition to vary their diet and are common in cities and towns, where they can be easily attracted by an offering of gray-striped sunflower seeds. If you want to give them a special treat, they find peanuts extremely appealing. Much of what we know about Blue Jays has been discovered while watching them at feeders. For example, we have learned that Blue Jays have the ability to carry several seeds at once in an area of their throat known as the crop. These seeds are later regurgitated so that they can be stored for future use in special places called caches. This practice allows Jays to survive when food becomes scarce and to feed during storms with minimal exposure to bad weather. In September, Blue Jays sometimes drive people crazy when they begin to store food for the winter because they empty the feeders so quickly. But have patience, Blue Jays stop storing food in large quantities once the cold weather arrives. So the next time you see this beautiful bird in the woods or at your feeder, remember it is not just another pretty face!

Northern Flickers

From mid-September to mid-October, large numbers of Northern Flickers are often sighted migrating south. Many of these birds are seen in city parks and people's back yards and are well worth looking for. Flickers are the strangest member of the Woodpecker family. Unlike other woodpeckers, which spend their time clinging to the sides of trees, Northern Flickers spend a good deal of their time on the ground. These Blue-Jay–size birds are mostly brown in colour and have a red patch on the back of their heads, and a big black slash around the front of their necks. In flight, they show yellow on the underside of their wings and tail; however, most people only see the large white patch at the base of their tail as the flicker flies away.

Dangers of Bright City Lights

Although I enjoy immensely the fall migration, I feel sad sometimes when I reflect upon certain discoveries from research. It has always been known that birds face numerous dangers while migrating and that some do not make it. However, a number of studies suggest that as many as 60 per cent of the birds that migrate south in the fall won't live long enough to return in the spring. This is an appalling figure, especially, when all indications are that the problem is getting worse.

One of the hazards birds face while on migration is bright lights. When migrating, birds are drawn to them, although they often become confused and are frequently killed. During fall migration in Halifax, Shawna Veinotte rescued a bewildered bird that was flying up against a lighted grocery store window in Clayton Park at about 10:30 P.M. The bird was very tame, allowing Miss Veinotte to catch it in her hands. Using a book and taking into account its tame behaviour, its location, and its general appearance, the bird was tentatively identified as a type of caged bird. After the bird didn't eat any of the typical seeds for caged birds, Miss Veinotte decided to have the bird's identification verified. Although similar in colour to some caged birds, the bird in question was a fall plumaged Blackpoll Warbler. After the bird was checked for injuries and fed, she released it at a location frequented by migrating Blackpoll Warblers in September.

This particular bird was lucky. In large cities, hundreds of birds can be killed in a single night, when, drawn by the bright lights, they often collide with tall buildings or other structures. Some die instantly, but many fall to the ground, stunned, and often meet their death before they have a chance to recover. Dazed and surrounded by bright lights and loud noises, these birds often become disoriented and get lost in a city's maze of steel and glass.

In Toronto, concerned citizens have decided to help the migrants. At night, they organize themselves in groups and patrol the city streets, looking for injured or dazed birds. They concentrate on downtown regions with the most lights. The rescued birds are taken a safe distance from the city and released. Perhaps a similar effort should be organized for the Halifax/ Dartmouth area.

Albinism

Albinism is the condition in which white feathers replace normally pigmented feathers. Causes for albinism vary. Although most albinistic birds are born lacking pigment, some acquire the condition. The most common form of acquired albinism occurs when a bird has been physically injured and white feathers grow in to replace the ones lost on the damaged areas of the bird's plumage. Severe shock can also cause a bird to suddenly grow white feathers. In Europe, a British ornithologist documented a case in which a male Blackbird moulted all its feathers and became pure white after nearly being killed by a cat. Albinism can also be the result of age. Some birds gradually acquire more white feathers as they grow older, just as people acquire more white hairs. Birds that exhibit albinism from birth are believed to have suffered a physiological disorder of dietary or circulatory deficiencies while their feathers were developing.

There are four types of albinism known to occur in birds. The most unusual form is total albinism, characterized by complete lack of colour in the bird's feathers, skin, and eyes. The bird's eyes often appear pink, when they are actually void of colour—a result of blood passing through the vessels of the eye, which is masked by the coloured irises of normal birds. Incomplete albinism is the second form, in which colour pigment is missing from the eyes, skin, or feathers, but not all three. The third form is imperfect albinism, recognized by reduced formation of pigment on any part of the bird but not a total lack of colour. The fourth and most common form is partial albinism, in which only certain feathers grow in white. In this case, it is common for the feathers to occur symmetrically on the bird's body; for example, two white feathers grown in the exact same location on each wing.

In Newfoundland, American Crows with one or two white feathers in each wing are noted on a fairly regular basis, but this is not true for Nova Scotia. Although albinistic birds may be seen during any time of year, they are frequently seen in September due to the recent crop of baby birds and the large number of migrants passing through the province.

Common Loons

Come mid-September, many loon lovers are sad to see the loons disappearing off their favourite lakes. Many people do not realize that the Common Loon can be enjoyed in the Metro area year-round. See February's "Winter Loons" selection for the full story.

Pied Billed Grebes

Pied Billed Grebes are small, ducklike birds that inhabit freshwater marshes. They are best separated from ducks by their straight, pointed bill. Pied Bills breed throughout eastern North America and winter from the southern United States to Argentina. In Nova Scotia, they are best seen in the Amherst region during the breeding season but can also be seen by the careful observer in smaller numbers in other parts of the province.

In Halifax County, late September and early October are opportune times to look for Pied Billed Grebes as they are in the process of migrating. As a result, they can be found over a wider area. When looking for grebes, keep in mind that they are often shy, so it is best to observe them from your car, which will act as a blind, allowing you to get longer and better looks at these skittish birds. Also remember that Pied Billed Grebes often swim with just their heads sticking out of the water. When they are feeling really vulnerable, they will sneak away by swimming with only the very tips of their bills above the surface of the water. This technique is called snorkelling, and unlike most waterfowl that have their nostrils at the bases of their bills, the Pied Billed Grebe's nostrils are located at the tip of their beaks.

Good places to check for Pied Billed Grebes are Three Fathom Harbour, Conrads Beach, Bisset Lake in Dartmouth, and perhaps the best place is Red Bridge Pond in Dartmouth.

Red Bridge Pond

From late September until the water freezes, Red Bridge Pond is one of the best places to view waterfowl. Each year, unusually large numbers of Ring Necked Ducks congregate there. In the fall, a visitor to this pond can expect to see a minimum of forty Ring Necked Ducks. Other species which have been observed there are Greater Scaup, Lesser Scaup, American Wigeon, Wood Duck, Green Winged Teal, Pied Billed Grebe, Hooded Merganser, American Black Duck, Mallard, Belted Kingfisher, and Great Blue Heron. No doubt more species will be discovered there, as this spot is still a relatively new area for birders.

Much of the credit for discovering the productivity of this pond should go to Liz Greenough. One day she telephoned me to say there were quite a number of Ring Necked Ducks at Red Bridge Pond in Dartmouth. I cautioned her that it would be unusual to see so many Ring Necks on such a small body of water. She revisited the pond later that day and assured me there were at least twenty–four. Intrigued, I visited the same spot near dusk and counted about seventy Ring Necked Ducks sleeping in the middle of the pond. Since then, up to a 150 Ring Necked Ducks have been sighted on this pond at one time. There are still opportunities to contribute to the knowledge about the Metro area's local birds.

Further Afield

....

September's Shorebirds

By September, many shorebird species are still present but in lower numbers than in previous months; however, four species become more prevalent in September. As luck would have it, Hartlen Point is a good spot to see all four.

Pectoral Sandpipers may be seen from July to October, but their numbers peak in September. Unlike other shorebirds that show a preference for feeding at the water's edge, the Pectoral Sandpiper will be seen feeding high up on the beach, off the piles of rotting seaweed. Its large size—20 cm to 23 cm (8 in. to 9 in.)—greenish legs, and breast streaks that are evenly cut along the bottom, make it an easy sandpiper to identify. A few of the tiny Least Sandpipers also feed high up on the shoreline with the Pectoral Sandpiper and look like miniature versions of the Pectoral. Pectoral Sandpipers are well distributed in September and may be seen at a variety of locations, providing they have access to piles of seaweed.

The American Golden Plover is harder to find but also peaks in number in September and may be seen along the shore feeding at low tide. Small flocks of these birds are most often sighted feeding on the Hartlen Point Golf Course. There,

•
S
E
P
T
E
M
B
E
R

they frequent the lower gullies where the ground is wetter, or grassy areas near the ponds (water hazards). These are the same places you are most likely to encounter one or two Buff Breasted Sandpipers. This sandpiper is well named as it is completely buff-coloured below. Although this shorebird is a readily identifiable species, only a few are seen each fall. Buff Breasts are sometimes spotted at the Conrads Beach mud flats as well.

The fourth species to look for at Hartlen Point in September is the Dunlin. Most Dunlins are in their winter plumage now and can be identified by their gray colouring and their downward drooping bills. The similar looking Curlew Sandpiper is almost never seen here, but if you are unsure of a single bird's identity, wait for it to fly and check to see if its rump is white. If it is, you have seen a Curlew Sandpiper. Normally, Dunlins occur in small flocks of half a dozen to a dozen birds. They may also be seen in October, November, or even December. Dunlins feed on both mud flats and sandy beaches but seem to favour the latter habitat later in the year, probably because the mud of exposed flats freezes faster than the sand on wave-washed beaches, thus preventing the Dunlins from probing that soil for insects.

Attracting Seabirds to your Boat

Although people often think of gulls as seabirds, true seabirds spend their lives on the ocean and come to land only for breeding purposes. If you are interested in watching seabirds, late August or September are the best times to discover the greatest variety. A boat leaving Halifax Harbour at that time of year can encounter a number of seabirds within an hour or two of clearing the harbour. Generally, the further out you get, the more seabirds you can observe, but the most important factor is where the food is concentrated. Just watch for fishing boats. Shearwaters and other seabirds often approach them in hope of finding food in the form of fish parts tossed over the sides. When fish parts are added to cod liver or vegetable oil, popcorn, puffed wheat, and/or other similar ingredients, they form a mixture known as chum, the secret formula used by birders to attract shearwaters and other seabirds to tour boats. It is dropped off the back of the boat in small amounts, creating an oil slick, which catches the attention of the birds and draws them in.

Gulls are always the first to discover the handout and will start to arrive singly or in pairs. Shortly, a cloud of gulls will be flying around the boat, helping to draw in other birds, some interested in food, others interested in what is happening. Shearwaters are generally the next group of birds to arrive. Like stealth bombers, they suddenly appear from nowhere, flying in fast and low, often just centimetres above the surface of the water. Smaller and less aggressive than the Great Black Backed and Herring Gulls, they rely on their speed to snatch up the smaller pieces of fish.

The most commonly encountered shearwater off the coast of Halifax is the Greater Shearwater, with hundreds seen on some days. Like most shearwaters, Greaters breed in the South Atlantic and come to the Metro area in their winter—our summer—to relax before going south again by early November to breed. Our second most common shearwater is the Sooty Shearwater, although on some trips it can be outnumbered by the smaller Manx Shearwater. Manx Shearwaters reach their peak numbers in July and August, while the Sooty Shearwater peaks in August. Our rarest annual shearwater is the Cory's. Only a few of these are reported each year, and waters between Halifax and Sable Island are considered the most reliable section of our offshore waters to see one of these birds. The Cory's Shearwater is the largest among shearwaters is likely to be encountered in August or early September, though it may be seen as late as October.

Shearwaters and petrels are the two groups most often seen during seabird trips. While most seabirds do a great deal of gliding, the tiny petrels flutter like little fairies just centimetres above the waves. It is a peaceful sight to see their tiny feet dabble on the ocean's surface as they dip their bill into the water to pick up food. Sometimes they will land for short periods to rest. Two common species are the Wilson's Storm Petrel, which readily comes to chum, and the Leach's Storm Petrel, which is more aloof. The Leach's breed in Nova Scotia, with Pearl Island the closest colony to the Metro area. The two petrels can be distinguished at a distance by remembering that Leach's bounce in flight like Common Night-hawks, while the smaller Wilson's fly more like swallows.

After the shearwaters and petrels, Northern Fulmars are the next species a birding party is likely to come across. These tough seabirds can fly against the strongest winds and withstand the coldest winter temperatures, so it is not surprising that this species is increasing in numbers in Nova Scotia and all along the eastern seaboard. Fulmars may be seen during any month. Two species of oceanic shorebirds which are also regulars on fall seabird trips are the Red Necked Phalarope and the Red Phalarope, both of which are common from July to September. Gannets are also frequently seen but are not considered a true seabird because they are often seen from land. Atlantic Puffins are a better treat as they are hard to see from land but are likely candidates on a seabird tour.

The really good birds to see are the jaegers and skuas. Three species of jaegers can be seen and two of skuas, which are, in order of likeli-hood: Pomarine Jaeger, Great Skua, Parasitic

Jaeger, South Polar Skua, and Long Tailed Jaeger. If only one of these species is seen on an outing, it is considered a good trip. If two of these species are seen, you have had an excellent trip, and if more than two species are discovered, it was an exceptional trip. Remote possibilities to see include the Black Capped Petrel, the Band Rumped and the British Storm Petrel, the Little and the Audubon's Shearwaters. Of course, an added bonus on these trips is the various species of whales, dolphins, sharks, and other sea creatures that could be encountered.

Great Blue Herons

The Great Blue Heron is the most common heron in the province and is often seen along the coast or on fresh water. It is often mistakenly called a crane, but an easy way to distinguish between these two similar kinds of birds is to remember that cranes spend most of their time in dry habitats like fields, while Great Blue Herons stick close to water. Another helpful tip is that cranes are rarely seen in Nova Scotia.

The Great Blue Heron appears to be more common than usual during the last two weeks of September because these large birds have begun their southward migration. At that time, literally hundreds of these herons can be viewed along the Eastern Shore, as well as in many other parts of the province. To a lesser degree, the Great Blue can also be found migrating in August, October, and November.

Yellow Billed Cuckoos

Worldwide, 127 distinct species of cuckoos are known to exist, of which 6 are native to North America. Four of those 6 breed only in the warmest regions of the continent, and 2 can be found as far north as Halifax County. Blacked

Billed Cuckoos breed here in very small numbers but rarely are seen because of their highly secretive nature. The Yellow Billed Cuckoo is occasionally encountered during the summer but is most often sighted during migration. Although it is rarer that the Blacked Billed Cuckoo, it is often seen more regularly as it is not quite as shy and is more likely to visit urban areas.

Cuckoos are long, slender, drab-coloured birds, named after their quiet, cooinglike calls. However, there may be something else "cuckoo" about these birds. I had my first look at a Yellow Billed Cuckoo in 1981, when a friend and I caught a brief glimpse of a distant one flying into a large patch of Japanese knotwood. We approached the patch, estimated where it had flown in, and proceeded to enter the patch ourselves. After our first steps, we were surprised and disappointed to find the cuckoo lying at our feet. Apparently, the bird had flown into one of the slender bamboolike shoots of the knotwood and broke its neck.

During the next four years, I came across three more lifeless Yellow Billed Cuckoos before having the pleasure of watching one enjoying life. Since then, I have had several encounters with lifeless Yellow Billed Cuckoos and I have come to think of them as extremely accident prone.

Black Billed Cuckoos seem to fare a bit better, but they, too, sometimes have accidents. In Tantallon, Michael Downing and Helen Blake saw their first Blacked Billed Cuckoo when it flew into their patio doors. Fortunately, the bird had only stunned himself, and a short while later he disappeared into a thick clump of cat–spruce and was never seen again. The greatest number of cuckoos pass through the Metro area in September and October. The best place by far to see one is at the Back Cove at Hartlen Point; however, both species, especially the Yellow Billed, may show up at almost any location.

Furry Caterpillars

Cuckoos' preferred food is caterpillars, especially furry caterpillars. I was quite mystified when I first learned this fact, as I had read that most birds learned to avoid furry caterpillars because their fur contains a chemical which can cause a burning sensation when eaten by birds. Besides burning, in most cases, this chemical causes the birds to get sick. I had also learned by that time, that when it came to birds, virtually every rule had an exception. So my question was not "if" but "how" could cuckoos regularly feed on furry caterpillars with apparently no ill effects. Although I searched many bird books at the time, I could not find an explanation.

I finally found the answer when I saw my first Yellow Billed Cuckoo at Birch Cove Park in Dartmouth. I followed the bird for over half an hour before I was able to watch him getting ready to dine on a furry caterpillar. After capturing a rather large one, he positioned it crossways in his bill, near the tip of his beak. I fully expected him to continue turning the bug around, swallow it head first, and that would be that. To my surprise, he quickly "de-furred" the insect by rapidly shooting the caterpillar back and forth through his bill; the scene resembled a cartoon character eating corn on the cob. Once all of the harmful hairs were removed, he safely swallowed the caterpillar. I stood there thinking to myself, "How simple yet clever nature can be at times."

American Pipits

American Pipits (previously called Water Pipits), breed in the Arctic and pass through the Metro area during the spring and fall migration. However, they are most frequently seen during the second half of September and during October. At this time, they usually are found along the coastline feeding on insects associated with clumps of kelp and other seaweed. Similar in appearance to a sparrow, they can be distinguished by their habit of pumping their tails continually while on the ground. They can also be recognized by the flash of their white outer tail feathers when they fly. Their very musical flight notes when flying overhead or taking off from the ground may also give away their identity. When walking the shoreline, keep in mind that pipits blend in well with the surrounding habitat, so it is not uncommon to spook a flock before you even realize they are present. Two good places to search for pipits are the Back Cove at Hartlen Point and Conrads Beach.

Eastern Kingbirds

The Eastern Kingbird is fairly common in Nova Scotia and is usually found in farmlands and other open areas. During migration, Kingbirds pass through urban centres but don't stay long. Throughout most of the year, the Eastern Kingbird is not seen in the Metro area. However, during the last week of August and early September, Eastern Kingbirds may be seen on roadside wires, in and outside city limits.

Flying insects make up the majority of their diet; however, kingbirds are also known to eat berries and fruit. Fruit is an extremely important part of their diet during the winter months that it spends in South America. In fall, Eastern Kingbirds migrate to the tropical regions of Peru and Bolivia, where they feed heavily on fruiting trees. Once the fruit trees are depleted, the birds move northward to the next batch of trees. This process continues until the birds reach Panama in mid-March. It is believed that a continuous fruit supply is critical to the kingbird's northern migration, and if too many sections of fruit trees continue to be removed along its migration routes, populations may decrease drastically. Like most flycatchers, the Eastern Kingbird is rather drab in colour—dark gray above and white below—however, they can be easily identified as they are the only medium-size bird in Nova Scotia with a white band running across the tip of an otherwise black tail.

Peregrine Falcons

September is an excellent month to see the powerful Peregrine Falcon. They may also be seen during the second half of August or the first half of October. Look for them in places where shorebirds gather, a favourite food of peregrines. Every fall peregrines are sighted at Hartlen Point and

Conrads Beach, so these are good locations to focus your attention on.

Serious declines in peregrine populations began after World War II. The increased use of pesticides, such as DDT, moved through the food chain to the Peregrine Falcon, causing egg thinning and resulting in few chicks. Since the ban of these poisons in North America in the early 1970s, the Peregrine Falcon has made a slow recovery. However, these magnificent birds of prey are still on the endangered species list. In recent years, several young falcons have been released into Nova Scotia by the Canadian Wildlife Service in an effort to re–establish the population.

Coats of Many Colours

. . . .

October's Autumn

Fall migration is one of the most spectacular
natural events to take place each year in Nova
Scotia. The excitement begins with a bang in
August as thousands upon thousands of sandpipers, plovers, and other shorebirds pour down
from their Arctic breeding grounds. In
September, they are joined by hundreds of species
of passerines, other land-breeding birds, and
seabirds. The sheer numbers make these months
an exciting time to do some birding.

By October, the migrators have diminished in
numbers, but looking for birds now can be just as
thrilling. After all, the reduction in numbers
makes it easier to pick out the rarer migrants
from the more common species. For this reason,
many birders find October and November an
even more interesting time of year to search for
unusual birds. A greater number of the remaining

O · C · T · O · B · E · R ·

migrants start to use feeders as a means of fuelling up during their journeys. Birders have a much better chance of seeing a rare and unusual bird just by looking out their windows. Back yards everywhere suddenly become hot spots where the careful observer can see interesting sights.

Song Sparrows, Dark Eyed Juncos, White Throated Sparrows, and Red Winged Blackbirds are four common migrants that visit feeders at this time of the year. Some of the rare birds one may see include Indigo Bunting, Brown Thrasher, Dickcissel, Carolina Wren, Varied Thrush, Rufous Sided Towhee, Eastern Phoebe, Northern Wheatear, Red Headed Woodpecker, and Red Bellied Woodpecker.

Along the shoreline, watch for migrating Great Blue Herons, Belted Kingfishers, and Northern Gannets. The grassy areas of beaches are also interesting places to check at this time of year. At Conrads Beach, one may see a few Horned Larks or Lapland Longspurs. Occasionally, an Eastern Meadowlark is seen. Over the years, Rainbow Haven Beach has been the location of several sightings of the extremely rare Seaside Sparrow. For this reason, from October to December, all sparrows at this location should be looked at carefully. Woodland walkers have a good chance of seeing Gray Jays and Ruby Crowned Kinglets as both species will be present in higher than usual numbers. If you are really lucky, you may see a Long Eared Owl. These owls pass through Metro in October and are rarely seen during other months. At Hartlen Point, rarity seekers should be alert for the presence of White Eyed Vireos. Records show that early October is the most likely time to see one. October is also an excellent month to enjoy hawk and waterfowl migrations.

City Birding

....

Sparrow Identification Made Easy

October is a great time for seeing various species of sparrows, often considered the most difficult types of birds to identify at feeders; they are simply dismissed as "LBJs" (Little Brown Jobbies). However, identifying sparrows at a feeder is not as hard as it first appears. The key to identifying most sparrows is to note the patterns on top of their heads and on their chests. There are eleven common species of sparrows in Nova Scotia, six of which visit feeders regularly. Of the six species, two have streaked breasts, two have plain breasts and a rusty cap, and two have plain breasts without a rusty cap. Below I have included a brief description of each of the six sparrows, indicating what to look for, but consult a field guide for complete descriptions.

The Song Sparrow is the only Metro area sparrow that is streaked underneath and has a large black spot in the centre of its chest. The other streaked feeder sparrow, the Fox Sparrow, is larger—almost as large as an Evening Grosbeak—and is very rusty all over, especially on the tail. The Tree Sparrow has a rusty cap and a plain breast with a dark spot and is usually seen only in the winter. The Chipping Sparrow, normally a summer resident, also has a rusty cap and a plain breast, but no black spot. The White Throated Sparrow has a white or off-white throat, a plain breast, and will have wide white or tan stripes alternating with black stripes on its head. The House or English Sparrow has a plain breast; the male sports a black bib while the female has a noticeable lightish stripe over her eye and no bib. Neither the male nor the female has streaks on top of their heads.

Within the urban areas, the House Sparrow is the most common sparrow, while in the suburbs the Song Sparrow is more prevalent. Many female finches resemble sparrows but can be distinguished by the fact that finches eat sunflower seeds, while sparrows prefer mixed seed or millet. The exception is the House Sparrow, a member of the Weaver Finch family, introduced from Europe in the 1800s.

As for identifying all of the types of sparrows you may see in October, I strongly recommend using the Peterson *Eastern Birds* guide. It illustrates six pages of sparrows and groups them according to unstreaked or mostly unstreaked breasts and streaked breasts. So, when you see a sparrow, to eliminate half the possibilities, check if it is streaked or unstreaked. When it comes to identifying birds accurately, the process of elimination is the name of the game.

Tall grassy areas, like the ones found at Rainbow Haven Beach and the Back Cove at Hartlen Point, are ideal places to find rare species of sparrows in October. Unfortunately, getting a good look at them in tall grass is difficult because most of the time, as soon as you get close enough to see them, they drop into the grasses. For this reason, I prefer to look for them along the shorelines at low tide, when they feast on insects from the piles of seaweed. The section of shoreline at Hartlen Point that faces Devils Island is a perfect location to see all kinds of sparrows. The pathway, a grassy muddy road that runs along the top of this shoreline, can also be good for sparrows. I have found that this pathway is best late in the day, when large numbers of sparrows come out of the dimly lit grass to feed on the weeds growing in it and to drink from the puddles. Another good place for viewing sparrows in October is the Fairview Cemetery.

Evening Grosbeaks

Although roving flocks of Evening Grosbeaks often consume large quantities of sunflower seeds, they are welcome additions to most back yards. The majority of Evening Grosbeaks nest to the north and west of us; however, small numbers of these beautiful birds do breed in Nova Scotia. Evening Grosbeaks belong to the Finch family, and like most finches, they are highly nomadic. In some winters, we may see many flocks from ten to three hundred birds, while in others there may be only small flocks of six to fifty birds scattered throughout the province. The first flocks of Evening Grosbeaks generally appear in Nova Scotia in October. These are not our winter birds but migrants on their way south. Researchers have noticed an interesting winter distribution pattern for Evening Grosbeaks. In the southern parts of their winter range, flocks have a greater number of females than males, while in the northern parts of their winter range, the flocks have a greater proportion of males. Nova Scotia falls roughly in the middle of the bird's winter range, and our winter flocks generally consist of 50 per cent of each sex.

Our Nova Scotia Evening Grosbeaks usually begin to arrive in late November and build in number throughout the winter, until they start to leave in March. There are slight variations in their migration times, so if you see a flock that you are uncertain about, simply count the male/female ratio and, as they say in the stock market circuit, "the numbers will tell the story."

If you are interested in attracting these birds to your yard, the following tips should help. While Evening Grosbeaks will feed very close to a house (i.e., on a deck or windowsill), they are still generally nervous birds and prefer to feed at feeders set further back from your home. Unlike many other feeder birds, Evening Grosbeaks generally don't require a lot of cover near their feeding stations and come quite readily to feeders placed in the open. There should be a tall tree or two nearby, though, as Evening Grosbeak flocks love to land in the tops of tall trees, especially deciduous ones. The type of feeder you use also determines how often they will frequent your yard. While they will use just about any size feeder, they generally prefer large wooden ones because they generally feel most comfortable at feeders where the whole flock can eat at once, or at least a good portion of it.

Mourning Doves

Although there are fifteen species of pigeons found in North America, when most people think of a pigeon, they think of the run-of-the-mill street pigeon. To birders, this is the Rock Dove, and to breeders it is the homing, carrier, or domestic pigeon. Regardless of what you call them, there are many people who don't like Rock Doves, or more precisely they don't like some of their habits. On the other hand, the Rock Dove's closest relative in the province, the Mourning Dove, is a favourite songbird of many.

Mourning Doves were first recorded in Nova Scotia in 1842. However, surveys of the province's bird population in 1856 and 1865 made no mention of the bird. In 1888, A. Down's recorded in his *A Catalogue of the Birds of Nova Scotia*, that although the Mourning Dove was once rare in Nova Scotia, it was then rather common. By 1962, when Robie Tufts' first edition of *Birds of Nova Scotia* was published, the Mourning Dove was once again considered rare. In 1984, Mourning Doves were regarded as uncommon in the province but growing in numbers. Though the status of the Mourning Dove has changed throughout Nova Scotia's history as their numbers fluctuated, it is likely that they will now continue to increase in the province. In recent decades, they have been going through a population explosion throughout North America.

There are several theories as to why this is happening. Studies have shown that a greater number of migratory birds die compared to sedentary birds due to the dangers and difficulties of migration. For most songbirds, evolution has determined whether they will migrate long before they are born. Interestingly, research has revealed that in recent years, a lower percentage of Mourning Doves are migrating. The presence of bird feeders in their summer breeding grounds appears to be the determining factor. If this is the case, it is the first record of feeders affecting the migration of a species of songbird. One possible explanation for this is that Mourning Doves probably had the abilities all along to survive northern winters but chose not to, until feeders gave them the extra edge needed to survive in large numbers.

Mourning Doves appear to be adapting in other ways as well. In the western United States, researchers have discovered that in many areas, they are now nesting on the ground, allowing them to expand into relatively treeless habitats and regions. Perhaps the most interesting theory on the expansion of the Mourning Dove population is that they are filling the ecological gap left behind when the Passenger Pigeon was decimated in North America. Whatever the reason, Mourning Doves are definitely on the rise.

Winter Warblers

Warblers are brightly coloured, tiny, insect-eating birds, with most species having some yellow in their plumage. In Nova Scotia, twenty–two species of warblers are considered fairly common

OCTOBER

and are best seen from May to September. Once September passes, the number of individuals of any one species seen diminishes significantly. However, three species of warblers—the Pine Warbler, the Yellow Breasted Chat, and the Orange Crowned Warbler—prove to be an exception to this rule. Each of these three species breeds outside the province but shows up every year in small numbers. They are best seen from October to December.

Although Yellow Breasted Chats are the largest warbler in North America and sport bright yellow on their throat and chest, they are a secretive and elusive bird, spending most of their time undercover in thick bushes. It is best to look for them in bushes that provide dense cover and berries. A good example is the multiflora rose, a favourite of theirs and many other species. The Yellow Breasted Chat is strictly a solitary species.

Orange Crowned Warblers are small and plump looking, mostly a dull greenish colour all over with yellow undertail coverts. They show no wing bars and almost never show an orange crown. They are often found feeding on the ground or close to the ground, at which times they are easily approached. While on the ground, instead of feeding like sparrows, which scratch, Orange Crowneds flit about from spot to spot like a warbler. They are often seen by themselves or travelling with a flock of chickadees, when they frequently feed high in the trees or at whatever height the chickadees are feeding. They may be seen anywhere flocks of chickadees are present; virtually every October, at least one Orange Crowned can be found with them at the Fairview Cemetery.

Pine Warblers are the easiest of these three kinds to find in Metro, for two reasons. The first is that in recent years, there has been a noticeable increase in their numbers. This is probably due in part to the fact that they now breed regularly in New Brunswick. They are seen more frequently than other winter warblers as they regularly come to feeders. Although they occasionally eat hulled sunflower seeds, their favourite food is peanut butter suet. This high-energy food will keep them coming back. Adult Pine Warblers have bright yellow throats and two white wing bars. The yellow may also extend down over the upper and lower chest, but their bellies are always white. Immatures may be grayish or brownish, and are distinguished from the similar looking fall plumaged warblers by their unstreaked backs.

The fourth warbler to see in October and all winter is the Yellow Rumped Warbler, also our most common summer warbler. In the winter, they may be found inside the city limits but are more common in areas where bayberries grow, a favourite winter food. The bushy areas and woods at Rainbow Haven, Conrads, and Martinique Beaches are regular winter locations for the Yellow Rumpeds. There, they may form their own flocks or be found with Golden Crowned Kinglets and sometimes Boreal Chickadees.

White Crowned Sparrows

The White Crowned Sparrow breeds to the north and west of Nova Scotia and is one of the province's uncommon fall migrants. Most south-bound White Crowns pass through the Metro area in October and may be seen at feeders, mixed in with migrating flocks of sparrows. A visit to the Back Cove at Hartlen Point in early morning gives you a good chance of seeing one of these birds.

Further Afield

....

Shorebird Surprises

By the time October arrives, most of the various species of shorebirds have left the Metro area, but there are a few notable exceptions. October is probably the best month to go looking in Metro for a Dunlin. American Golden Plovers are still fairly common as well. For more information on both of these species check out September's "Shorebirds."

To see a different side of the Common Snipe, try walking through a brackish marsh in October. Like saltwater marshes, they are located along the coast but still have enough fresh water flowing into them to allow cattails to grow. If you are unable to find a brackish marsh, there is one located in the Back Cove at Hartlen Point. As you weave your way along the edge of the cattails, be prepared for the high-speed takeoff of a Common Snipe. This bird will bolt well ahead of you and will utter a sharp cry that sounds like "skipe" or "scaip." A few steps farther and a second snipe will explode up from the ground. Often, others fly off shortly after. Why they do not all leave at once in such a small area is a mystery; perhaps they are eternal optimists. The fact that they do not flee simultaneously is good for birders—after the first one flies off, a birder is better prepared to see the others. They are fast moving birds with a zigzagging flight, so they can be difficult to see through binoculars. They can be identified without binoculars by the combination of their calls, their long bills, and long pointed wings hooked back along their bodies. It is even possible to see the diagnostic white stripes on their backs or the rust on their tails as they whiz by.

The American Woodcock is another shorebird that moves through the Metro area in large numbers in October. Unfortunately, because they are highly secretive, solitary migrators, it is difficult to note their migratory movements. Each year hundreds pass through our region but only a few are actually seen. In Windsor Junction, long-time resident Mary Vaughan finally saw one when it hit a window of her house. Hearing the "thunk," she rushed outside and saw this odd looking bird sitting in her deck chair. Just momentarily stunned, the bird quickly flew away. Although this is one way to see a Woodcock, your best chance is to check small isolated patches of moist woodlands that have lots of leaf litter. Birch Cove Park and the Urban Wilderness Park are two locations that are representative of the type of sites they choose. At these locations, I have been able to closely view one of these peculiar looking birds. You have to keep your eyes open though, as their buffy coloration closely matches the colour of dead leaves. Besides camouflaging, areas with lots of leaf litter are home to earthworms, the main food item of a Woodcock's diet.

Conrads Beach often hosts a few late shorebirds. In October, the seaweed piles along the beach are a good place to see Pectoral Sandpipers. At low tide, keep an eye on the marshy area along the road leading to the Conrads Beach parking lot. There, at low tide, Hudsonian Godwits can be seen. Another spot for late shorebirds, especially unusual ones, is Hartlen Point. For example, the only Metro record for Little Stint (a European shorebird) occurred in October at Hartlen Point.

Snow Geese

Snow Geese breed in the Arctic and winter in the southern United States and Mexico. Each fall, thousands fly over Canada on their southward trek. This migration begins in August and is completed by the end of November. Each province has a part of the Snow Goose population pass through it, the greatest numbers occur in Quebec. Birders have counted up to 100, 000 Snow Geese at Cape Tourmente, 15 km (25 mi.) northeast of Québec City. The annual visit of the Snow Geese at that location is so spectacular that it has become a popular tourist attraction, drawing people from all over the world. The appeal in a group of these large white birds is understandable since the beauty of just one individual is impressive. I can only image how breathtaking it must be to see a flock so large that it seems as if Cape Tourmente is suddenly covered by a moving blanket of snow.

In Nova Scotia, only a few Snow Geese are sighted each fall. They may be sighted on their own, but in most cases they prefer the company of other geese. For this reason, always check through flocks of Canada Geese for these delightful birds. Nearly all fall sightings have occurred between the last week of September and the last week of November.

Snow Geese can be distinguished from regular white domestic geese by their larger size, more graceful appearance, and most importantly, their pure black wing tips. Flocks of Snow Geese are almost unheard of in Nova Scotia, but at a distance they can be distinguished from Canada Geese by the way they fly. Instead of the typical "V" formation used by the Canada Geese, they prefer to fly in a long curved line.

Another rare goose to look for amongst the Canada Geese is the Greater White Fronted Goose. Only a few records exist for Halifax County, but if you are scanning flocks of Canada Geese anyway, you might as well watch for them. They are most likely to be seen during October and November. Look for a gray goose with a pink bill and yellow or orange feet.

Goodbye and Good Riddance to Grackles!

Many people are happy to see large numbers of
Common Grackles exiting Nova Scotia during
the latter part of September and early October.
They are aggressive birds which can dominate
summer feeders, driving all other birds away. Even
Blue Jays can be forced to back off when grackles
arrive in numbers. Common Grackles often breed
in colonies and travel in large flocks, although fortunately, the majority of the grackle population
does not enjoy our metropolitan winters.

Enthusiastic birders make sure they check
through large flocks of grackles, starlings, and
Red Winged Blackbirds in the fall, as every year,
more than one person discovers something
unusual amongst these flocks. In most cases, the
odd bird is a less common species of blackbird.
The most likely species to be seen in one of these
flocks is a Rusty Blackbird. However, we also
have several reports in the Metro area of the rarer
Yellow Headed Blackbird and Brewers Blackbird.
Although the latter are extremely rare for this
area, they are a possibility.

Just Another Little Brown Bird

It was a cool October day in the middle of the
month, but a good-size group of new birders had
gathered in the early morning to go on an
instructional birding trip that I was leading. The
purpose of the walk was to learn how to identify
birds easily and quickly. One of the highlights of
the trip was a female Indigo Bunting. The bird
was foraging with a flock of Dark Eyed Juncos on
a field adjacent to Tantallon Junior High School.
This bird presented an interesting challenge for
the participants to identify, as female Indigos are
smooth brown birds with no other readily noticeable markings. At first this sounds like a difficult

bird to identify, but in fact it is very easy because we only have one other markless brown songbird in the province—the female Brown Headed Cowbird, a species that is quite a bit larger than the petite goldfinch–size Indigo.

Once the participants realized what species of bird they were looking at, this plainly coloured bird sparked a new interest, and they began to notice other things about it. They observed that whenever the bird moved, it gave a sharp "spitz" note. This call note of the Indigo Bunting is distinctive and is a great way to discover female Indigos and the bright blue males—a useful tip as these birds often hide and feed in tall grass.

On this particular day, both the Dark Eyed Juncos and the Indigo Bunting avoided the grassy areas on the field and chose instead to forage along the narrow boundaries between the grass and the bare patches of ground. Although no food was readily detectable to human eyes, the birds appeared to be feeding actively. Insects or very tiny seeds from pineapple weeds, which rimmed most of the bare patches, may have been their source of nourishment. This experience is a typical example of what happens when you take the time to observe birds. It not only provides interesting discoveries but reveals mysteries for future exploration.

Indigo Buntings pass through the province in increasing numbers each spring and fall. Although most Indigos are reported in the spring, it is likely many go unnoticed in the fall because much of the bright blue plumage of the male is obscured by brown-edged feathers.

Any time from September to November, Indigos may be seen in Metro. However, October is the month of most fall sightings. Back yard feeders and Hartlen Point are the best places to find Indigo Buntings in October. To find them at Hartlen Point, go to the Back Cove and walk through or along the edge of the tall grass lining the cove. On an exceptionally good day at Hartlen Point, you may first hear and then see up to a dozen Indigos, some still showing a little of the bright blue. On most days in October, at least one Indigo will be present.

Waterfowl Migration

October is the best month for viewing the fall waterfowl migration, a busy one that can be divided into three major groups of birds. The first group is the summer breeders in Nova Scotia. Although a few individuals from this group will stay in the Metro area during the winter, the majority head for warmer waters, such as Pied Billed Grebes, Double Crested Cormorants, Blue Winged Teals, Green Winged Teals, American Wigeons, Ringed Necked Ducks, Wood Ducks, Northern Pintails, Northern Shovelers, Gadwalls, and Ruddy Ducks.

The second group of waterfowl migrants is the ducks that occur in numbers in the Metro area year-round but peak during the fall or spring migration. This group consists of American Black Ducks, Common, Red Breasted and Hooded Mergansers, Common Eiders, and, to a lesser extent, Common Loons.

The third group is those species that breed to the north of Metro but gather in Metro during the winter months. These species begin to arrive in October at about the same time as our summer waterfowl are exiting. Included in this group are the Red Throated Loons, Horned and Red Necked Grebes, Greater and Lesser Scaups, Black, Surf and White Winged Scoters, Common and Barrow's Goldeneyes, Oldsquaws, and Buffleheads. In October, this third group does not concern local birders as these species can be seen at any time in the Metro area during the winter months. In fact, most are easier to find once the colder weather arrives. Likewise, the species categorized as year-round residents are of only minor interest. (One exception is Hooded Mergansers as they are harder to find during the rest of the year.) This is also true for many of the province's breeding waterfowl as the Metro area has very little in the way of breeding marshes when compared to other parts of the province, such as Amherst. In addition to these local breeders, there is also a chance that species from the west may be found amongst the regulars.

Perhaps Metro's two most interesting waterfowl spots in October are Red Bridge Pond and Bissett Lake. At these spots, amongst the gathering Ring Necked Ducks, many unusual species may be observed. Red Bridge is a productive little pond, located on Braemar Drive, opposite Micmac Lake. The nice thing about this pond, especially on cooler days, is that most of the species present can be viewed without leaving your car. All you have to do is park off Braemar in the little parking lot that lies between the road and the pond. Occasionally, some species are hidden from view but may be seen by driving towards the Parclo (formerly the Dartmouth Rotary), turning left onto Maple, taking the first left onto Plymouth, and the second left onto Cranbrook. At the end of Cranbrook you can clearly see the back corner of the pond.

Larger than Red Bridge Pond, Bissett Lake attracts an even greater volume of waterfowl. The drawback created by its size, at least as far as birders are concerned, is that the birds can be difficult to view up close. When planning to visit this location, it will be worthwhile to bring a birding scope along. There is a healthy population of American Black Ducks present in this lake, which helps to attract other species of puddle ducks; however, this lake appears to be particularly popular with the freshwater divers.

October is also a good time to start checking Sullivans Pond for new arrivals. This pond becomes even more productive in November. See "Birding Sullivans Pond" in the "Places" section for details on what species may be observed there.

In October, Hooded Mergansers may be encountered at The Puddle, Whynauchts Cove and the mouth of the Sackville River. Hooded Mergansers are the smallest and shyest species of Mergansers found in Nova Scotia. In the summer, they inhabit quiet backwater areas and wooded lakes but move out to saltwater areas in the fall and winter. At most locations, only the occasional Hooded Merganser may be seen. However, in the fall these three places have produced exceptional numbers of Hooded Mergansers. Up to a dozen birds may be seen at each of these spots.

The Puddle is a small cove of water that lies immediately to the west of Black Point, towards Queensland Beach along Route 3. Whynauchts Cove can be observed from the power plant at St. Margarets Bay or from Whynauchts Point Road in Tantallon. As many as thirty Hooded Mergansers have been counted at this sight. The Hoodeds at the mouth of the Sackville River may be easily observed from Shore Drive in Bedford.

Hawk Migration

Migration is just one of the many fascinating aspects of birding, with hawk migration of particular interest for many people. In Nova Scotia, hawk migration begins slowly in mid–August and continues until about the end of October for southbound birds leaving the province. During this time, nine species of hawks are fairly common in the Metro area, but more than a dozen may be seen.

Many of these species follow the natural contours of the coastline and often concentrate along headlands and inshore islands. Other hawks, especially members of the Buteo family will often choose inland routes to take advantage of thermals and updraughts associated with mountains and ridges—mountains close to the coast are especially productive areas for viewing large numbers of migrating raptors. At such locations you could see a hundred or more hawks in one day. Unfortunately, no really good hawk-watching places have been discovered in the Metro area. There are several high places around the Metro area that have the potential, they just have to be visited by the right person at the right time of year.

The time of day for watching hawks is crucial as well. Since thermals are very important to hawk migration, the best time to see the greatest number and variety of hawks is from about 11:00 A.M. to 3:00 P.M., when the thermals are at their best. For those who are not early risers, hawk-watching is the perfect type of birding. If you do decide to try it, be sure to pick up a copy of the book *Hawks In Flight.* This excellent book is full of information on how to identify flying hawks even at a distance. Another good guide is Peterson's *Hawks*, which contains a lot of additional information on hawk identification not found in the standard field guides. It is particularly useful for identifying perched birds of prey.

October marks the peak of the Red Tailed Hawk migration and is the easiest time of year to see them in the Metro area. Like most hawks, they are more frequently seen outside the city limits. Look for them near open grassy locations. This is also an excellent time to keep your eyes open for the rarely seen Red Shouldered Hawk. It is about the size of the Red Tailed and is generally seen in the province during fall or spring migration. The "red shoulders" of the Red Shouldered Hawk are a rufous section found on each wing of adult birds and can best be seen on the top side of the bird when it is in flight. When viewed from below or front-on, its most impressive features are closely spaced, reddish–orange bands on its chest and belly. However, this is not a good field mark to identify a Red Shouldered Hawk as three other species of hawks—the Sharp Shinned, the Broad Winged, and the Coopers—show very similar bands. To seemingly complicate identification, these three species, like the Red Shouldered, show black-and-white bands on the tail. The Red Shouldered's unique design gives the appearance of narrow white lines on a black tail; the reverse is true of the other three species, so that the tail bands alone can be used to distinguish the Red Shouldered from the others.

Another rare hawk is the Coopers Hawk. September and October are the most likely times to see one in Metro. Even then, caution should be exercised as Sharp Shinned Hawks look very similar and are much more common.

N·O·V·E·M·B·E·R

A Month of Transition

Metro's Green Areas

One of the great things about birding is that each month offers a special treat, that is, if you know where to watch. In November, you do not necessarily need to go far to see interesting birds. Try looking carefully at the birds attending your feeder and especially at the birds poking about in your yard. Some of the best birders in the province make it a rule to spend time checking the feeders of neighbours and friends during this time of year; the chances of seeing something exciting are quite good.

November is the best time to visit city parks and other green areas in Metro to see unusual birds. In past Novembers, Point Pleasant Park, Fairview Cemetery, the Music Conservatory, and Conrose Park at the end of Waegwoltic Street in Halifax (also known as The Horsefields) have been particularly productive. In Dartmouth, some good places to visit are Birch Cove Park, Findlay

Park, Sullivans Pond, Bissett Lake, and Red Bridge Pond. A visit to one or more of these parks will be well worth your while. At these parks, pay particular attention to birds in bushy areas or those mixed in with the flocks of Black Capped Chickadees. By doing so, your chances are very good that you will see at least one uncommon species. Some of the rarities regularly encountered at this time are Yellow Breasted Chats, Rufous Sided Towhees, Pine Warblers, Orange Crowned Warblers, and Northern Orioles, but a lot of other possibilities exist. Anywhere in the city watch for flocks of House Sparrows. The House Sparrows themselves may not interest you, but each year in November and December a few of the flocks have a Dickcissel with them.

Outside the city limits, watch for Western Kingbirds. These beautiful flycatchers breed in western Canada and the United States, but winter on the east coast, in Florida and points southward. Each year in early November, at least one or two of these birds pass through the Metro area. In some years, as many as a dozen of these kingbirds may be sighted. They are best seen outside the city limits, as they feed over open areas, often from roadside wires.

Shorebirds are scarce in November but a few stragglers can be seen. Pay special attention to any dowitchers you encounter as this is the one time of year that the bird is more likely to be a Long Billed rather than a Short Billed Dowitcher.

In November, one good location to see waterfowl is Three Fathom Harbour. This is especially true for the second half of the month. Although Ruddy Ducks are a rare migrant in the Metro area, nearly every November for the past ten years, one or two of these unusual looking ducks have shown up there. This is also a good spot to see Buffleheads, Pied Billed Grebes, Greater Scaups, and the occasional Hooded Merganser. The

Ruddy Ducks are often mixed in with the flocks of Buffleheads, so look at each bird carefully.

I grew up in Dartmouth and was always proud that I lived in a city with plenty of trees. However, because most of Dartmouth has very few protected green areas, I have seen a majority of my favourite birding spots disappear to development. Although it is necessary for the growth of our economy, it is equally true that green areas are important to the well being of city occupants. They not only make neighbourhoods more attractive to birds but also to most people, and protected green areas help to ensure the lasting beauty of a neighbourhood. Also the combination of plants, birds, and animals in these areas contribute in numerous ways to a healthier environment for our day-to-day living. Some may argue that Metro has plenty of green areas, but as long as we take them for granted, they will disappear—a lesson that fellow bird lovers have learned the hard way in England, much of the eastern United States, parts of Ontario, and even here in Nova Scotia. Even as I write this book, I am painfully aware that some of the places I have mentioned, although protected, are deteriorating. Others have no protection at all and will someday likely disappear. I hope those who visit the locations mentioned in this guide will grow attached to them and take an active interest in their future. It is not enough to enjoy looking at birds; each of us must help protect them. I believe such efforts are the mark of a true birder.

You may choose to start your own effort to protect an area or become involved in programs such as "Adopt A Park," in which a group of people help to watch over a park, help keep it clean, and may even become involved with planning events. You can even join an organization that focuses on such activities. Good local organizations include the Sackville River Association, Friends of McNabs Island, the Halifax Field

Naturalists, the Clean Nova Scotia Foundation, the Nova Scotia Bird Society, and many others. The Nova Scotia Bird Society, for example, runs a Raptor Rehabilitation Program, helps to organize Christmas Bird Counts, and owns several pieces of property around the province. They also have a committee that deals with conservation issues.

The Halifax Field Naturalists is by far the most active conservation group in the Metro area and has spearheaded and taken part in hundreds of programs to help wildlife. Their efforts have led to improvements in local parks, such as Hemlock Ravine and Point Pleasant. They also help to implement many national programs through their affiliation with the Canadian Nature Federation, the most broad-based conservation organization in Canada. For the address of these organizations and others, see the listing of resources at the back of this guide. Efforts from each of us can make a difference, however small.

In October, we may see the first of our winter birds, but November is truly the time of transition between fall and winter. It is in this month that fall migration reaches its final stages and gives way to the pressures of the encroaching winter.

City Birding

....

Cardinals in Nova Scotia

Have you ever been told that there are no cardinals in Nova Scotia? I have. Although they are not as numerous here as they are in other areas, Northern Cardinals are spotted every year in the province. However, there are reasons why the news of cardinals in Nova Scotia is not well known. First of all, although they can be found here during any season, most visit us in the fall and winter, when cardinals are the most difficult to detect because of changes in their behaviour. In the spring and summer, the loud and continuous song of both the male and female makes it relatively easy to find a cardinal as it sings from its exposed perch. Nests too, are comparatively easy to find as they are often built in low bushes close to or in urban areas. Unfortunately, few cardinals have nested in Nova Scotia, and after the breeding season, all the flamboyant behaviour of the male as he tries to impress the female is gone. Cardinals transform into quiet, shy birds that prefer to spend the majority of their time poking about in thick bushes after breeding season. Under those circumstances, bright red cardinals can be surprisingly difficult to see, even when you know they are at a particular location.

A pair of Northern Cardinals was first sighted in Nova Scotia in 1871, but no other sightings were recorded until 1957, when a female was identified. Since then, cardinals have been sighted annually in the province. Historically, the southwestern counties of Digby, Yarmouth, and Shelburne have been the best places to see cardinals, but they have also been recorded throughout the province; the Halifax/Dartmouth area is one of the regions where they are more frequently seen. In the fall, flocks of cardinals are observed occasionally, but most often they travel alone or in pairs. Cardinals are very fond of berry bushes that have red berries—multiflora rose is their favourite.

Search for Northern Cardinals in places that have lots of these bushes, especially if they are near feeders. Some places in Metro that have an abundance of multiflora rose bushes are Conrose Park, Findlay Park, Shore Drive in Bedford, the end of Silvers Road in Dartmouth, and Hallmark Avenue in Sackville.

The Year of the Cardinal

For many, 1994 will be remembered as the Year of the Cardinal. Unusually high numbers of cardinals in the spring and summer were the result of warm weather the previous November and December, which encouraged between 50 and 100 of these birds to spend the winter in this province. November and December are the two best months to see cardinals as this is the period when they migrate through Nova Scotia. Warm weather during those months can encourage cardinals to stay in greater numbers. This was the case in the winter of 1993–94, when we did not have cold temperatures until just before Christmas.

Cardinals invaded Nova Scotia previously, during the winter of 1973–74, when nearly fifty Northern Cardinals were sighted around the province. The following summer, several were present and a few pairs even bred in Yarmouth, Digby, and Shelburne Counties. It was thought then that maybe the Northern Cardinal had finally established itself in the province. However, by 1976, sightings had diminished to about a dozen per winter, which continues to be the average winter number. Again in 1994, it was hoped that the Northern Cardinal had established its beachhead in Nova Scotia, but again their numbers slowly dropped to previous levels. In the winter of 1995–96 numbers again rose to above average, especially in the Metro area. Cardinals are continuing to extend their range northeastward from the United States and will in the near future be a regular breeder in the province.

Identifying Northern Orioles

Northern Orioles are an exciting and regular fall migrant in the Metro area. Hundreds pass through in September, but most people see them in

November and December when they start to show up at city parks and feeders. Fall Northern Orioles can be difficult to identify, as they can vary from bright orange individuals to those with only small patches of orange. However, two things are consistent about these birds. First, they always have a long pointed bill, which is usually light gray in colour or sometimes it appears black and resembles a Blue Jay's, although a little smaller. The second consistent feature is the presence of yellow–orange plumage, similar to the colour of an egg yolk, somewhere on the bird. Even the dull individuals will show some orange, usually in the throat or on the rump patch, the patch immediately above where the base of the tail meets the back. Keep this in mind, and you will never have any problems identifying a fall-plumaged Northern Oriole.

Although most Northern Orioles spend their winters in Mexico and northern South America, every winter a few can still be found lingering in the province. Orioles are not typical cold weather birds; normally, their main diet consists of caterpillars and other live insects. This makes it difficult for orioles to survive a winter in the Northern Hemisphere. However, the Northern Oriole appears to be a highly adaptive species, and increasing numbers are learning to survive the rigours of a colder climate.

Feeders are playing a major role in their survival, allowing orioles to find food, even during the hardest parts of the winter. Normally, fruit and berries would make up less than 20 per cent of the Northern Oriole's diet, but in winter, fruits and seeds are its mainstay. Berries of ornamental bushes are important to orioles. But virtually all of those that survive our Nova Scotia winters do so by visiting feeders. When desperate, orioles will eat cracked corn and sunflower seeds from feeders, although they do show a special fondness for grapes.

Paula McCluskey always has great success attracting Northern Orioles. She has found that whenever they are present, they showed a preference for red grapes over green. I have further discovered that if the grapes are broken open, they are more readily sampled by these birds. Also, grapes appear to work well in helping weak individuals regain their strength. Pieces of apples, pears, and orange halves have all been eaten by orioles at feeders, as well as suet and peanut butter. Some people have attracted orioles by using grape or apple jelly.

For those of you who have feeders, and even those of you who don't, making some sort of fruit available in your yard for the orioles, and other species such as warblers, mockingbirds, and robins, could save the life of a bird. It is estimated that about half of the Northern Orioles that attempt to overwinter in Nova Scotia survive. The percentage of survivors is increasing each year as more people put out special food for them. Some people, like Eva Urban, make an extra effort. To increase one oriole's chances, she set up special accommodations for him, including his very own crate to feed from. The crate was laid on its side so it could easily get in out of the wind, and it was loaded up with his favourite foods—grapes, orange halves, and sugar water. Not only did this box provide him with the finest of foods, it allowed him to come and go as he pleased, and best of all, his "room" included heat so neither he nor his food would freeze!

American Coots

Coots are small, ducklike birds with rounded bodies and very large lobed feet to aid in swimming. These oversized feet also allow the coot to walk on top of aquatic vegetation, a truly amazing sight. In the water, coots are conspicuous as they pump their heads forward while swimming. They also dive frequently to reach their favourite foods, the roots of aquatic plants. They will eat small fish, insects, and even land grasses. In the south and the west, American Coots have been increasing in numbers, and they may someday be a common bird in Nova Scotia. Each year, a few more American Coots arrive in the province from points westward and southward. In fact, the coot now breeds in Nova Scotia in very small numbers, but during the summer months it is likely to be seen only in the Amherst region. In Canada, its status is currently recorded as a scarce and local breeder east of the Prairies, with large populations in the western part of the country.

The American Coot's closet relative is the Common Moorhen (previously known as the Common Gallinule). The Common Moorhen, in shape, colour, and actions, resembles the American Coot so closely that the two species have interbred on the odd occasion. Coots are a uniform bluish-gray with a white bill and forehead shield, while Common Moorhens are grayish–brown above, bluish–gray below, and have a bright red bill. Young Common Moorhens lack the red bill but can still be recognized by their white side stripe, a feature that is also noticeable in the adult. The absolute best place in Metro to see American Coots and the Common Moorhen is Sullivans Pond. Every year one or two coots show up in November at Sullivans Pond, and on rare occasions, a Common Moorhen is present. Both the coots and the moorhens can be picked out from the numerous ducks at Sullivans Pond by their smaller size and their shared habit of vigorously pumping their heads forward as they swim. Coots have also been seen at the Albro Lakes (Big and Little) and Bissett Lake.

Barred Owls

The cawing of crows is not usually considered one of the more musical or even pleasant sounds of nature, but it can be of interest to a birder. For example, listening to crows is one of the best ways to see owls during the daytime. Crows are especially keen-eyed and often spot owls in their daytime sleeping places. Once they discover an owl, they will caw constantly, causing other crows to gather to scream at, dive-bomb, and generally pester the owl. This behaviour is called mobbing and often alerts birders to the presence of an owl. In Halifax, B. J. Edmondson realized that there were suddenly more crows than usual in her neighbourhood, and they were making an awful lot of noise. Upon investigating, she noticed that the centre of their attention was a Barred Owl. When Evanne O'Leary recognized that the crows in her Lower Sackville neighbourhood were making an usual amount of racket, she investigated in hopes of seeing an owl. She soon spotted a Barred Owl getting mobbed by crows and Blue Jays.

Barred Owls feed primarily on mice and other small rodents and pose no threat to a crow; however, crows will generally harass this or any other species of large owl. The suggested reason for this behaviour is that Great Horned Owls will occasionally raid crow roosts at night for a quick meal. However, crows will also mob any species of hawk they come across, and they will even attack a Bald Eagle. One might conclude from their behaviour that either they can not tell one bird of prey from another, or they harass all of them just for the fun of it. Regardless of why they do it, knowledge of crow behaviour is beneficial to those interested in seeing owls.

Point Pleasant Park

Point Pleasant Park is a place where crows and owls gather. Visitors to the park during the daylight hours may see and hear crows sending out an alarm over an owl that causes all other crows within earshot to gather. The new crows also send out the alarm and so it spreads. Soon, anywhere from twenty to two hundred crows are gathered around an owl, calling as loud as they can. Some believe that the strategy of the crows is to force or encourage the owl to move on by harassing it. In most cases, though, they can not persuade the owl to move far. What they can do, however, is bother the owl as much as possible so it does not get much sleep. This is significant, for a sleepy owl has a difficult time hunting once night falls, and some individuals prey on crows.

Most years in November, a Great Horned Owl shows up at Point Pleasant Park and quite often spends the winter there, catching Norway rats along the shore and around the forts. Almost every winter at least one Black Backed Woodpecker can be seen and in some winters, there is also a Barred Owl present in the park.

During November, all kinds of rare birds show up in Point Pleasant Park. A walk anywhere in the park may turn up an unusual species. However, one of the most productive areas in November is the path that runs along the outer perimeter of the park; the section starting at Black Rock Beach is perhaps the most interesting. Some of the surprises that have been found there in past Novembers include Western Kingbirds, Scarlet Tanagers, and Eastern Phoebes. If it is a cold morning, each of the species may be feeding off the flies from the seaweed scattered along the shore. Late migrating shorebirds, such as the Ruddy Turnstone, may also be seen feeding on this seaweed, so keep your eyes open!

Mockingbirds

Much of the year Northern Mockingbirds are
solitary creatures, and unlike most birds, which
maintain only a summer or breeding territory,
mockingbirds also set up a fall and winter territory that are sought out after the mockingbirds
complete their fall moult. It may or may not
cover the same area as their summer territory.
The purpose of a fall/winter territory is to ensure
that each mocker will have enough food to survive the winter months. Individuals guard their
territories from perches, which provide a good
view of their domain. Though occasionally a pair
will share a winter territory, most mockers will
try to drive out any others that wander into their
territory and any other berry–eating birds, such
as American Robins, Starlings, and waxwings.
Although noticeably noisy in the summer, mockingbirds are usually quiet in the winter, using only
the occasional scolding note to warn intruders, followed by dive-bombing or a chase, if necessary.

Red Bellied Woodpeckers

Red Bellied Woodpeckers are year-round residents of the eastern United States, with their
range running from Eastern Texas, north to the
Great Lakes region. Studies show the Red Bellied
is continuing to increase its range northward. This
is partly due to its habit of wandering widely when
food supplies become scarce in its home range.

Like most woodpeckers, Red Bellieds scour
trunks of trees for the larvae of wood-boring
insects. However, they also frequently feed on the
ground, hunting for ants, beetles, and especially
acorns. Beech nuts and some berries are also
eaten by Red Bellieds. In the South, they occasionally become a pest when they attack oranges
in commercial orchards. In both urban and rural

areas, Red Bellieds will visit feeders and often eat sunflower seeds or carry them away to store in secret caches.

They are noisy woodpeckers with many calls. For this reason, they are often heard before they are seen. When seen, their red bellies are hardly noticeable, looking more like a faint reddish tinge on the lower belly. However, males can be identified easily by their zebra backs and red on the top of the head and back of the neck. Females also have the zebra-banded back but have red only on the back of the neck. By the end of 1984, there were nine records of Red Bellied Woodpeckers occurring in Nova Scotia. In recent years, however, it seems the bird is becoming more prevalent, especially in the Metro area. Every fall, one or two of these rare woodpeckers are sighted in the area. Although they may be seen in the fall, winter, or spring, November appears to be a particularly good month to watch for these birds.

Further Afield

....

Leach's Storm Petrels

Leach's Storm Petrels are robin–size birds, which spend most of their time on the open ocean and normally come to land only to breed. However, during severe storms, they can be forced or carried many kilometres landward by strong winds and are often deposited, exhausted, on land, where they frequently die before they have a chance to recover. In Bedford, stormy weather was responsible for the Leach's Storm Petrel which landed in Paula Richardson's living room. The bird had come in through an open patio door after being dazed when it flew into the side of her apartment building. This particular Leach's Storm Petrel was lucky. Mrs. Richardson not only provided the bird with the rest he needed, he also had the full run of the bathtub, where blended sardines had been added to simulate the bird's natural feeding environment.

After providing the bird with food and rest, Mrs. Richardson took it to the Department of Natural Resources, where it was checked for injuries and then released. That bird was one of five Leach's Storm Petrels brought to Natural Resources that week. All five birds recuperated enough to be released at Lawrencetown Beach, where they could gain quick access to the open ocean.

Petrels gain their name from the apostle Peter because like him, they can walk on the surface of the water for short periods of time. Technically, though, petrels don't walk on the water, they fly just above it and let their small webbed feet patter against the surface. Once in this position, the petrels use their bills to pick up tiny organisms floating on the surface of the ocean. Small fish, crustaceans, and animal refuse make up the largest part of their diet. Leach's Storm Petrels occur off our coast from early April to early November.

Red Throated Loons

Red Throated Loons migrate through the Metro area each fall. They are most often sighted from the middle of October to about the end of December. In January and February, Red Throated Loons are only rarely seen, but by mid-March their numbers are again on the rise as they begin their spring migration. I have found that Red Throats are most easily seen in March, but they are well worth looking for during the fall to catch a glimpse of their silvery winter plumage. Coastlines facing the open ocean, such as Hartlen Point and Cow Bay, are good places to watch for these birds. See the March chapter for more details about spring migration.

Horned Grebes

Horned Grebes are found in the Metro area only during our winter months and are best seen feeding in saltwater environs in the St. Margarets Bay region or along Fergusons Cove Road. Horned Grebes may also be seen at other local coastal birding spots, especially in November during their fall migration. Unlike other grebe species, Horned Grebes often feed in small groups with two or more birds scattered along a small section of shoreline.

Fergusons Cove Road is also one of the best spots for viewing the Horned Grebe's larger cousin, the Red Necked Grebe. This side-by-side comparison can make it easier for newer birders to identify both species. Keep in mind that by November both species will be in their winter plumage.

Cattle Egrets

Egrets are those large, stately, white birds that Canadians in general associate with Florida and other parts of the South. When one is spotted in Nova Scotia, it often draws the attention of the public at large. Such was the case one November, when a Cattle Egret visited a field adjacent to the Moir's Chocolate Factory. Employees of the factory located in Woodside, a community on the outskirts of Dartmouth, were the first to spot the bird, and word of its presence was spread quickly. Even more people became aware of the Cattle Egret when it was featured on a local television broadcast. I am told that as a result, many people took advantage of the Remembrance Day holiday to see the bird, which continued to feed in the field most of that day.

Many people were curious as to why this Cattle Egret was feeding in the field and not along the water as most egrets do. Some were even concerned that the bird was injured or sick and that it should not be in the province at all. It is great to see people concerned enough about wildlife to ask those questions. Showing concern for nature is a good first step toward improving a badly damaged environment. It can be argued that as we watch out for and protect animals, we are protecting ourselves since to accomplish the former, we need to protect our shared environments. Protecting green spaces, which help detoxify our air and water, results in better health for Canadians, and it helps to save millions of dollars spent annually combatting problems linked to environmental damage.

This Cattle Egret's appearance in a field in Metro in November was not because the bird was sick or injured. Cattle Egrets, unlike other species of egrets, prefer to feed on dry land because their favourite foods are grasshoppers, crickets, and earthworms. They pass through Metro in the fall in October and November, with most birds seen outside city limits. Cattle Egrets have a completely white plumage, except during their breeding season, when they sport patches of orange on the head, chest, and back. They are members of the Heron family, but unlike all other egrets and herons, they are often found feeding on solid ground, sometimes kilometres away from water. In fact, fields are their preferred habitat.

While their relatives are getting their feet wet, slogging through swamp water in search of food, Cattle Egrets are strolling along green pastures having others find food for them. For centuries, they have been taking advantage of the free service provided them by cattle. When cattle walk through a field grazing, they disturb numerous insects, so all a Cattle Egret has to do is walk beside a cow and grab any insect that moves. An average cow is said to stir up enough insects to easily feed one to three Cattle Egrets a day.

Studies show that Cattle Egrets eat a variety of

insects and even some very small animals, but their favourite food is the grasshopper. Of course, Cattle Egrets are not totally dependent on cows for their food. They can find their own food, but this is much more difficult. Allowing cattle to flush out their food has worked so well for them that Cattle Egrets are the most widespread egret in the world. Originally an Old World species only, the Cattle Egret immigrated to South America in the 1800s and as of 1952, they were found in every continent except Antarctica. Since its self-introduction to South America, Cattle Egrets have continued to expand their range northward and now breed sporadically as far north as Maine. The Cattle Egret's current status in Nova Scotia is that of a rare visitor.

'Tis the Season

A Winter Land of Activity

As a young boy, with my limited knowledge of birds, I thought that nearly all birds flew south in the fall to areas of warmer weather and did not return again until the spring. I viewed winter as a cold, drab season, which was almost devoid of birds and other wildlife. Furthermore, winters were too long and I waited eagerly for the coming of spring.

As my knowledge of birds grew, I realized that although we have fewer birds here in the winter than during the summer, I could still find lots of them if I looked in the right places. I soon learned that winter, like the other seasons, provided unique opportunities. Although I still enjoy the warmer seasons most of all, I have come to respect and even appreciate the cold winter.

It is surprising just how many species of birds have been observed in the province during

D·E·C·E·M·B·E·R

December—in total, over 250 have been observed at one time or another. This list includes many out of season birds, uncommon species, and rarely seen birds. If a tally were made of only the more common species, there would still be about 90 species of birds to look at—that's a lot of birding! Unfortunately, in December, most people do not have a lot of time to go looking for birds; even hard-core birders do not get in as much birding as they would like because it is such a busy time of year. The good news is that most of the species here in December can also be found in January.

During December and January, the largest groups of birds are the various species of water birds. Most of these can be seen by exploring a number of locations around Halifax Harbour. See "Sewer Stroll" in January for more details.

December is probably the one month when the largest volumes of seed-eating birds are present. Variety is fairly high as well. Many of these birds can be attracted to feeders, which benefits the birds and helps us to better enjoy winter. December is also a good time to see owls in the city and to participate in a Christmas Bird Count.

Old Christmas Tree

This year when you take down your Christmas tree, instead of throwing it away, give it to those who need it—the birds! A Christmas tree is an excellent way to draw more birds to your property and to better protect the ones you have.

Birds need trees in order to survive since they provide them with food, a place to nest, and most importantly in winter, protection from hungry predators and harsh winter conditions. Many songbirds are so strongly dependent on trees that, generally, the closer your feeder is to a tree, the more birds that will come to it. If you can not move your feeders closer to trees, why not move a tree closer to your feeders by propping up your old Christmas tree next to them. You can even hang a feeder right on it. You will be amazed how the birds will respond, it is as if it were a live one. An old Christmas tree is especially great for those living in new subdivisions. Just think, you no longer have to wait for your newly planted trees to become large enough to hang feeders on; you can just prop up your "insta–tree," and voilà, you are all set to put up feeders.

If you already have your feeders hung in a tree, your old Christmas tree can still be of value by providing extra cover for the birds in your yard. As far as most feeder birds are concerned, there is no such thing as too much cover. An additional benefit of your old Christmas tree, if it was an evergreen, is that some species of birds are more strongly attracted to a feeder hung in an evergreen tree than one hung in a deciduous tree. Dark Eyed Juncos and Pine Siskins are two common examples.

However, if you already have plenty of standing evergreens in your yard, your old Christmas tree does not need to be wasted. An old Christmas tree that is laid down creates a wonderful foraging place for ground-feeding birds. In fact, if you can get three or more old Christmas trees, you can build a nice brush pile in your yard, and all kinds of birds will use it, some will even sleep in it nightly. So, use those Christmas trees wisely as they still have a lot of life to give.

City Birding

....

The Upside–down Bird

Red Breasted Nuthatches are tiny birds which can often be seen high in evergreen trees, busily extracting seeds from cones that are almost as big as they are. Evergreen cones are a favourite food of these birds, and from time to time, when large cone crops occur in the province, literally thousands of Red Breasted Nuthatches may stage a winter invasion of the Metro area.

Like woodpeckers, nuthatches find it easy to cling to trunks of trees; unlike woodpeckers, nuthatches always travel down the trunks of trees head first. This unusual behaviour is found only amongst members of the Nuthatch family and has earned them the nickname of "upside-down birds." This peculiar method of feeding allows them to spot insects in places that are missed by the right side up woodpeckers.

The upside-down bird's official name, nuthatch, is a derivative of "Nut-Hack." The name was given by early Europeans because of its habit of wedging nuts in crevices, then hacking them open.

Two species of nuthatches are found in Nova Scotia. The most common, the Red Breasted, is blue above and reddish–orange below. The White Breasted Nuthatch is blue above and white below. It is much less common than the Red Breasted, but it is the dominant species in areas of the city where there are plenty of hardwood trees. Red Breasted Nuthatches, on the other hand, prefer softwood areas. In Point Pleasant Park, both species of nuthatches may be encountered. Nuthatches are a favourite of mine as they are fairly friendly and will, with a little patience on our part, feed from an outstretched hand.

Yellow Shafted Flickers

Historically, Yellow Shafted Flickers are rarely seen in the Metro area during the winter months; however, since 1990, winter flicker reports have been higher than normal. Perhaps this is because they are learning to benefit from bird feeders. Each winter in the Metro area, about a dozen people report flickers coming to their feeders to eat peanuts and hulled sunflower seeds. They usually do not go to suet feeders as other wood-peckers do.

Pheasants in the City

Ring Necked Pheasants are common in the Annapolis Valley and are often associated with farms and fields. Surprisingly, they can be found in several neighbourhoods in Metro and most of the large towns in the province. A number of fac-tors may contribute to the presence of pheasants in urban areas. Hunting pressures can force pheasants to seek safety around urban homes, and it is well known that major power lines often act as corridors for wildlife to penetrate city or town limits. Once inside urban areas, the greater the area of suitable habitat available, the better the bird's chances are of finding the necessities of life—food, water, and shelter. Even small urban green areas may be used by a pheasant if they are close to a larger green area sporting open or semi–open habitat, especially if they are physical-ly joined to a larger area, even by a thin strip of trees or bushes. Also Ring Necked Pheasants are commonly raised by hobbyists who often release them near urban centres. Feeders help urban pheasants to find food and supplement their diets, especially during times when natural food sup-plies become scarce. As a bird that spends most of its time on the ground, urban pheasants do come into contact with cats. However, male pheasants have been seen on more than one occasion successfully defending themselves against cats, and I have heard more than once that a male pheasant was spotted chasing a cat! Ring Necked Pheasants are most common in urban areas during the fall and winter seasons.

Barred Owls

There are six species of owls that breed in Nova Scotia, and of those, the Barred Owl is the most common. Unfortunately, people rarely get a chance to see a Barred Owl because, like many owls, it spends the daylight hours sleeping in the cavities of trees. Old growth trees are the Barred Owl's preferred habitat; however, due to a scarcity of such prime forests, they are often forced to use other types. Fall and winter are the times of the year when such forced excursions often take place, usually triggered by the need for food. As Barred Owls search for food, they frequently venture closer to urban areas. It is then that people are more likely to come in contact with one. The birds seen are usually ones that were born in the spring of that year. These post-season dispersals most often take place in November, December, and January.

Rufous Sided Towhees

Rufous Sided Towhees breed all along the east coast, from Texas to southern Maine. In winter, most retreat to the South and are found no further north than Massachusetts. In their typical winter range, flocks of up to twenty–five birds may be seen. In Nova Scotia, large flocks usually consist of one, maybe two birds. For this reason, the Towhee is classified as a rare winter visitor to Nova Scotia. One of the best times of year to see Towhees in Metro is in December, when they show up at feeders. These are shy ground-feeding birds that like to scratch vigorously on the ground for their food. They usually stay close to bushy cover and are often found rummaging about in dead leaves under hedges. They are at times solitary birds, but in the winter they are more often found feeding with flocks of Dark

Eyed Juncos or White Throated Sparrows.

T. C. Haliburton was the first person to report a Rufous Sided Towhee in the province—in 1825, he recorded a Chewink on his list of Nova Scotian birds. "Chewink" was a popular name for the Towhee, a name that is still used by some today, as it refers to its call note. Bird calls do not sound the same to everyone, and many people believe that the Towhee's "chewink" call sounds more like "toe–hee." Regardless of the way it sounds to us, Towhees use this call to keep in contact with each other while they are looking for food. This auditory way of keeping tabs on their own kind means that they do not have to be within sight of one another and allows them to focus their attention on their food search.

The western race of the Towhee, called the Spotted Towhee, has a call note that is slightly different from its eastern cousins. It is said this sounds similar to the meow of a cat. However, the main feature that separates the eastern and western races are the rows of white spots running vertically along the back of the Spotted Towhee. The Towhees in the west also have two white wing bars which the eastern birds lack. Males of both subspecies share the black hood, black back, bright rufous sides, white bellies, and distinctive red eyes. The scientific name for the Towhee is *Pipilo erythrophthalmus*, which translates to "red-eyed chirper." Perhaps when researchers gave the Rufous Sided Towhee its scientific name, they were not aware that the southern race of the Rufous Sided, which is found along the south Atlantic coast and Florida, has white eyes.

As expected, it is members of the eastern race that show up in the Metro area most often, but western individuals have been seen, and a sighting of the southern subspecies is not out of the question. Hybridized individuals may also be seen as all three subspecies will interbreed.

Bohemians

One of Metro's winter highlights is the Bohemian Waxwing. Bohemian means "wanderer," and that is exactly what these birds are as Nova Scotia's most nomadic winter songbird. During the winter months, these western birds gather in large flocks and wander across the country in search of berry-producing bushes. Their search normally carries them eastward, and a few always make it as far as Nova Scotia. In exceptional years, large numbers of Bohemians come pouring into the province. When this happens, hundreds of people in the Metro area get to see these fascinating birds.

Bohemians are sometimes mistaken for female Northern Cardinals as they have a cardinal–like crest with some red on it. A good way to distinguish the two positively is to check the bill. Female cardinals have large red-coloured bills, while the waxwing's is slightly smaller and all black.

Bohemian Waxwings may also be mistaken for their close relatives, the Cedar Waxwings. Both Cedar and Bohemians are medium-size birds, about 19 cm (7 in.) long, with a black mask and a brown crest on top of the head. They both also sport a wide yellow band across the tip of the tail. The Bohemians can be distinguished by the fact that they are slightly broader and grayer than Cedars, and they have a yellow stripe and white markings on each wing, which the Cedars lack. In addition, Bohemians have a rusty red section under their tails. If you are unable to get a good look at the waxwing in question, the time of year may identify the bird for you. As a general rule of thumb, Cedar Waxwings are rarer in the winter and Bohemian Waxwings are nonexistent in summer. Caution should be exercised, though, as in recent years we have been finding small numbers of Cedar Waxwings during the winter months.

If you are hoping to see Bohemian Waxwings, the surest method is to plant winter berry bushes in your yard, and they will eventually show up for a feast. If you do not have berry bushes of your own, keep your eyes open for bushes with berries, especially red berries. Upon locating one, the waxwings will feed on it intensely for several days or perhaps a week, depending on its size, and once they have stripped it of food, they will quickly depart in search of more berries. A good way to tell if waxwings have been feeding at a particular bush is to look at the snow or earth under the plant— as it is usually covered with red stains if waxwings have been feeding.

Winter Finches

All of the province's winter finches have a reputation for roaming like the Bohemian Waxwings. This results in their numbers fluctuating from winter to winter. Usually by the end of December, nomadic patterns start to become apparent for most species. It is then possible to determine how common or rare a certain species will be in that season. Winter songbirds whose numbers are affected most frequently include American Goldfinches, Purple Finches, Common Redpolls, Pine Siskins, Red Breasted Nuthatches, White Breasted Nuthatches, Pine Grosbeaks, White Winged Crossbills, Red Crossbills, Snow Buntings, Brown Creepers, Brown Headed Cowbirds, Evening Grosbeaks, and American Tree Sparrows.

Winter population fluctuations of other species such as Blue Jays, Black Capped Chickadees, and House Sparrows are unrelated to nomadic patterns; therefore, they occur less often.

Christmas Traditions

December is a month steeped in traditions, which bring people together to spread cheer and to work for the common good. Each year, hundreds of thousands of volunteers from across North America join forces to complete a continent-wide bird survey. The survey covers fifty states and all of Canada, including the territories. The observations of winter bird populations have led to valuable information about distribution of species, population trends, and even migration patterns This event, known as the Audubon Christmas Bird Count (CBC), has always taken place during the Christmas season.

The first CBC took place in the eastern United States in 1900 and quickly caught on. Nova Scotia has supported the CBCs since 1913, when twelve species were counted by two observers. As a result of this modest beginning, more than 217 species of birds have been observed during the holiday season in Nova Scotia. Although a CBC is completed in one day, it usually gives a reasonably accurate picture of what bird species are currently in the area and in what numbers. It is always interesting to learn what birds were seen on a Christmas count; when combined with information gained from previous Christmas counts, it can provide some very valuable data.

Christmas counts help to document both old and new patterns in bird populations. For example, I can remember when it was quite a surprise for someone to discover a Northern Mockingbird on a Metro Christmas count. Today, it would be quite a surprise if someone did not discover one. In addition to the long-term benefits of a Christmas count, the information gained from a count gives local bird lovers a better idea of what bird species are in the region and an opportunity to compare those sightings with what they have been seeing on birding excursions or at their feeders.

Three of the biggest Christmas counts in the province are held in the Metro area. Besides counting the species of birds, all CBCs keep track of the number of each bird species they see. Participants divide up into parties of two and endeavour to cover as much territory as possible while keeping their eyes open for all types of birds and recording numbers and species of birds seen. Afterwards, the teams get together and over some hot food, compare notes and tally up the day's results. Although the information gained about our winter bird species is the most important part of the count, aiming for the highest numbers possible helps to encourage people to do their best, and it keeps the count fun and interesting.

You can contribute to a CBC by birding an area within a count circle, or by keeping notes on the birds attending your feeder on a count day. Making sure your feeder is well stocked through-out December and especially on count day is also helpful.

If you would like to be involved in one of the Metro counts or to learn more about them, you can write to the following addresses: for the Halifax/Dartmouth count, contact the coordina-tor, Fulton Lavender, 3207 Hemlock Street, Halifax, N.S., B3L 4B5, telephone: (902) 455–4966; for the Halifax East or the Halifax West counts, contact the Nova Scotia Bird Society, c/o the Nova Scotia Museum, 1747 Summer Street, Halifax, N.S., B3H 3A6. New volunteers are always needed and appreciated, and they usually have a good time learning about and helping our local birds.

The Christmas Bird Count is followed closely by a second tradition, which should be prepared for in December. Come January 1, a number of birders like to start off the New Year by trying to see as many species as possible. Those seen are usually recorded on a list known amongst birders as a year list. It is a record of all birds seen in any given year. The magic of this list is that every year it is exciting, at least for a moment, to see even such common species of birds as crows and starlings since any species you see is a new bird for your list. This New Year's Day birding tradition is part of the reason why so many interesting birds are sighted at the beginning of January. If you were unable to go birding on the first, pick another day to start your year list; chances are, you will be surprised by how many species of birds you encounter in the run of a year. The first bird you see in the New Year starts your list. With a bit of luck and some enforced tunnel vision, I have been able to start off a few of my year lists with a Bald Eagle! For more information on year lists, refer to the introduction in the January chapter.

Urban Migration

In December, we start to see a phenomenon that I call urban migration. While this is not a true migration, it is one in the sense that we begin to notice a variety of birds moving from their current locations into a new area—the city. This happens every year and is triggered by the settling in of colder weather, which encourages some birds to move away from the cooler countryside and towards the warmer confines of the city. Many people recall from their school days that large bodies of water, like the Halifax Harbour absorb heat in the summer and give off heat in the winter. This heat combined with the by–product heat generated by the city make the Halifax/Dartmouth region the second warmest part of the province during the winter months.

The more delicate species such as Pine Warblers, Orange Crowned Warblers, and Yellow Breasted Chats are amongst the first to begin this migration. The urban migration in December provides additional opportunities for Metro residents to see unusual species, such as Northern Orioles, Dickcissels, and Rufous Sided Towhees. Although urban migration begins in December (some years in November), it continues throughout the winter. As winter progresses, an increased number of species will move into the city. Dark Eyed Juncos, White Throated Sparrows, Mourning Doves, American Tree Sparrows, and American Robins are some of the species that will respond in this manner. Other birds, such as Snow Buntings, only come into the city for a short time, during or immediately after bad periods of weather, and then quickly disperse again.

American Black Ducks

The American Black Duck, or the Black Duck as it is often called, is the most common freshwater duck in the province. In Metro, this bird is found everywhere, both in freshwater habitats and saltwater environments. It is a year-round resident and although wary during the fall hunting season, it will readily come for hand-outs in any month. Fairly trusting by nature, these ducks will quickly learn to eat from an outstretched hand. Many Metro residents have fed these ducks and most have seen them but relatively few know their name or how to distinguish them from other species of waterfowl. They are fairly easy to identify, and once you learn how to recognize Black Ducks, you will begin to discover how interesting they can be. For example, in this species, only the females quack as the male's voice is limited to a low croak.

Although males and females have identical plumages, they can quickly be distinguished by the colour of the bills. The male's beak is yellow, while the female's is an olive green colour and often has black spots. Black Ducks are not black at all but appear to be mostly dark brown. They can be easily separated from other brown-coloured ducks by noting the colour of the Black Duck's head. Unlike other species, its head and upper neck are noticeably lighter brown than the rest of their body. Another good field mark is the colour of their speculum, a small patch of colour on the wings of ducks that can be seen both in flight and while the bird is sitting or swimming. The Black Duck has a purple speculum, while the similar looking female Mallard has a bright blue speculum. Black Ducks eat a variety of aquatic plants and seeds. During the summer months, aquatic insects are their favourite food. Besides helping to keep the insects under control, they also readily eat leeches, a habit from which people and animals benefit.

In the Metro area, most Black Ducks build their nests in April. They may use either fresh-water areas or salt marshes for breeding. Their nests are usually well concealed, and it is not uncommon for a nest to be built a couple of kilo-metres from water. The females normally lay eight to ten eggs but may produce as many as twelve. In May, we see the first newborn duck-lings, which are able to swim almost immediately after birth. At first, the downy young are mainly yellow in colour but as each week passes, they acquire more and more of their brown plumage.

These little ducklings are so cute that most people cannot resist feeding them. Remember, though, that young ducklings should not be fed bread for two reasons. The first and most impor-tant is that the pieces of bread can swell up in their throats and choke them. Second, bread does not have many of the nutrients needed for these young birds to develop properly. If you want to feed them, a good choice is finely cracked corn.

An endearing quality of these birds is their maternal instinct. If something should happen to the mother duck, her chicks will be quickly adopted by another female, even if her own chicks are not the same age. Although young ducklings can feed themselves from day one, they depend on the adult for guidance and protection for at least their first sixty days.

Some people point an accusing finger at Black Ducks as they, like all freshwater ducks, can carry a parasite that causes swimmers' itch. This parasite becomes abundant in warm water where large numbers of waterfowl gather. Swimmers' itch crops up almost every summer in Metro. One main problem area is Lake Banook, which lies immediately adjacent to Sullivans Pond, commonly called the Dartmouth Duck Pond. However, it is not the Black Ducks that are causing the problem. While it is true that large numbers of wild Black Ducks gather in this pond during the winter months, they exit this body of water before the water warms enough for the parasites to multiply and spread to these ducks. The problem birds are the ducks that spend all summer in the Sullivans Pond area. The majority of these birds are nonmigratory domestic ducks and hybrids between Black Ducks, domestic ducks, and Mallards. While it is nice to have some tame ducks in this pond during the summer, too many have been released into this small body of water. The combination of overcrowding and warm summer water make perfect conditions for the production of the swimmers' itch parasite and other waterfowl diseases.

This situation can be improved by decreasing the number of tame ducks currently in Sullivans Pond. Now, I am not suggesting that any of the birds be harmed in any way. On the contrary, some of these birds should be moved to other locations in order to prevent an outbreak of a fatal waterfowl disease. Right now, the conditions in this pond are ripe for just such a disaster. Of course, if we choose not to take steps to solve this problem, nature will, and the resulting

•
D
E
C
E
M
B
E
R

deaths will be unfortunate and unnecessary.

TAPA (Taking Action to Protect Animals) is a local organization that is trying to help the birds at Sullivans Pond and is eager to hear from people interested in the pond area or who would like to know more about birds and plants found there. For further information, write to TAPA, RR 2, Site 21, Box B-O, Porters Lake, N.S., B0J 2S0.

Further Afield

Rough Legged Hawks

Rough Legged Hawks are large birds of prey that visit Nova Scotia during the winter months. Despite their large size, they have weak feet and are limited to catching very small mammals. These hawks are generally found in open areas where they search for their favourite food, the meadow vole. Rough Leggeds are said to have such good hearing that they can actually hear the meadow voles running through their tunnels under the snow.

One of the best areas for seeing Rough Legged Hawks in the province is the dykelands at Grand Pré. Locally, favourite winter haunts are Hartlen Point, the adjacent Devils Island, the fields surrounding the Shearwater Airport, the fields in the Woodside Industrial Park, Wedge Island (which can be seen from the end of the Seaforth Causeway Road), and Conrads Beach.

They are often distinguished from Nova Scotia's most common large hawk in the winter, the Red Tailed Hawk, even at a great distance, by their habit of frequently hovering—a hunting technique not normally employed by the Red Tailed.

Boreal Chickadees

The Boreal Chickadee is less well known than its close cousin, the Black Capped Chickadee. With its readily recognizable call, its acrobatic behaviour, and its friendly nature, the Black Capped is by far one of the favourite and best-known birds in Metro. Like the Black Capped, Boreals are found year-round in the Metro area but are considered to be slightly less common. Their preferred habitat is coniferous forests, where they forage for various insects and seeds from the cones of the balsam fir. Unlike the Black Capped Chickadee, Boreals do not normally come to feeders, but in years that fir cones are scarce, they may pay a visit. Pairs or small flocks of Boreals may come to feeders on their own, but they are more likely to be seen travelling with Black Cappeds or Golden Crowned Kinglets. While the Black Capped Chickadees prefer sunflower seeds, the Boreal's favourite feeder food is suet. To recognize a Boreal, look for its brown, not black, cap or listen for its shorter and more nasal "chick–a–dee" call, which could be likened to the sound of a Black Capped singing with a stuffed-up nose!

The Boreal Chickadee is well named as it is truly a citizen of the boreal forest. Outside the city limits, this species is abundant and may be found in a great number of locations. They are present anywhere evergreens dominate the landscape; they can be found inside the city limits, where pockets of this habitat still exist. One of the best locations to see Boreal Chickadees, and my personal favourite, is Point Pleasant Park. There it is possible to get both species of chickadees to feed right out of your hand. It is truly a special feeling when something so little is willing to trust you so much. Building a bond with a wild creature is one of my favourite aspects of birding. Hand-feeding chickadees is not only exciting, but it gives you a new opportunity to learn about these birds. For instance, the first time I hand-fed chickadees, I quickly discovered that the Boreals are a gentler species. Even with my eyes closed, I could tell if it was a Black Capped or a Boreal that was taking the seed from my hand.

The purpose of this section is not to mention all the birding sites found in Halifax County. Rather, it includes enough specific locations to provide users with a wide array of birding experiences. It is meant to be used in conjunction with the main text and not as a summary of the locations of different bird species. The sections are organized from the most frequently birded areas—City Parks and Green Areas, the Eastern Shore, and Granite Coast—to the less birded but highly productive areas further from Metro—Routes 253 and 349: Fergusons Cove to Sambro through to Route 357: Musquodoboit Harbour to Elderbank. You will need to refer to a provincial map as directions cite route numbers labelled there.

City Parks and Green Areas

For the purpose of this guide, any park that lies within the boundaries of Bedford, Dartmouth, Halifax, or Lower Sackville is considered a city park. The majority of these can be located on any current Metro map. For parks that are not currently illustrated, directions are provided. Generally, during the spring and fall migrations, almost any park or green area can suddenly attract and temporarily shelter different species of birds, making these areas valuable to birds. Even unlikely places, such as Citadel Hill and different playgrounds, have produced interesting birds, so it pays to stay alert when walking in or driving past these areas. Of course, the most interesting are the parks that consistently attract a variety of birds.

When it comes to birds, parks can be grouped into five categories, which can all be found in the Metro area. These classifications are based on what time of year a park appeals the most to birds and birders; we have seasonal and year-round

P • L • A • C • E • S •

parks. Our spring parks are good spots to see a number of different species in May. Some of our better-known spring areas are the Frog Pond, Fleming Park (also called the Dingle), the Public Gardens, Kearney Lake Trail, and Shubie Park. All of these locations are also good summer parks. See May and June for details on these areas and what species you might encounter.

The Kearney Lake Trail, a good spring and summer trail, is not marked on local maps but can be reached via Kearney Lake Road. As you near the Atlantic Acres Industrial Park, watch for Blue Mountain Drive. At the very end of this road, the trail, also called the Blue Mountain Drive Trail, begins. One fork of this trail leads to a breath-taking view at the top of Blue Mountain. This site has the potential to be a good hawk-watching spot. See October for more information on this subject.

Other summer parks in Metro are Spectacle Lake, Admirals Rock, Jack Lake Trails, the Urban Wilderness Park, Golden Acres, and Powder Mill Lake. Spectacle Lake Park is not labelled on all Metro maps but Spectacle Lake is. Entrances to the park are located on Spectacle Lake Drive in Burnside. Lakeside birds, such as the Common Yellowthroat, can be found here as well as all the species associated with open shrubbery wood-lands and bogs. This is also a great place for berry picking. Golden Acres Park, also called Martin Lake Park, is located in north end Dartmouth and has trails that run between and around Albro and Martin Lakes. It is similar in composition but also has some larger trees, thus it is home to a greater number of forest species, such as the Ruffed Grouse and Black Throated Green Warbler.

Admirals Rock Park, also called Admirals Cove Park, can be accessed from Shore Drive in Bedford or from Snowy Owl Drive. The Snowy Owl path leads straight to Eagle's Nest or Eagle's

Rock, a large boulder perched on top of a vertical cliff. The view from there is beautiful, and it is a great place to listen to bird songs in May and June. Admirals Rock Park is an important breeding area for many Metro birds. Feeder birds, such as Pine Siskins, Purple Finches, Black Capped Chickadees, plus virtually all the other summer feeder birds, breed in this woods. This park is also home to large numbers of Hermit Thrushes, American Robins, and Northern Flickers.

The Urban Wilderness Park is a small, heavily wooded park, located in Dartmouth on Nantucket Avenue between the Dartmouth High School and the Sportsplex. American Redstarts, Yellow Warblers, and Song Sparrows are a few of the city woodland birds that breed there. This site has great potential but is also subject to periodic vandalism.

Powder Mill Lake Park is just a road side park, but because it has deciduous woodlands nearby, it has become a place where Great Crested Flycatchers have been seen and heard several times.

Birch Cove Park is another location that has had breeding Great Crested Flycatchers. Eastern Wood Pewees were once common there as well, but in recent years both species have disappeared. This park has a beautiful natural stand of partially dying beech trees that provide important cavities for cavity nesters, such as chickadees, nuthatches, and three species of woodpeckers. This park is also a good place to see the beautifully constructed nests of the Red Eyed Vireo. Their hanging nests are smaller than the Northern Orioles, but are just as interesting. The unusual sounding Gray Catbird can also be heard calling here during the summer.

Birch Cove Park becomes an even more exciting place in the fall. Starting in September and continuing into October and November, this park has many species of migrating passerines pass through its boundaries. Part of the appeal of the park is that it contains many large hardwood trees near a city centre that has few green areas.

Another city green area that is a good fall birding spot from September to November is Fairview Cemetery, almost a miniature reflection of Hartlen Point for bird species. The same migrants that are seen passing through Hartlen Point also fly through Fairview Cemetery at the same time. This parallel can be seen almost any fall day by visiting both locations. The main difference is that Hartlen Point receives much larger numbers of those same species. Hartlen Point's variety is slightly greater as well, but Fairview Cemetery still receives enough diversity to make it the best migrant trap inside city limits. However, as the graveyard continues to expand and trees and bushes are lost, its appeal to the birds is diminishing.

An unusual feature of the Fairview Cemetery is that there is frequently a fair amount of bird activity around noon, a feature not normally seen at other fall migration sites in the Metro area. You may find birds anywhere in the cemetery, but the best section can be most easily reached by taking the Windsor Street entrance nearest Connaught Avenue. Park along the straight stretch just inside the entrance. To your left you will see a small wooded hill. This section of the cemetery produces the most and the rarest birds. Check here first, then, as with all fall migration locations, find the Black Capped Chickadees and stick with them. At this location be particularly respectful of the final resting places.

In November, city areas like the Music Conservatory, Conrose Park, and Findlay Park start to become good places to see passerines. Northern Orioles, Mockingbirds, Yellow Breasted Chats, Orange Crowned Warblers, and Pine Warblers are some of the highlights at each of these locations. All of these birds like bushes, so pay special attention to this type of vegetation when searching for them. The Music

Conservatory birders refer to is located on Gorsebrook Avenue in Halifax. Its grounds have a variety of different bushes and abut onto the Canadian National Railway property and a section of undeveloped woodland at the end of Robie Street. The three pieces of land combine to create an interesting, diverse habitat that has attracted some unusual birds. At Conrose Park, a little bit of exploring will lead you to trails that will connect you to the surrounding green areas of St. Mary's Recreation Centre and the CN Railway cutting. Conrose Park is regularly on the maps. Findlay Park, sometimes labelled on Metro maps, is a small but very productive park that lies between Sullivans Pond and Lake Banook.

Two other city parks become interesting areas for birders in the fall—Sullivans Pond (see the following section) and Red Bridge Pond (see September). Instead of passerines for the big draw, various species of waterfowl are the main attraction. Besides Sullivans Pond, other winter parks that are good places for waterfowl are mentioned in the Sewer Stroll in January. One that is not mentioned, though, is First Lake in Sackville. Two locations on the lake produce interesting winter birds. The first is the Murdock MacKay Memorial Park, the other is where Sucker Brook exits the lake. The memorial park is good for gulls and ducks, while Sucker Brook is especially attractive to ducks because the running water stays open, no matter how cold the temperature gets. One of the rarer duck species to frequent this location is the Wood Duck. Another pond that turns up the occasional interesting duck in late fall to early winter is Morash Pond, the small pond located on Woodlawn Road in Dartmouth.

It is also noteworthy that in the winter Mount Saint Vincent becomes home to about ten thousand crows. This crow roost is the largest in the Metro area; starting about two hours before dark, crows can be seen gathering here from

Dartmouth, Bedford, Halifax, and Sackville.

The three year-round Metro parks are Point Pleasant Park, McNabs Island, and Hemlock Ravine. For complete details on these sites see the sections following Sullivans Pond.

Birding Sullivans Pond

Sullivans Pond is widely known as "the Duck Pond." However, few people realize just how many exciting species of birds can be encountered there. During the summer months, only domestic ducks and various tame hybrids are present. In November the pond starts to become much more interesting as various species of wild ducks begin to arrive. They gather here to escape hunting pressures and to enjoy the pond's open waters. At first, these new arrivals are rather nervous and scatter when you raise your binoculars, as if they expect you to shoot at them. Soon they realize that this is a safe place, and they start to settle down. This is when the magic begins. Sullivans is the only place in Nova Scotia that I know where you can feed the normally shy Wood Duck from your hand. Here it is possible to take amazing photographs with an ordinary camera of beautiful birds like the American Coot and the Northern Pintail because you can get so close to them. The tiny Green Winged Teal and the American Wigeon are regularly present in this pond.

However, it is often difficult, especially for new birders, to pick out the really unusual species present because of the large numbers of Black Ducks, Mallards, and domestic ducks. Here are a few tips to help your visit to this pond be more productive. When expert birders arrive at this pond, the first thing they do is quickly scan through the birds to look for any that stand out. Size, shape, and actions are the keys to identification. For example, the American Coot is often located by the action of pumping its head as it swims, differentiating it from Black Ducks. The small size of the Green Winged Teal, about half the size of the Black Duck, causes it to stand out.

Next, experienced birders look at individual ducks. They also take the time to completely circle the pond at least once, often twice. They know from past experiences there is a high probability that more than one species of unusual waterfowl will be present in Sullivans. In fact, almost every species of freshwater duck seen in the province has visited this pond at one time or another. Even saltwater species, such as the Black Scoter and Oldsquaw, have been blown into Sullivans. Before or during stormy weather, it is not uncommon to see other waterfowl come voluntarily from the salt water to Sullivans.

As you walk around the pond, pay particular attention to certain areas. There is a fast-flowing stream that connects Sullivans Pond to the tail end of Lake Banook. Newly arriving species sometimes first arrive at this tiny piece of Lake Banook, and occasionally an American Coot feeds here. Along the banks of the stream, the Wood Duck may be found. Where this stream flows into Sullivans, there is an island. Check the shores of this island carefully as it is a favourite resting place of the Wood Duck, the American Coot, and other species. To the right of the stream, in the corner of the pond, there can be seen a small trickle of water. Check there for the Green Winged Teals. On the lawns surrounding the pond, watch for ducks eating the grass. Black Ducks will do this, but it is the favourite food of the American Wigeon. When resting, wigeons like to sleep on the section of cement wall on the Prince Albert Road side of the pond. The deeper water near the dam is the favourite site of the diving ducks, such as the Ring Necked. The shoreline of the island that is near the dam should be inspected as unusual ducks, especially shyer individuals, often rest there. When trying to identify the ducks in Sullivans, ignore any whose plumage colours look blotchy—they are the hybrids. The wild ducks will have sharp looking plumages, meaning the borders between colours are sharply defined. Also, the birds themselves look sleek, not chubby.

Next, try looking through the flock of gulls that gather along the Crichton Park side of the pond. Mixed in with the Herring and Great Black Backed Gulls will be lots of Ringed Billed Gulls. There are usually a few Black Headed Gulls present and occasionally Bonapartes. Mew and Lesser Black Backed are two rare species that are sometimes present as well. Also watch for the pure white Iceland and Glaucous Gulls. Remember, many of the birds in Sullivans fly between there and the harbour, so if they are not present at one time of the day, try another, perhaps when the tide has changed.

Hemlock Ravine Park

This nearly 80 ha (200 acre) park can best be reached from the Bedford Highway by driving to the end of Kent Avenue, where a good-size parking lot is maintained year-round. The five trails in the park are also easily accessible throughout the year.

Hemlock Ravine Park is aptly named, for within the confines of the park lies a deep ravine with one of the most ancient stands of eastern hemlocks in the province. Here, visitors can see trees which are over three and a half centuries old and tower a height of 24 m to 30 m (80 ft. to 100 ft.) above the ground. The park is also home to a very impressive list of animals and is known as the best place within the city limits to view such species as Yellow Spotted Salamanders, Little Brown Bats, and Northern Flying Squirrels, all of which are most active after dark.

Although Hemlock Ravine is not one of the

better birding spots in our area, even quieter sites such as this hold a few points of interest for a birder. The hemlocks are a favourite tree of the Dark Eyed Junco, which loves to feed on the seeds buried inside the hemlock cones and may be seen in the park year-round. Juncos are a favourite amongst bird lovers as they are one of the few species that are easily identified in flight without the aid of binoculars. Simply watch for one to flash its four pure white outer tail feathers. There are two located on each side of its gray tail. Visit the park on warm, sunny days in March and April, when the males begin their spring song. See March to understand why the Dark Eyed Junco's melody is worth listening for. Other highlights to watch for in the life of the Dark Eyed Junco occur in the park from May to August while the Juncos are breeding. See May for details on where to look for Junco nests. In June, the first batch of young Juncos are out of the nest and active throughout the park. This is a good time to learn how to distinguish between the plumage of the male and female and the adult and immature Juncos. By July, the Juncos have started raising their second brood of chicks. Amazingly, these younger birds will be flying just as well as their older siblings by the end of August.

This park is also a good place to become familiar with the lives of some of the other year-round bird residents. See what you can discover about the Black Capped Chickadee, the Red Breasted Nuthatch, the Golden Crowned Kinglet, or the Yellow Rumped Warbler. On a regular basis, a Pileated Woodpecker briefly visits this park. Two other woodland bird species that occasionally wander into the park are the Barred Owl and the Great Horned Owl. In the fall, birds such as the Great Blue Heron and the Belted Kingfisher stop by for food at the heart-shaped pond. Even a Great Egret has fished at this romantic location. During the winter, you can try tracking the Ruffed Grouse through the hard-wood section of the park. These are just a few of the birds awaiting discovery at this location.

McNabs Island

Islands the world over are noted as places where bird populations differ from those found on the adjacent mainland. Sometimes those differences are quite striking, as in the Galapagos Islands, while in other circumstances they are less noticeable.

McNabs Island is no exception to this rule. Although it is situated very close to the mainland, it does support a slightly different mixture of birds. In summer, McNabs Island is an important breeding area for sensitive species, such as the Great Blue Heron, which seeks out isolated areas to establish breeding colonies. These colonies can range in size from a few pairs of nesting birds to hundreds of individuals. Surprisingly, Great Blue Herons usually build their nests in the tops of trees. Unfortunately, these nests are rather flimsy by nature, and a single visit to a heron colony by a careless person can cause many eggs and young birds to tumble to the ground when the adults are spooked off their nests. Roger Pocklington, a local birder who has been visiting the island for twenty–five years, reported that McNabs hosts a wide diversity of bird life. He says, "One would have to get in their car and drive quite a distance to see the same variety of birds they would see on McNabs Island."

Besides a variety of woodland birds, McNabs has also attracted a number of waterfowl to a small freshwater pond, including such unusual species as the Northern Shoveler. In fall, a wide array of birds use the island as a migratory stopover—some are common species while others are rarities, such as the Peregrine Falcon. Fall is also the time when you can often see small birds

fly across the water from McNabs to Point
Pleasant Park. The island contributes to the
diversity of birds found in Point Pleasant by act-
ing as a giant stepping stone or gateway into the
park. In the winter, both Great Horned and
Barred Owls sally over from the island to capture
small rodents found at Point Pleasant. Winter is
also the time of year to visit McNabs for viewing
sea ducks, which are often difficult to see from
the mainland. This is one of the main reasons
that McNabs Island has been included each year
in the Christmas Bird Counts.

Regardless of the season, a trip to the island
has the potential to produce interesting birds for
a visitor. At least eight other islands in Nova
Scotia are famous for their bird life. Three of
them, Pearl Island (see pages 121–22) and the two
Bird Islands in Cape Breton, are noted for their
value to Atlantic Puffins and other breeding
seabirds.

Point Pleasant Park

This 75 ha (186 acre) park, located in the south
end of Halifax with its variety of habitats, contains within its boundaries so many great birding
opportunities for all types of birders that I could
probably write a book on this location alone!
Suffice it to say here that this park is well worth
visiting during any month. However, its most
productive period starts in September with fall
migration, peaks in November, and continues
until roughly the end of May when spring
migrants are abundant. In winter a diverse and
healthy population is present.

If you are new to the Metro area or are from
out of town, you can reach the park by driving
south on Robie Street towards the downtown
area, turning left onto Inglis Street then right
onto Tower Road. At the end of Tower Road you
can either go straight from the Stop sign to the

parking lot directly ahead, or turn left onto Point Pleasant Drive and follow the road to the lower parking lot. The latter allows quicker access to the coastal area of the park, while the former borders the woodland trails. Besides being a great place to hand-feed birds, this park offers free parking, a canteen during the summer months, washrooms, benches, and plenty of trails.

The Eastern Shore

Dartmouth to Jeddore

Metro residents are fortunate to live so close to an area that is currently considered one of the most productive birding zones in the province. Of particular interest to local birders is the chunk of shoreline from Hartlen Point to West Chezzetcook Marsh.

Hartlen Point can be reached via Pleasant Street (Route 322) in Dartmouth. Follow the road through Woodside and into Eastern Passage. There, Route 322 curves to the left, but to reach Hartlen you must continue straight ahead. You can not get lost if you remember to keep the water on your right-hand side at all times; all you are doing is following the contours of the harbour. Almost immediately on your right you will see a large, white sand beach that birders refer to as the Eastern Passage Beach, locals often call it McCormicks Beach. It has a large parking lot and a nice boardwalk that winds through a grassy area. In the summer, lots of Savannah and Sharp Tailed Sparrows are present in the grasses. This beach provides a wonderful view of Lawlor Island, where Osprey nests can be seen. In the evenings, white-tailed deer often swim over from this island to feed along the beach, an area that is of most interest to birders as a good place to see shorebirds at low tide during the fall migration.

The gulls present always get the once-over as well, since both Mew and Laughing Gulls have been sighted here.

As you continue along the road, past the beach, you will see one or two noticeable spots to pull over. They are used by many people to enjoy the view of the water and by birders in particular to scan for waterfowl. A little further you will come to the beginning of the Hartlen Point Golf Course. On your left you will see a gravel road that is the old entrance to the golf course and is now used as a service road for maintenance staff. The road has a gate that is open most weekdays but is closed and locked in the evenings and much of the weekend. This road crosses the golf course, allowing one to drive directly to the famous Back Cove at Hartlen Point. Although it is currently permissible to drive the length of this road, I do not recommend it. It is an inconvenience to the golfers and potential for future conflict. If you choose to do so, remember, golfers hit the ball across this road in two locations and have the right of way, so you must wait for them to finish their plays, unless they wave you through.

Instead of driving across the golf course, I suggest driving only the first section of this road that leads up the hill to the old clubhouse, where you can scan the part of the golf course that often has interesting birds. What birds you may see depends upon the time of year. During the colder months, hawks and owls may be seen, while in the fall, there are often uncommon species of shore-birds present.

Returning to the main road, watch for a cart track or dirt path running perpendicular from the road to the shoreline. This trail follows along the top of the shoreline and faces a low flat island called Devils Island. A walk along this trail may produce a wide variety of birds on the shoreline and in the water during any month. However, it reaches its peak productivity from July to

October, during the fall migrations. Be sure to carefully check the mouth of the small stream, the clump of willows, and the patch of Japanese knotwood.

Returning to your car, you can drive to a large locked gate that runs across the road and park your vehicle. (Be sure to park far enough back from the gate to allow it to swing freely either way and to permit large vehicles to pass through.) This road is owned by the Department of National Defence and "No Trespassing" signs are posted. The gate and the signs were added in recent years because of garbage dumping and vandalism. The military police patrol this road regularly. I have been told that the signs are there in order to legally deal with trouble-makers. Despite the signs, people are unofficially allowed to walk this road, although they are technically trespassing and do so at their own risk. Although this road is a popular way to reach the Back Cove, I can not recommend you travel it. Back Cove can also be reached by parking at the new clubhouse and walking down along the edge of the golf course until you reach the shoreline. If you take the road, it leads to a tower, from which you can walk a path down over the hill to the shoreline. The road and the path often have interesting bird species along them, but the best birds are at the cove itself.

From late August to early November just about any bird imaginable could be and probably has been seen at the Back Cove, making this location the hottest birding spot in Metro and one of the best in the province. However, you do have to get to this location early in the morning. The time from about half an hour after dawn to approximately 10:30 A.M. is the best time, after which the migrating birds often settle down for a rest and are just about impossible to find. Be sure to wear boots as the U-shaped road that hugs the cove is often very muddy and many of the birds present are seen by walking back and forth along it.

While walking, if you come across a flock of chickadees, you will find many of the regular and rare migrants with them. Also, be sure to walk down any of the side trails that lead to the cove itself. Early in the morning check the cove, the grassy areas, the marsh, and the trees that line the cove. Take note of what trees the sun shines on, and check these spots well. The sun's warmth causes the insects to be active and they, in turn, attract the birds. You may want to visit this site on the weekends as it is a good time to meet other birders. You will find most of us are friendly and helpful, so don't be shy!

From Hartlen Point you can rejoin Route 322, and it will lead you to Rainbow Haven Beach. On the way, watch for and take Cow Bay Road for a brief side trip. On your right you will not be able to miss a large statue of a moose, a good place to stop and check the waters of Cow Bay for water-fowl. This is an especially good spot to see the Red Throated Loon. At the bottom of the hill, on the opposite side of the road, is a lake that some-times attracts rare ducks. Canvasbacks and Eurasian Wigeons have been sighted there. Further along, on the water side of the road, you will sight a small white building, which is the local community centre. It is an excellent place to see Northern Gannets. The seaweed along the shore should be checked at this location as well for American Pipits and shorebirds.

Cow Bay Road is a loop that brings you back to Route 322. Turning right will take you to Rainbow Haven Beach, also referred to as the Cole Harbour Dykes. This location has a variety of birds year-round. Some highlights include migrating Canada Geese, Whimbrels, and Hudsonian Godwits. In the winter, check for Horned Larks, Short Eared Owls, Yellow Rumped Warblers, and if you are lucky, you may even see a Seaside Sparrow.

Upon leaving Rainbow Haven Beach, turn right onto Bissett Road. On the left is the Halifax County Rehabilitation Centre. From the back of the hospital, you can see Bissett Lake, a productive waterfowl location in November and December. Bissett Road takes you to Cole Harbour Road, Route 207.

Route 207 is also known as Portland Street, Lawrencetown Road, and Marine Drive. Whatever you call it, the road takes you to all the other birding sites along the Eastern Shore. The first stop is the West Lawrencetown Marsh, bordered on one side by the West Lawrencetown Road and on the other side by Conrads Road. This marsh is best viewed by walking the old railway bed that runs between the two. It can also be partially viewed from the shoulder of the main road at three places. A wide variety of birds may be seen at this marsh, a place that has also attracted many rarities. Although this site is interesting year-round, it is at its best from April to November, when most of the marsh is not frozen. Conrads Road borders this marsh and runs down to Conrads Beach, a site that plays host to species too numerous to mention here. It crops up frequently in the main text and is also worth visiting year-round.

Return to Route 207 (Marine Drive) and turn right, continuing until you reach the spot where the Lawrencetown River crosses the road. On the right is Stoney Beach and on the left Lawrencetown Lake. At low tide, this is a good place to check for shorebirds. Over the years, a number of unusual birds have been seen here, including Eurasian Ruff and Franklin's Gull. If you have the time, try walking the old railway bed to get a better view of Lawrencetown Lake. Further down the road, you will see Lawrencetown Beach on the right, a great place for swimming and large waves, but not a very good place for birds. Instead, focus your attention on the various pools of water on the left side of the road. They don't look like much, but these pools are natural gathering places for herons, sandpipers, and ducks and have produced all kinds of fascinating birds. Egrets are frequently seen there, and super rarities like the American Avocet seem to find these pools almost every year.

The next stop is the Rocky Run Bridge. This spot is always worth a quick check for the unusual wanderer. Immature Yellow Crowned Night Herons have been seen here for a number of years. Just on the other side of the bridge is a road running to the right that you should turn onto. On the right you will see a harbour and on the left a small pond, often called Teal Pond as large numbers of Green Winged Teals gather here during migration. Most of the pond can be seen from the side of the road, but the best section for viewing birds is hidden in the right-hand corner. Approximately opposite a side road called Spruce Court Road is a short walking path from which you can view this hidden corner. Here, Solitary Sandpipers are frequently seen as well as other species of shorebirds.

As you continue driving, take note of the only left-hand turn—it leads to Three Fathom Harbour—but you should continue straight. Almost immediately after this intersection, you will come to a low-lying area, which is a black spruce bog. Gray Jays live there year-round, and in the summer, Palm and Blackpoll Warblers are common. This road continues for another half kilometre. You will see a sign to indicate that the road ends at 150 m (492 ft.). Just after this sign is a pull-over spot large enough for one or two cars to park. If you pull in, you will be facing Lower Three Fathom Harbour. Although there is no particular bird to look for here, it is always worth a peek.

Return to the aforementioned intersection and take the road leading to Three Fathom Harbour.

As you crest the hill, you will be overlooking a picturesque horse farm and the harbour itself. After a quick scan from this advantageous viewpoint, continue to the bottom of the hill for a look at the rest of the harbour. In November, this is a good place for Pied Billed Grebes, Ruddy Ducks, Buffleheads, and Greater Scaups. At other times of the year, it is less active but can still be interesting. In the late '80s, migrating Black Terns would pass through this site during the Labour Day weekend. Perhaps they will return again someday.

Travel another 1.5 km (1 mi.) and watch for a mailbox on the left with the number 540. Across from the mailbox is a private driveway, which people are welcome to walk (but not drive) down. This driveway leads to Smelly Cove, also called Stinky Cove, and is an excellent site for shorebirds. Your nose will immediately detect the strong odour there that comes from rotting piles of seaweed. This location is often at its best two and a half to three and a half hours after high tide.

Three Fathom Harbour Road returns you to Route 207. Turn right and travel to the entrance of Seaforth Causeway Road. The two most interesting birding sites are found at the very end of the road and where the actual causeway lies. The end of the road provides a good view of Wedge Island, where Rough Legged Hawks are often seen. The winter waters here are also good for waterfowl. The causeway is a good place to observe shorebird migration and waterfowl.

Back on Route 207, turn right. On the left there will be a pond and across the road to the right lies a barrier beach. During and shortly after rough weather, sea ducks sometimes gather in this pond. Further along on your right, near the Seaforth Community Centre, is a small triangular pond. This small pond has attracted rare species of ducks and is an ideal location for Cattle Egret.

At the next right turn-off, watch for the Dyke Road (previously called the Grand Desert Dyke Road), which provides excellent views of one of our most productive local saltwater marshes, the West Chezzetcook Marsh. By returning to Route 207, you will come to another right, which is Shore Road. This road provides several additional views at other parts of this large marsh. High numbers of Canada Geese gather here during their spring migration. It also is a good place to see various species of swallows, Northern Pintails, Blue Winged and Green Winged Teals, and the occasional Northern Shoveler. In the fall, huge numbers of shorebirds pass through the marsh, and past sightings have included rarities such as Eurasian Ruffs and Curlew Sandpipers. This is one of the few Metro sites that also attracts shorebirds in the spring—Black Bellied Plovers, Greater Yellowlegs, and Least Sandpipers are three species I have seen there more than once.

When driving along Shore Road, be sure to make lots of stops to scan each section of the marsh. When looking with just your eyes, this marsh can appear deceptively quiet, so don't forget to raise those binoculars to find out what is really there. After reaching the end of Shore Road, most birders either take Highway 107 back to Dartmouth or retrace their path along Route 207. If I have the time, I prefer to go back the way I came as things have often changed enough that I frequently see a few new birds for the day. If you choose to return via Highway 107, turn right at the Stop sign at the end of Shore Road and travel less than a kilometre. Route 207 ends here and you must turn left to reach the No. 7 West Highway. Turn left onto the No. 7 and immediately start to watch for a large sign indicating a left turn to reach Highway 107. All these left turns may seem as if I am directing you to drive in circles, but trust me, these directions will get you home!

The section of the Eastern Shore from Dartmouth to West Chezzetcook is currently the most intensely birded shoreline in Halifax County. If you wish to continue your birding trip, the following are the most frequently visited sites. In the late summer, early fall flocks consisting of hundreds of shorebirds can be observed on the large mudflat located at the end of the East Chezzetcook Road. The East Petpeswick Road leads to Martinique Beach, an excellent birding area, but do not be in too great a hurry to get there as the East Petpeswick Road often has interesting birds along it. In the water, White Winged Scoters, Oldsquaws, and Red Breasted Mergansers are often present year-round, and an Eared Grebe from the west was once discovered there. During their migration or after storms, Northern Garnets have been sighted and on more than one occasion, a Parasitic Jaeger has been seen. Small-hawk migration can be observed along this road and Snowy Owls haunt the area in winter.

Martinique Beach provides good bird-watching opportunities year-round. Untold numbers of shorebirds visit this large white sand beach and the mudflats that lie behind it. It is also known for its large concentrations of Canada Geese (thousands), American Black Ducks, and Northern Pintails. Martinique is one of the most reliable places to see the Ipswich race of the Savannah Sparrow and provides important breeding habitat for the endangered Piping Plover. In the winter, Northern Harriers, Yellow Rumped Warblers, Snow Buntings, Horned Larks, Lapland Longspurs, Golden Crowned Kinglets, and Boreal Chickadees are all plentiful. Bald Eagles frequent the area year-round as do Gray Jays in the adjacent spruce bogs. A long list of rarities have been sighted at Martinique Beach, including Little Blue and Tricolored Heron, Gull Billed Tern, and Golden Eagle.

Like Martinique Beach, Musquodoboit Harbour is known for its large numbers of Canada Geese and Bald Eagles. It also has an active Arctic Tern colony on Sterring Island. Many winter ducks gather here. The most regular species are Common Goldeneyes, but Red Breasted Mergansers, all three scoters, and Greater Scaups are usually present as well.

Ostrea Lake Road is used each year by a variety of south-bound passerines and shorebirds. At the end of the West Jeddore Road, one can see Whimbrel, Great Horned Owl, Olive Sided Flycatcher, and Bay Breasted Warbler. Breeding Bay Breasted Warblers can also be found in the woodlands surrounding Jeddore.

The Shore of Islands

....

The Eastern Shore Continued

Starting at Clam Bay, the rest of the eastern Halifax County shoreline takes on a decidedly different look—all of a sudden the inshore waters are peppered with hundreds of islands. Drumlins, which make up most of the islands in Mahone Bay and the soft headlands along the first stretch of the Eastern Shore, are rare along this section of the coast. But this area is highly productive for birds, containing important features such as pro-tected inlets, salt marshes, and extensive growths of eelgrass and other important seaweeds; how-ever, it is not as heavily travelled by birders as the section of Eastern Shore closest to the Metro area.

The Shore of Islands, also known as Bay of Islands, begins with the large Clam Bay and runs along Highway 7, also called Marine Drive. Here, watch for Bald Eagles and Gray Jays. A vast vari-ety of shorebirds use this bay during migration, including our two largest, the Whimbrel and the

Hudsonian Godwit. The next productive birding site is Tangier. The drive between Clam Bay and Tangier is scenic but uncharacteristically quiet when it comes to birds. The inlands near Tangier host breeding colonies of Double Crested Cormorants, Great Blue Herons, and most importantly, all of the Common Eiders.

Your next stop should be Taylors Head Provincial Park, a phenomenal area for birds. Here, Spruce Grouse are as easy to see as barn-yard chickens and Gray Jays hang around the picnic tables waiting for hand-outs. Boreal species abound, and birds such as Boreal Chickadees and Pine Grosbeaks are virtually guaranteed. In the summer, Black Backed Woodpeckers, Great Horned Owls, Yellow Bellied Flycatchers, Winter Wrens, Canada Warblers, Arctic Terns, and breeding Fox Sparrows can be seen. In the winter, watch for sea ducks, Red Throated Loons, and Purple Sandpipers.

Flocks of Whimbrels pass through the park in the fall; in the spring, the tip of Taylors Head is one of the few places in the area that experiences heavy migration. Two of the most exciting reports to come from Taylors Head were of an Eared Grebe and a flock of over forty Caspian Terns. Sheet Harbour, most noted for Bald Eagles and also the most southerly breeding colony of Great Cormorants along our shore, is worth checking out.

The next place of interest is Sober Island, a rarity hot spot, which is connected to the main-land by a short causeway. In the winter, Harlequin Ducks and King Eiders are often present. During the summer, breeding Black Guillemots can be found as well as a few Roseate Terns and Least Sandpipers (suspected of breed-ing there). Fall migration is incredible; the few visits there by birders in the fall have turned up rarities like White Eyed Vireo, Prairie Warbler, Northern Oriole, and Upland Sandpiper.

Dufferin Mines is a good spot to see a lot of the wood warblers and Great Horned, Barred, and Saw Whet Owls. From Port Dufferin to Moser River, Black Poll Warblers can be found along any of the little side roads. These roads are also good places to see Arctic and Common Terns. Check for Great and Snowy Egrets, too.

European Brambling, Blue Grosbeak, Varied Thrush, Brown Thrasher, and Red Bellied Woodpecker are just some of the rare birds that have shown up at Moser River over the years. From Necum Teuch to Ecum Secum Bridge, the last community in Halifax County, the coastal bogs are home to the usually hard to find Wilson's Warbler. The clear cuts house the rare Mourning Warbler. After storms, Leach's Storm Petrels are often seen here as their burrows are located on the nearby Halibut Islands.

The Granite Coast

The entire piece of land that lies between Halifax Harbour and St. Margarets Bay is underlain by a massive layer of thick granite. This granite creates a very different coastline from that found on the Eastern Shore. This hard-rock coast is known for well-elevated headlands, a scarcity of islands, and few beaches. The beaches that do exist are composed of white sand derived from the granite; the islands and knolls are the result of submerged granite headlands.

Large sections of the coastal land are covered by almost treeless bush-dominated barrens, evergreen bogs, and old fire barrens. The granite has given this entire region what is known as a "deranged drainage pattern." This means that the many lakes, streams, and bogs lying on its surface are interconnected by erratically wandering, slow-moving streams.

•
P
L
A
C
E
S

Routes 253 and 349:
Fergusons Cove to Sambro

This shoreline is most productive during the winter months. Details on what species to look for and where to find them can be found in January, under Sewer Stroll. In April and May, especially after stormy weather, the South Point and Bald Rock Roads are excellent places to check for storm-blown strays. See April for details on what species may be seen. In the spring, the pond behind Your Corner Store should be checked for rarities. Any time of the year Chebucto Head is an interesting place to visit. This site is constantly changing and is a good place to just sit and watch. In the summer, the rest of this shoreline is relatively quiet, but in the fall it heats up again. From September to November, it's worth stopping to look at any flocks of birds you encounter along this route. Many of the same species that pass through Hartlen Point can also be found scattered along this shoreline.

The Purcells Cove Road (Route 253) is one of several exits off the Armdale Rotary and runs along the Northwest Arm to the mouth of Halifax Harbour. The entrance to Fleming Park, also called the Dingle, lies 1.5 km (0.9 mi.) from the rotary. About a kilometre farther you can find the Frog Pond, which has a large parking lot and several hiking trails conducive to spring and summer birding. Melvin Road can be found 2.5 km (1.5 mi.) farther on the left and provides an excellent view of water birds at Point Pleasant Park. The start of Fergusons Cove Road, 2 km (1.2 mi.) ahead, turns off Route 253 and rejoins the highway just past the entrance to York Redoubt. Turn left and travel 2.5 km (1.5 mi.) to reach the Herring Cove Look-off. Upon leaving the look-off parking lot, turn left and drive a kilometre before turning left onto Village Road. Just 300 m (327 yds.) past the intersection is Harrigans Road;

opposite this is a narrow cove—a good winter bird spot. Another 300 m (327 yds.) on the left is Stonewall Road. Drive a half kilometre to the end of Village Road, where you turn left on Route 349. The start of South Point Road is 5.5 km (3.4 mi.) farther. Chebucto Head Road (also called Duncans Cove Road), East Road (in Ketch Harbour), and Sandy Cove Road all run off to the left and are several kilometres apart. Bald Rock Road is the next short left with Atlantic View Drive just beyond and then the pond behind Your Corner Store on the right. Drive through Sambro to the signs for Government Wharf Road on the left. Route 349 ends at the far edge of the village. A left turn will take you to East and West Bull Point Roads, a short kilometre away. You can take Route 349 (also called Herring Cove Road) back to the Armdale Rotary or turn right on Village Road and return via the more scenic Route 253.

Route 333: Goodwood to Tantallon

This route winds through some of the South Shore, also known as the Lighthouse Route. The scenery becomes a barren landscape littered with large boulders, called erratics, which are debris left behind by receding glaciers during the end of the last ice age. The bordering shores are lined with granite boulders polished by sea waves.

Departing Halifax through the Armdale Rotary, travel south on Route 3, exiting onto Route 333, and continue travelling towards Goodwood. At Goodwood there are plenty of hiking opportunities with four major trails that begin in the community and take you in just about any direction you desire. Goodwood is an excellent place to experience spring warbler migration. Local bird expert Fred Dobson has taken people to this area for many years to see these migrants. Special sightings include

•
P
L
A
C
E
S

Blackburnian and Bay Breasted Warblers and Barred Owls.

Nearby Hatchet Lake is a good area for the Black Throated Blue Warbler, Saw Whet Owl, and Pileated Woodpecker. Continuing to Brookside, both Great Horned and Barred Owls are frequently seen, and from the end of Brookside Road runs a trail where Spruce Grouse have been found. Gray Jays are common in Whites Lake. Woodcock breed along the first half of Terence Bay Road, left off Brookside Road. At the end of the Terence Bay Road, breeding Double Crested Cormorants from a nearby colony are easily seen.

Continuing along Route 333 you will see the turn-off to Prospect, an excellent place to view Purple Sandpipers, most members of the Alcid family, Whimbrels, and Harlequin Ducks, especially from the Indian Point Road, which is further along the route. Just after the turn-off to Prospect is Shad Bay, where the trail leading to Camperdown Hill is home to Black Backed Woodpeckers.

Past Bayside, turn on the road to Black Point where you can see Blackpoll Warblers, Pine Grosbeaks, Hermit and Swainson's Thrushes, Boreal Chickadees, and various waterfowl in the winter. One of the few places along the Halifax County coast where breeding Canada Geese can be found is in this area of Blind Bay.

The large barrens at McGraths Cove, located farther along Route 333, support breeding populations of Lincoln's Sparrows and Palm Warblers. The cemetery at West Dover has had nesting Gray Catbirds, and Willets may be seen on the coastal side of the road between West Dover and Peggy's Cove. The list of birds that can be found at Peggy's Cove during the summer months includes Black Guillemots, Arctic Terns, Common Yellowthroats, Savannah Sparrows, Yellow Rumped and Blackpoll Warblers. During the winter you can see Purple Sandpipers, Dovekies, and Black Legged Kittiwakes. An even better place to view kittiwakes is nearby Indian Harbour. There, many of our winter sea ducks are commonly seen and rarities, such as the Common Murre and the Western Kingbird, have been sighted. Paddys Head, connected to the mainland by a short causeway, is an excellent place to see fall migrants and Purple Sandpipers. Further along the route, Hacketts Cove is frequently visited by both White Winged and Red Crossbills. In Glen Margaret, watch out for Willets and Red Necked Grebes. The trail opposite Woodens Cove provides the woodland walker with the chance to see Cape May and Blackburnian Warblers.

In Seabright there are two main sites of interest for birders. The first is the Irwin Hubley Road, a regular gathering place for winter puddle ducks when the water along this road is ice free. The second, Wedge Island, housed one of the most important tern breeding colonies in Halifax County. There, the endangered Roseate Tern could be found breeding with the Arctic and Common Terns. At least that was the case until the gulls began to destroy their eggs and young. Tern numbers dropped, the Roseate Terns disappeared, and the others would have, too, if local bird lovers Blair Smith and Simon Krasemann hadn't interfered. Placing a grid barrier over the tern nesting sites allowed the terns but not the gulls to pass through. Using tape recordings to draw in terns, the colony is recuperating. From the McDonald Point Road in Seabright, one can get a wonderful look at the Wedge Island tern colony, especially if a birding scope is used. Rare birds are sometimes sighted along the McDonald Point Road as well, with the rarest to date being a Scissor Tailed Flycatcher. Eastern Bluebirds have also been seen between Seabright and Upper Tantallon in the spring. On average, an Eastern

Bluebird is reported from this area one out of every two springs. Horned Grebes may be seen anywhere along this section of our coast, but the most consistent location has been French Village Harbour.

In Glen Haven, the Indian Point Road has a good supply of multiflora rose bushes, a favourite food of many berry eating species. A variety of waterfowl, including Buffleheads, Dovekies, Common Goldeneyes, and Hooded Mergansers can be seen there as well. These same species and others can be seen in Whynachts Cove in Tantallon. These less common species of ducks are often mixed with the huge numbers of American Black Ducks present. This cove has produced such rarities as Little Blue Heron and Snowy Egret.

At Upper Tantallon you can return to the city via the scenic, meandering Route 3, or use the faster route, Highway 103.

Highway 103: Halifax to Hubbards

Our 100 series highways are the largest highways in the province. They allow quick travel but the traffic noise, created by high speed limits and large volumes of traffic, combined with limited access provide few birding opportunities.

Highway 103 can be reached by leaving the Metro area and travelling towards the South Shore. Between the Halifax city limits and Exit 4, few birds of interest are sighted from the highway, except the occasional hawk or other large, readily identified species. At Exit 4, from the off-ramps, two uncommon species, the Fox Sparrow and the Northern Waterthrush, can be found. At Exit 5, a large Osprey nest can be seen situated on top of a power line pole. Common Loons may be observed in the lakes between the two exits. Approximately 3 km (2 mi.) past Exit 5 is a small area of water on either side of the road.

Immediately after this water, a road crosses the highway and may be travelled in either direction. The left extension, on the coastal side of the highway, is called the Mill Lake Road; the right extension, on the inland side of the highway is called the Mersey Paper Road. The Mill Lake Road is best known for Black Throated Blue Warblers, Common Loons, breeding Common Mergansers, and Barn Swallows. The Mersey Paper Road has gates across it, which are usually closed for a brief period in early spring to prevent damage to the roads. Birders most often drive this road slowly, stopping frequently to look and listen, but it may also be walked. Along the first part of the road you will see Little Indian Lake. Here, Wood Duck boxes have been erected and the occasional rare bird has been observed. Good examples of past rarities are the Great Egret and an unconfirmed Reddish Egret.

Less than a kilometre farther, the road forks. A short distance up the left fork will take you to a massive sawdust pile. This pile has numerous nesting tunnels dug by Bank Swallows and a pair of Belted Kingfishers. Unfortunately, the same sawdust piles are used by dirt bikes and all-terrain vehicles so the Bank Swallow numbers have dropped drastically over the years. The right fork in the road takes you to Sandy Lake, where one of our rarer breeders, the Eastern Phoebe, has been found nesting near the dam.

Approximately half a kilometre up the right fork is a short road that runs to Wrights Lake. Watch for an area of dead trees, where you may spot breeding American Kestrels or you may discover them hunting over the nearby barrens where Lincoln Sparrows are relatively common. Other species that live along the Mersey Paper Road include Common Nighthawk, Pileated Woodpecker, Great Horned Owl, Palm Warbler, Winter Wren, and Black Backed Woodpecker.

Where the Ingram River crosses Highway

103, there is another logging road nearby. However, the gate across this road can be locked without warning, so do not take your car in unless you have a key. The birds along this trail are similar to the ones found along the Mersey Paper Road, minus the more exciting species. The rest of the distance between Exit 5 and Exit 6 is uneventful except that Pileated Woodpeckers are often seen flying across the highway. Exit 6 leads to Hubbards. Gray Catbirds breed in the road side bushes. From Hubbards you can return to the city by either Highway 103 or Route 3. (See the following route for further information on Hubbards.)

Route 3: Beechville to Hubbards

Route 3 parallels Highway 103 on the South Shore of Halifax County from Beechville to Hubbards. This route takes you on a leisurely excursion through many of the local communities, passing by several parks and stretches of sandy beaches.

The section of road between Beechville and Exit 4 is an excellent place to watch for Broad Winged Hawks, as the woodlands near the Timberlea area are the best place along the coastal part of Halifax County to find these breeding hawks. These woodlands are also home to Pileated Woodpeckers, Yellow Bellied Sapsuckers, Barred Owls, and Ruby Throated Hummingbirds. Just before Exit 4 lies Cranberry Lake. Stop here to see Common Snipes, American Woodcock, Spotted Sandpipers, Swamp Sparrows, or the occasional unusual waterfowl, such as the Pied Billed Grebe or Wood Duck. Just past Exit 4 is Sheldrake and Five Island Lakes, both of which should also be checked quickly. Next is Big Hubley Lake Road, at the end of which Wilson's Warblers have been sighted. Continuing on, the next noteworthy place to stop is Lewis Lake Provincial Park. A variety of woodland birds may be observed there, including three normally hard to find species: the Black Throated Blue Warbler, the Canada Warbler, and if you are lucky, the Barred Owl. The flashy Red Winged Blackbird is common along the lake.

Approximately 2 km (1.2 mi.) farther on Route 3, the road crosses over Route 333, and approximately another kilometre past this intersection is a narrow cove and the St. Margarets Bay Power Station. The water here stays ice-free year-round and is a magnet for all kinds of waterfowl. All three species of mergansers can be found here as well as both species of goldeneye, Black and White Winged Scoters, Greater Scaup, Canada Geese, American Wigeons, Northern Pintails, and of course lots of Black Ducks. Check all of the birds carefully—waterfowl as rare as the Canvasback have been attracted to this oasis. A pair of Bald Eagles are also present year-round.

On Todds Island, connected to Route 3 via a short causeway, one can readily see a large bank of red soil. This site is home to Bank Swallows and Belted Kingfishers. Hooded Mergansers may also be seen in the waters surrounding the island. Further along, roads, feeders, and woods near the tip of Boutiliers Point should always be checked carefully. This site has produced exceptional rare species such as a Varied Thrush and a Carolina Wren. Where the Ingram River crosses under Route 3, watch the narrow cove for Dovekies, Oldsquaws, and Belted Kingfishers. Between Black Point and Cleveland Point lies a small cove called The Puddle. On the inland side of Route 3 at this location is a small body of connecting water, also referred to as The Puddle. Both are a popular staging area for migrating Hooded Mergansers. The Black Point Picnic Park is usually fairly quiet bird-wise, but it is a nice place to have a snack, and a rare Glossy Ibis was seen there once.

Next stop is Queensland Beach, a medium-size white sand beach. A small number of shorebirds use it during migration. A typical sighting would be a small flock of six Sanderlings or a couple of Semipalmated Plovers. The occasional Semipalmated and Least Sandpiper have been viewed here as well. The Halifax County part of Route 3 terminates at Hubbards. Very little bird knowledge has been accumulated about Hubbards, but we do know that Fox Sparrows pass through here in the spring. Hubbards is an under–birded area that has great potential. All along Route 3, Red Necked and Horned Grebes are commonly seen, as well as Dovekies, other Alcids, and Surf and Black Scoters. If you want to return to the Metro area you can do so by travelling east along Highway 103 or retracing your path along Route 3.

The Interior

....

Introduction

The interior part of Halifax County could be described as an ecotone in the sense that it is a transitional zone between two very different birding regions in the province—the Atlantic shore and the Annapolis Valley. However, most ecotones are richer in bird life than either of the two zones which border them. This is not true of the inland areas of Halifax County only because our coastline has a very diverse mixture of bird life, consisting of individuals that are strongly dependent on saltwater environments, so the inward extensions of their range are extremely limited.

Our land-based coastal birds fall roughly into three categories: birds that can survive equally well on the coast or inland; birds that are best adapted to coastal living but can exist inland in smaller numbers; and those birds that occur on the coast but are more plentiful inland. While there are no species of birds in the interior parts of Halifax County that cannot be found along the coast, certain groups of birds certainly become more prominent and thus easier to find the further inland you go.

Distinct birding regions are marked by noticeable changes in the landscape. For example, the predominant farmland of the Annapolis Valley looks very different from the extensive marshlands of the Amherst area or the wind-swept coastal forest of the Atlantic shoreline. In transitional zones like the interior of Halifax County, changes are much more subtle, where elements from adjacent birding regions are intermixed in much smaller proportions than those found in their own distinct region. This intermixing gives a transitional zone a variable landscape with only small patches of distinct habitat; therefore, the inland portions of Halifax County are made up of the same jumbled terrain, regardless of which route you choose to follow.

The following routes take in sites that show the greatest diversity of the inland parts of Halifax County. Throughout the interior you will notice there is slightly more farmland and hardwood habitat than along the coast, but coniferous species will still be common with a great deal of mixed woodland present. Unlike the Halifax County coast, which has three distinct sections, each with its own unique make-up of birds, the bird populations of the interior region are basically the same throughout. The greatest variation can be detected in the same patches of pure habitat and at the extremities of the county, where the slight effects of bird populations outside of Halifax County influence those inside county lines.

Route 224:
Cooks Brook to Sheet Harbour

This route can be accessed from Exit 10 on Highway 102 or by travelling east on Highway 7 from Dartmouth. This road between Cooks Brook and Sheet Harbour connects the marine surroundings of Sheet Harbour to the green valleys of Upper Musquodoboit and the Shubenacadie River, offering a variety in scenery and bird life.

The section of Route 224 from Cooks Brook to Upper Musquodoboit has more farmland and abandoned farmlands along it than any other part of Halifax County, and this is reflected in the bird life. American Kestrels and Red Tailed Hawks love to hunt over the oldfields in search of mice and insects. In the winter, another predator, the Northern Shrike, is common in this area. Watch for young spruce trees in fields. White spruce are one of the first trees to colonize oldfields, and as far as Chipping Sparrows are concerned, the isolated trees are the ideal place to build a nest. Where the fields meet the woodlands, especially if the latter is hardwoods, a tangled bushy border exists, where different bird species can be seen, such as Gray Catbird, Brown Headed Cowbird, Chestnut Sided Warbler, Eastern Kingbird, and occasionally an Eastern Bluebird.

In the larger hardwood stands, Pileated Woodpeckers are often present as are Veerys, Saw Whet Owls, and a few Rose Breasted Grosbeaks. Common Mergansers breed in the larger rivers of the area and on any body of water. Keep in mind that Cliff Swallows are easier to find here than in most other parts of Halifax County. Blue Winged and Green Winged Teals, Wood Ducks, and breeding Canada Geese are other water-loving birds representative of this area. The section of Route 224 that runs from Upper Musquodoboit to Sheet Harbour is an isolated area, but it is an excellent place to hear and see Great Horned, Barred, and Saw Whet Owls. This stretch of road also has a very good selection of wood warblers, making it easy to find over a dozen species in an hour or two.

This latter leg of Route 224 runs parallel to a road that leaves the highway at Elmsdale and passes through Mooseland on the way to the Atlantic Coast. This Mooseland Road takes you through a wonderful example of a productive boreal bog. Here, there are a lot of Rusty Blackbirds and Blackburnian Warblers, two species which can normally be difficult to find. Also one can reasonably expect to see Black Backed Woodpeckers, Boreal Chickadees, Pine Grosbeaks, and Gray Jays.

Route 212 and the Halifax International Airport

The interesting challenge here is to see how many birds you can identify while your plane is waiting to land or in the process of landing or taking off. I think you will be surprised by just how many different species can be seen. Some of the more appealing ones located at the airport are Red Tailed Hawks, present year-round; Snow Buntings in the winter; and Cliff and Barn Swallows in the summer.

Route 212, also known as the Old Guysborough Road, holds two sites of interest for the Halifax County birder: Dollar Lake Provincial Park and Lake Egmont. The larger hardwood trees at Dollar Lake are home to Northern Goshawks, Sharp Shinned and Broad Winged Hawks, and the occasional Coopers Hawk may also be seen in the park or along Route 212. While in the park, birders may encounter a Veery, Eastern Wood Pewee, Barred Owl, Ruffed Grouse, a variety of warblers, Yellow Bellied Sapsucker, White Breasted Nuthatch, and

Pileated Woodpecker. In the evergreen areas of the park, the Blackburnian Warbler and the Northern Parula can be sighted.

Lake Egmont is an incredible place for birds, with some nice surprises. The biggest surprise yet is breeding Sharp Tailed Sparrows, which normally breed in salt marshes along the coast. The breeding colony at Lake Egmont is currently the only known inland nesting site in the province. The variety and number of waterfowl found at Lake Egmont are more reminiscent of lakes in Cumberland County. At Lake Egmont, Wood Ducks and Blue Winged Teal are just as common as they are in the Amherst area. There are also a lot of Pied Billed Grebes, and Soras are fairly common.

As evening approaches, the air at Lake Egmont comes alive with singing American Bitterns and Pied Billed Grebes; Saw Whet Owls are often heard as well. Other waterfowl species present that are more typical of Halifax County include American Black Duck, Green Winged Teal, and Ring Necked Duck, all of which appear in healthy numbers. Adding to the variety are other common lake birds, such as Great Blue Heron, Belted Kingfisher, Spotted Sandpiper, and American Woodcock. Woodcock are fairly common all along Route 212, as are Common Snipes and the tiny Saw Whet Owl. Also keep an eye open for Alder Flycatchers, Lincoln's Sparrows, Olive Sided Flycatchers, Wilson's Warblers, and Northern Waterthrushes.

Route 374: Liscomb Game Sanctuary

Route 374 begins in Sheet Harbour and passes through Malay Falls, Lochaber Mines, and the Liscomb Game Sanctuary, ending outside Halifax County in Stellarton.

My first trip, many years ago, to the Liscomb Game Sanctuary proved to be quite a disappointment. I expected the area to be protected, and it is—from hunting—but logging and mining are allowed. Mature trees line Route 374 as it passes through the sanctuary, but just behind the thin layer of trees there are massive clear cuts of various ages. You are not allowed to hunt the animals, but you can cut down the trees, forcing them to go elsewhere. Sounds like a poor excuse for a sanctuary to me.

Another feature of this area is the massive and dangerous quaking bogs. They look safe to walk on but will support the weight of a person in only a few spots. You will know when you start to step on one as the land will undulate in front of you from the pressure of your footstep. In the boggy areas, watch for Palm and Blackpoll Warblers. In the more wooded sections of the bog, you may find Rusty Blackbirds, or if you are really lucky, a Greater Yellowlegs. This is the only place in the province outside northeastern Cape Breton where breeding Greater Yellowlegs can be found. Stands of dead trees along this route often have Black Backed Woodpeckers in them, especially if there are some mature evergreens nearby. In the larger evergreens, search for Swainson's Thrush and Blackburnian Warblers, as well as the occasional Pileated Woodpecker. Amongst the middle-aged evergreens, there are Yellow Bellied Flycatchers. Mixtures of fir and spruce in this area attract Bay Breasted and Blackburnian Warblers. Cape May Warblers are common in the clear cuts, where the evergreens are starting to regenerate.

Route 357: Musquodoboit Harbour to Elderbank

On Route 357, just outside Musquodoboit Harbour, you will come to a section of highway that is bordered by a hill of large hardwoods, called Jerusalem Hill. At an elevation of approximately 107 m (350 ft.), it is the highest point of

•
P
L
A
C
E
S

land in the area. This site is favoured by large numbers of Barred Owls, Pileated Woodpeckers, Yellow Bellied Sapsuckers, and Black Throated Blue Warblers, as well as a number of the more common woodland species, such as Ovenbirds and Black and White Warblers.

Near Lower Meaghers Grant, look for Canada Warblers in the wet woodlands, and in the roadside bushes watch for Catbirds. Chipping Sparrows breed in the town of Meaghers Grant. The Meaghers Grant Back Road leads to a boreal bog where Nova Scotia's second rarest breeding owl, the Long Eared Owl, can be found. In Elderbank, there is a large marsh, which is an incredible place to see a variety of birds. Besides the common ducks, Blue Winged Teal, American Wigeon, Wood Duck, Hooded Merganser, and Pied Billed Grebe can be found here. There are also a lot of swallows, Red Winged Blackbirds, American Bitterns, Soras, Northern Harriers, Woodcock, and Common Snipes. In the adjacent field, Bobolinks breed, and a Sandhill Crane was once spotted.

This checklist is the newest and most comprehensive listing of each wild bird species observed in Nova Scotia. You may wonder why a book about Halifax County birds has a checklist that covers all of Nova Scotia. The answer is simply that the greater Metro area is such a productive place to look for birds that, with the exception of three species—Gray Partridge, Rock Ptarmigan, and Willow Ptarmigan—all of these birds can be seen here and most of them have been.

At first glance, this checklist may look typical, but several innovations have been made to create an easier, faster, and more convenient tool for the use of all birders. In order not to upset the ornithological establishment too much, I stayed with the general outline of a standard checklist, which starts with loons and grebes and ends with finches and sparrows.

However, this bird checklist differs in two significant ways. First, birds with similar characteristics have been grouped together. This means that Part I of the checklist, "Water-loving Birds," starts with the Loon family, and since loons are swimmers, they are followed by each of the other families of swimmers. Next in the list are all of the water-loving birds that commonly fly over or around water, referred to collectively as aerialists (i.e., gulls, terns, etc.). They are followed by the waders, birds such as herons and rails, that walk in the water. They come just before the shorebirds, those species that are usually found walking around the edges of bodies of water. Like waders, shorebirds may occasionally walk into the water. Next, you will find all of the larger land birds, birds of prey such as eagles, hawks, and owls, and the game birds, such as grouse and pheasant.

After this group, the checklist moves into Part II, "Smaller Land Birds." The organization of the second part loosely parallels the order of the first, with some notable exceptions. The main purpose of the parallel is to help users remember where certain species may be found. Since there are no loon–type smaller land birds, Part II begins with those smaller land birds that are commonly seen diving into the water (i.e., kingfishers). Next are the aerialistic types, those species that gather most of their food while in flight, such as swallows, flycatchers, and hummingbirds. Next, one can find the waders/shorebirds, namely pipits. They are followed by the only songbirds that also eat or prey on other songbirds (i.e., shrikes). After the shrikes, there are no categories to which the small land birds can be compared because they have evolved more so than their water-dependent relatives, placing them higher on the evolutionary scale. The evolutionary scale is the basis from which bird checklists are designed—they begin with those species that have changed the least over the years and end with those birds that have shown the greatest evolution.

Part III of the checklist, "Smaller Land Birds Continued," again follows the same general outline of a standard bird list but with several improvements, including such things as listing the Snow Bunting with the other buntings; placing the Starling family next to the Blackbird family because of their similar appearance; and separating the sparrows from the finches. A comparison to a standard checklist will reveal other changes that make this revised checklist easier to use.

The second significant difference between this checklist and a standard one can be seen by the arrangement of the birds under their respective families. Instead of being listed in what appears as a haphazard order, the names are listed alphabetically within families to allow you to find a particular bird quickly. Each species is alphabetized by its last name, so that in complex families such as the sandpipers, all three curlews are together, all the godwits are together, and all the phalaropes are together. This approach also prevents such inconveniences as Greater Yellowlegs being listed under "G" and Lesser Yellowlegs under "L."

Like many checklists, this one has a status rating to give users some idea of how common each species may be. Most checklists that include symbols generally use letters such as "O," "C," "H," "R," "A," and "U" to stand for "occasional," "common," "hypothetical," "rare," "accidental," and "uncommon." These terms can be helpful but do not always mean the same thing to each person, and the particular definitions are sometimes hard to remember, especially for newer birders.

In this checklist, one asterisk (*) is used for birds commonly seen in the Metro area; two asterisks (**) indicate the harder to find bird species; and three asterisks (***) represent bird species rarely seen in the province. In other words, the more asterisks, the rarer the bird in Nova Scotia.

On the checklist, you will notice eleven species marked unconfirmed, usually meaning a bird has been seen only by one person who did not get a photograph of the bird or provide a detailed written report of the sighting. This status does *not* mean the bird was not seen in the province, it just means it is unconfirmed by other observers. Also, a particular species may be listed as unconfirmed if there is some doubt as to whether the bird in question is truly wild. For example, in July 1981, a Scarlet Ibis showed up near Metro, in the Rocky Run/Three Fathom Harbour area. Many birders saw the bird and it was photographed. However, since there was a very good chance the bird escaped from captivity, it was listed as an unconfirmed or hypothetical species. The Hoary Redpoll was added to the unconfirmed list for Nova Scotia after it was suggested that only the Greenland race of the Hoary Redpoll, which is about the size of a Purple Finch, was a true species. The rest of the Hoary

•
C
H
E
C
K
L
I
S
T

Redpolls are thought now to be races of the similar Common Redpoll; however, there are some experts who disagree. Since no one knows for certain if any of the Greenland Hoary Redpolls have been seen in Nova Scotia, this species was placed on the unconfirmed list. So, if you happen to see one of these unconfirmed species, grab your camera, document it, and try to have as many people as possible view the bird!

A species commonly seen in Halifax County. You have a good chance of seeing this bird if you look in the right place at the right time.

**A species less commonly seen in Halifax County.*

****A species rarely seen in Nova Scotia. Double-check the identification, and then spread the news!*

? Unconfirmed status.

Part I: Water-loving Birds

....

Swimmers

Loons:
___ Arctic Loon   *Gavia arctica*   ***?
___ Common Loon   *G. immer*   *
___ Pacific Loon   *G. pacifica*   ***
___ Red Throated Loon   *G. stellata*   *
___ Yellow Billed Loon   *G. adamsii*   ***?

Grebes:
___ Eared Grebe   *Podiceps nigricollis*   ***
___ Horned Grebe   *P. auritus*   *
___ Pied Billed Grebe   *Podilymbus podiceps*   **
___ Red Necked Grebe   *Podiceps grisegena*   *
___ Western Grebe   Aechmophorus occidentalis   ***

Auks or Alcids:
___ Black Guillemot   *Cepphus grylle*   *
___ Dovekie   *Alle alle*   *
___ Common Murre   *Uria aalge*   **
___ Thick Billed Murre   *U. lomvia*   *
___ Atlantic Puffin   *Fratercula arctica*   **
___ Razorbill   *Alca torda*   **

Cormorants:

___ Double Crested Cormorant
    Phalacrocorax auritus   *

___ Great Cormorant *P. carbo*   *

Swans:

___ Tundra Swan *Cygnus columbianus*   ***

Geese:

___ Brant *Branta bernicla*   **

___ Barnacle Goose *B. leucopsis*   ***

___ Canada Goose *B. canadensis*   *

___ Greater White Fronted Goose *Anser albifrons* ***

___ Snow Goose *Chen caerulescens*   **

Whistling Ducks:

___ Fulvous Whistling Duck *Dendrocygna bicolor*   ***

Marsh Ducks:

___ American Black Duck *Anas rubripes*   *

___ Wood Duck *Aix sponsa*   **

___ Gadwall *Anas strepera*   **

___ Mallard *A. platyrhynchos*   *

___ Northern Pintail *A. acuta*   *

___ Northern Shoveler *A. clypeata*   **

___ Blue Winged Teal *A. discors*   *

___ Cinnamon Teal *A. cyanoptera*   ***

___ Green Winged Teal *A. crecca*   *

___ American Wigeon *A. americana*   *

___ Eurasian Wigeon *A. penelope*   ***

Diving Ducks:

___ Bufflehead *Bucephala albeola*   *

___ Canvasback *Aythya valisineria*   **

___ Common Eider *Somateria mollissima*   *

___ King Eider *S. spectabilis*   **

___ Barrow's Goldeneye *Bucephala islandica*   *

___ Common Goldeneye *B. clangula*   *

___ Harlequin Duck *Histrionicuc histrionicus*   **

___ Oldsquaw *Clangula hyemalis*   *

___ Redhead *Aythya americana* ***
___ Ring Necked Duck *A. collaris* *
___ Greater Scaup *A. marila* *
___ Lesser Scaup *A. affinis* **
___ Black Scoter *Melanitta nigra* *
___ Surf Scoter *M. perspicillata* *
___ White Winged Scoter *M. fusca* *
___ Tufted Duck *Aythya fuligula* ***

Stifftails:
___ Ruddy Duck *Oxyura jamaicensis* **

Mergansers:
___ Common Merganser *Mergus merganser* *
___ Hooded Merganser *Lophodytes cucullatus* **
___ Red Breasted Merganser *Mergus serrator* *

Coots, Gallinules:
___ American Coot *Fulica americana* *
___ Purple Gallinule *Porphyrula martinica* **
___ Common Moorhen *Gallinula chloropus* **

Aerialists

Albatrosses:
___ Black Browed Albatross *Diomedea melanophris* ***
___ Yellow Nosed Albatross *D. chlororhyncnos* ***

Shearwaters, Petrels:
___ Northern Fulmar *Fulmarus glacialis* *
___ Black Capped Petrel *Pterodroma hasitata* ***
___ Bulwer's Petrel *Bulweria bulwerii* *** ?
___ Audubon's Shearwater *P. lherminieri* ***
___ Cory's Shearwater *Calonectris diomedea* **
___ Greater Shearwater *Puffinus gravis* *
___ Little Shearwater *P. assimilis* ***
___ Manx Shearwater *P. puffinus* *
___ Sooty Shearwater *Puffinus griseus* *
___ Band Rumped Storm Petrel *Oceanodroma castro* ***
___ British Storm Petrel *Hydrobates pelagicus* ***

___ Leach's Storm Petrel   *Oceanodroma leucorhoa*   *
___ Wilson's Storm Petrel   *Oceanites oceanicus*   *

Tropicbirds:
___ White Tailed Tropicbird   *Phaethon lepturus*   ***

Pelicans:
___ American White Pelican
Pelecanus erythrorhynchus   ***
___ Brown Pelican   *P. occidentalis*   ***

Gannets, Boobies:
___ Brown Booby   *Sula leucogaster*   ***
___ Northern Gannet   *Morus bassanus*   *

Frigatebirds:
___ Magnificent Frigatebird   *Fregata magnificens*   ***

Jaegers, Skuas:
___ Long Tailed Jaeger   *Stercorarius longicaudus*   **
___ Parasitic Jaeger   *S. parasiticus*   **
___ Pomarine Jaeger   *S. pomarinus*   **
___ Great Skua   *Catharacta skua*   **
___ South Polar Skua   *C. maccormicki*   **

Gulls:
___ Bonaparte's Gull   *Larus philadelphia*   *
___ Common Black Headed Gull   *L. ridibundus*   *
___ Franklin's Gull   *L. pipixcan*   ***
___ Glaucous Gull   *L. hyperboreus*   *
___ Great Black Backed Gull   *L. marinus*   *
___ Herring Gull   *L. argentatus*   *
___ Iceland Gull   *L. glaucoides*   *
___ Ivory Gull   *Pagophila eburnea*   ***
___ Laughing Gull   *Larus atricilla*   **
___ Lesser Black Backed Gull   *L. fuscus*   *
___ Little Gull   *L. minutus*   ***
___ Mew Gull   *L. canus*   **
___ Ring Billed Gull   *L. delawarensis*   *
___ Sabine's Gull   *Xema sabini*   ***

___ Yellow Legged Gull *Larus cachinnans* ***
___ Black Legged Kittiwake *Rissa tridactyla* *

Terns:
___ Arctic Tern *Sterna paradisaea* *
___ Black Tern *Chlidonias niger* *
___ Caspian Tern *Sterna caspia* **
___ Common Tern *S. hirundo* *
___ Forster's Tern *S. forsteri* **
___ Gull Billed Tern *S. nilotica* ***
___ Least Tern *S. antillarum* ***
___ Roseate Tern *S. dougallii* **
___ Royal Tern *S. maxima* ***
___ Sandwich Tern *S. sandvicensis* ***
___ Sooty Tern *S. fuscata* ***

Skimmers:
___ Black Skimmer *Rynchops niger* ***

Waders

Herons, Bitterns:
___ American Bittern *Botaurus lentiginosus* *
___ Least Bittern *Ixobrychus exilis* ***
___ Cattle Egret *Bubulcus ibis* **
___ Great Egret *Casmerodius albus* **
___ Little Egret *Egretta garzetta* ***
___ Reddish Egret *E. rufescens* ***
___ Snowy Egret *E. thula* *
___ Great Blue Heron *Ardea herodias* *
___ Green Heron *Butorides viriscens* **
___ Little Blue Heron *Egretta caerulea* **
___ Tricolored Heron *E. tricolor* **
___ Black Crowned Night Heron
   Nycticorax nycticorax **
___ Yellow Crowned Night Heron
   Nyctanossa violacea **

Ibises:
___ Glossy Ibis *Plegadis falcinellus* ***

___ Scarlet Ibis *Eudocimus ruber*   *** ?
___ White Ibis *E. albus*   ***
___ Roseate Spoonbill *Ajaia ajaja*   *** ?

Flamingos:
___ Greater Flamingo *Phoenicopterus ruber*   ***

Cranes:
___ Sandhill Crane *Grus canadensis*   **

Limpkins:
___ Limpkin *Aramus guarauna*   ***

Rails:
___ Corn Crake *Crex crex*   ***
___ Black Rail *Laterallus jamaicensis*   ***
___ Clapper Rail *Rallus longirostris*   ***
___ King Rail *R. elegans*   ***
___ Virginia Rail *R. limicola*   **
___ Yellow Rail *Coturnicops noveboracensis*   ***
___ Sora *Porzana carolina*   **

Shorebirds

Oystercatchers:
___ American Oystercatcher *Haematopus palliatus* ***

Stilts:
___ American Avocet *Recurvirostra americana*   ***
___ Black Necked Stilt *Himantopus himantopus*   ***

Plovers:
___ Killdeer *Charadrius vociferus*   *
___ Northern Lapwing *Vanellus vanellus*   ***
___ American Golden Plover *Pluvialis dominica*   **
___ Black Bellied Plover *P. squatarola*   *
___ Common Ringed Plover *Charadrius hiaticula*   ***
___ Greater Golden Plover *Pluvialis apricaria*   ***
___ Piping Plover *Charadrius melodus*   *
___ Semipalmated Plover *C. semipalmatus*   *

___ Wilson's Plover *C. wilsonia* ***

Sandpipers:

___ Eskimo Curlew *Numenius borealis* ***

___ Eurasian Curlew *N. arquata* ***

___ Long Billed Curlew *N. americanus* ***

___ Long Billed Dowitcher *Limnodromus scolopaceus* ***

___ Short Billed Dowitcher *L. griseus* *

___ Dunlin *Calidris alpina* **

___ Bar Tailed Godwit *Limosa lapponica* ***

___ Hudsonian Godwit *L. haemastica* **

___ Marbled Godwit *L. fedoa* ***

___ Common Greenshank *Tringa nebularia* ***

___ Red Knot *Calidris canutus* **

___ Red Phalarope *Phalaropus fulicaria* **

___ Red Necked Phalarope *P. lobatus* **

___ Wilson's Phalarope *P. tricolor* **

___ Common Redshank *Tringa totanus* ***?

___ Spotted Redshank *T. erythropus* ***

___ Ruff *Philomachus pugnax* **

___ Sanderling *Calidris alba* *

___ Baird's Sandpiper *C. bairdii* **

___ Buff Breasted Sandpiper *Tryngites subruficollis* **

___ Curlew Sandpiper *Calidris ferruginea* ***

___ Green Sandpiper *Tringa ochropus* *** ?

___ Least Sandpiper *Calidris minutilla* *

___ Pectoral Sandpiper *C. melanotos* *

___ Purple Sandpiper *C. maritima* *

___ Semipalmated Sandpiper *C. pusilla* *

___ Solitary Sandpiper *T. solitaria* *

___ Spotted Sandpiper *Actitis hypoleucos* *

___ Stilt Sandpiper *Calidris himantopus* *

___ Upland Sandpiper *Bartramia longicauda* **

___ Western Sandpiper *Calidris mauri* **

___ White Rumped Sandpiper *C. fuscicollis* *

___ Common Snipe *Gallinago gallinago* *

___ Little Stint *Calidris minuta* ***

___ Rufous Necked Stint *C. ruficollis* *** ?

___ Ruddy Turnstone *Arenaria interpres* *

___ Whimbrel *Numenius phaeopus* *

___ Willet *Catoptrophorus semipalmatus* *

___ American Woodcock *Scolopax minor* **

___ Greater Yellowlegs *Tringa melanoleuca* *

___ Lesser Yellowlegs *T. flavipes* *

Birds of prey

American Vultures:

___ Black Vulture *Coragyps atratus* ***

___ Turkey Vulture *Cathartes aura* **

Kites:

___ American Swallow Tailed Kite
   Elanoides forficatus ***

___ Mississippi Kite *Ictinia mississippiensis* ***

Accipiters:

___ Northern Goshawk *Accipiter gentilis* **

___ Cooper's Hawk *A. cooperii* ***

___ Sharp Shinned Hawk *Accipiter striatus* *

Buteos, Eagles:

___ Bald Eagle *Haliaeetus Ieucocephalus* *

___ Golden Eagle *Aquila chrysaetos* ***

___ Broad Winged Hawk *Buteo platypterus* *

___ Red Shouldered Hawk *B. lineatus* ***

___ Red Tailed Hawk *B. jamaicensis* *

___ Rough Legged Hawk *B. lagopus* *

___ Swainson's Hawk *B. swainsoni* ***

___ Zone Tailed Hawk *B. albonotatus* ***

Harriers:

___ Northern Harrier *Circus cyaneus* *

Osprey:

___ Osprey *Pandion haliaetus* *

Falcons:

___ Peregrine Falcon *Falco peregrinus* **

___ Gyrfalcon *F. rusticolus* **

___ American Kestrel *F. sparverius* *

___ Eurasian Kestrel *F. tinnunculus* ***

___ Merlin *F. columbarius* *

Owls:

___ Barred Owl *Strix varia* **

___ Boreal Owl *Aegolius funereus* ***

___ Common Barn Owl *Tyto alba* ***

___ Eastern Screech Owl *Otus asio* ***

___ Great Gray Owl *Strix nebulosa* ***

___ Great Horned Owl *Bubo virginianus* **

___ Long Eared Owl *Asio otus* **

___ Northern Hawk Owl *Surnia ulula* ***

___ Northern Saw Whet Owl *Aegolius acadicus* **

___ Short Eared Owl *Asio flammeus* **

___ Snowy Owl *Nyctea scandiaca* **

Game birds

Grouse:

___ Ruffed Grouse *Bonasa umbellus* *

___ Spruce Grouse *Dendragapus canadensis* **

___ Rock Ptarmigan *Lagopus mutus* ***

___ Willow Ptarmigan *L. lagopus* ***

Quail:

___ Gray Partridge *Perdix perdix* **

___ Ring Necked Pheasant *Phasianus colchicus* *

Part II: Smaller Land Birds

....

Kingfishers:

___ Belted Kingfisher *Ceryle alcyon*   *

Swallows:

___ Purple Martin *Progne subis*   **

___ Bahama Swallow *Tachycineta cyaneoviridis*   *** ?

___ Bank Swallow *Riparia riparia*   *

___ Barn Swallow *Hirundo rustica*   *

___ Cave Swallow *H. fulva*   ***

___ Cliff Swallow *H. pyrrhonota*   **

___ Northern Rough Winged Swallow
      Stelgidopteryx serripennis   **

___ Tree Swallow *Tachycineta bicolor*   *

___ Violet Green Swallow *T. thalassina*   ***

Swifts:

___ Chimney Swift *Chaetura pelagica*   **

Goatsuckers:

___ Common Nighthawk *Chordeiles minor*   *

___ Chuck Will's Widow *Caprimulgus carolinensis* ***

___ Whip Poor Will *C. vociferus*   **

Flycatchers:

___ Acadian Flycatcher *Empidonax virescens*   ***

___ Alder Flycatcher *E. alnorum*   *

___ Ash Throated Flycatcher *Myiarchus cinerascens* ***?

___ Fork Tailed Flycatcher *Tyrannus savana*   ***

___ Great Crested Flycatcher *Myiarchus crinitus*   **

___ Least Flycatcher *Empidonax minimus*   *

___ Olive Sided Flycatcher *Contopus borealis*   **

___ Scissor Tailed Flycatcher *Tyrannus forficatus*   ***

___ Vermilion Flycatcher *Pyrocephalus rubinus*   ***

___ Willow Flycatcher *Empidonax traillii*   ***

___ Yellow Bellied Flycatcher *E. flaviventris*   *

___ Eastern Kingbird *Tyrannus tyrannus*   *

___ Gray Kingbird *T. dominicensis* ***

___ Tropical Kingbird *T. melancholicus* ***?

___ Western Kingbird *T. verticalis* **

___ Eastern Wood Pewee *Contopus virens* **

___ Eastern Phoebe *Sayornis phoebe* **

___ Say's Phoebe *S. saya* ***

Hummingbirds:

___ Black Chinned Hummingbird
   Archilochus alexandri ***

___ Ruby Throated Hummingbird *A. colubris* *

___ Rufous Hummingbird *Selasphorus rufus* ***

Pipits:

___ American Pipit *Anthus rubescens* *

Shrikes:

___ Loggerhead Shrike *Lanius ludovicianus* ***

___ Northern Shrike *L. excubitor* *

Part III: Smaller Land Birds Continued

....

Jays, Crows:

___ American Crow *Corvus brachyrhynchos*   *

___ Fish Crow *C. ossifragus*   ***

___ Eurasian Jackdaw *C. monedula*   ***

___ Blue Jay *Cyanocitta cristata*   *

___ Gray Jay *Perisoreus canadensis*   *

___ Black Billed Magpie *Pica pica*   ***

___ Common Raven *Corvus corax*   *

Titmice:

___ Black Capped Chickadee *Parus atricapillus*   *

___ Boreal Chickadee *P. hudsonicus*   *

___ Tufted Titmouse *P. bicolor*   ***

Kinglets:

___ Blue Gray Gnatcatcher *Polioptila caerulea*   **

___ Golden Crowned Kinglet *Regulus satrapa*   *

___ Ruby Crowned Kinglet *R. calendula*   *

Wrens:

___ Carolina Wren *Thryothorus ludovicianus*   ***

___ House Wren *Troglodytes aedon*   **

___ Marsh Wren *Cistothorus palustris*   **

___ Rock Wren *Salpinctes obsoletus*   ***

___ Sedge Wren *Cistothorus platensis*   ***

___ Winter Wren *Troglodytes troglodytes*   *

Nuthatches:

___ Red Breasted Nuthatch *Sitta canadensis*   *

___ White Breasted Nuthatch *S. carolinensis*   *

Creepers:

___ Brown Creeper *Certhia americana*   *

Woodpeckers:

___ Northern Flicker *Colaptes auratus*   *

___ Yellow Bellied Sapsucker *Sphyrapicus varius*   **

___ Black Backed Woodpecker *Picoides arcticus* **
___ Downy Woodpecker *P. pubescens* *
___ Hairy Woodpecker *P. villosus* *
___ Pileated Woodpecker *Dryocopus pileatus* *
___ Red Bellied Woodpecker *Melanerpes carolinus* ***
___ Red Headed Woodpecker *M. erythrocephalus* **
___ Three Toed Woodpecker *Picoides tridactylus* ***

Pigeons, Doves:
___ Common Ground Dove *Columbina passerina* ***
___ Mourning Dove *Zenaida macroura* *
___ Rock Dove *Columba livia* *
___ White Winged Dove *Zenaida asiatica* ***
___ Band Tailed Pigeon *Columba fasciata* ***

Cuckoos:
___ Groove Billed Ani *Crotophaga sulcirostris* ***
___ Black Billed Cuckoo *Coccyzus erythropthalmus* **
___ Yellow Billed Cuckoo *C. americanus* **

Mimic Thrushes:
___ Gray Catbird *Dumetella carolinensis* *
___ Northern Mockingbird *Mimus polyglottos* *
___ Brown Thrasher *Toxostoma rufum* **

Thrushes:
___ Eastern Bluebird *Sialia sialis* **
___ Mountain Bluebird *S. currucoides* ***
___ Fieldfare *Turdus pilaris* ***
___ Eurasian Redwing *T. iliacus* ***
___ American Robin *T. migratorius* *
___ Townsend's Solitaire *Myadestes townsendi* ***
___ Bicknell's Thrush *Catharus bicknelli* **
___ Gray Cheeked Thrush *Catharus minimus* **
___ Hermit Thrush *C. guttatus* *
___ Swainson's Thrush *C. ustulatus* *
___ Varied Thrush *Ixoreus naevius* ***
___ Wood Thrush *Hylocichla mustelina* **
___ Veery *Catharus fuscescens* *
___ Northern Wheatear *Oenanthe oenanthe* ***

Waxwings:

___ Bohemian Waxwing *Bombycilla garrulus*   *

___ Cedar Waxwing *B. cedrorum*   *

Vireos:

___ Philadelphia Vireo *Vireo philadelphicus*   **

___ Red Eyed Vireo *V. olivaceus*   *

___ Solitary Vireo *V. solitarius*   *

___ Warbling Vireo *V. gilvus*   **

___ White Eyed Vireo *V. griseus*   ***

___ Yellow Throated Vireo *V. flavifrons*   **

Wood Warblers:

___ Yellow Breasted Chat *Icteria virens*   *

___ Ovenbird *Seiurus aurocapillus*   *

___ Northern Parula *Parula americana*   *

___ American Redstart *Setophaga ruticilla*   *

___ Bay Breasted Warbler *Dendroica castanea*   *

___ Black and White Warbler *Mniotilta varia*   *

___ Blackburnian Warbler *Dendroica fusca*   *

___ Blackpoll Warbler *D. striata*   *

___ Black Throated Blue Warbler *D. cearulescens*   *

___ Black Throated Gray Warbler *D. nigrescens*   ***

___ Black Throated Green Warbler *D. virens*   *

___ Blue Winged Warbler *Vermivora pinus*   ***

___ Canada Warbler *Wilsonia canadensis*   **

___ Cape May Warbler *Dendroica tigrina*   **

___ Cerulean Warbler *D. cerulea*   ***

___ Chestnut Sided Warbler *D. pensylvanica*   *

___ Connecticut Warbler *Oporornis agilis*   ***

___ Golden Winged Warbler *Vermivora chrysoptera* ***

___ Hermit Warbler *Dendroica occidentalis*   ***

___ Hooded Warbler *Wilsonia citrina*   ***

___ Kentucky Warbler *Oporornis formosus*   ***

___ Magnolia Warbler *Dendroica magnolia*   *

___ Mourning Warbler *Oporornis philadelphia*   **

___ Nashville Warbler *Vermivora ruficapilla*   *

___ Orange Crowned Warbler *V. celata*   *

___ Palm Warbler *Dendroica palmarum*   *

___ Pine Warbler *D. pinus*   *

___ Prairie Warbler *D. discolor*   **

_____ Prothonotary Warbler *Protonotaria citrea* ***

_____ Swainson's Warbler *Limnothlypis swainsonii* ***

_____ Tennessee Warbler *Vermivora peregrina* *

_____ Townsend's Warbler *Dendroica townsendi* ***

_____ Virginia's Warbler *Vermivora virginiae* ***

_____ Wilson's Warbler *Wilsonia pusilla* **

_____ Worm Eating Warbler *Helmitheros vermivorus* ***

_____ Yellow Warbler *Dendroica petechia* *

_____ Yellow Rumped Warbler *Dendroica coronata* *

_____ Yellow Throated Warbler *D. dominica* ***

_____ Louisiana Waterthrush *Seiurus montacilla* ***

_____ Northern Waterthrush *S. noveboracensis* **

_____ Common Yellowthroat *Geothlypis trichas* *

Starlings:

_____ European Starling *Sturnus vulgaris* *

Blackbirds:

_____ Brewer's Blackbird *Euphagus cyanocephalus* ***

_____ Red Winged Blackbird *Agelaius phoeniceus* *

_____ Rusty Blackbird *Euphagus carolinus* **

_____ Yellow Headed Blackbird
     Xanthocephalus xanthocephalus **

_____ Bobolink *Dolichonyx oryzivorus* *

_____ Brown Headed Cowbird *Molothrus ater* *

_____ Boat Tailed Grackle *Quiscalus major* *** ?

_____ Common Grackle *Q. quiscala* *

_____ Great Tailed Grackle *Q. mexicanus* ***

_____ Eastern Meadowlark *Sturnella magna* **

_____ Western Meadowlark *S. neglecta* ***

_____ Black Cowled Oriole *Icterus dominicensis* ***

_____ Northern Oriole *I. galbula* *

_____ Orchard Oriole *I. spurius* **

Tanagers:

_____ Scarlet Tanager *Piranga olivacea* **

_____ Summer Tanager *P. rubra* **

_____ Western Tanager *P. ludoviciana* ***

Finches:

___ Brambling *Fringilla montifringilla*   ***

___ Indigo Bunting *Passerina cyanea*   **

___ Lark Bunting *Calamospiza melanocorys*   ***

___ Painted Bunting *Passerina ciris*   ***

___ Snow Bunting *Plectrophenax nivalis*   *

___ Northern Cardinal *Cardinalis cardinalis*   **

___ Chaffinch *Fringilla coelebs*   ***

___ Red Crossbill *Loxia curvirostra*   *

___ White Winged Crossbill *L. leucoptera*   *

___ Dickcissel *Spiza americana*   **

___ House Finch *Carpodacus mexicanus*   **

___ Purple Finch *C. purpureus*   *

___ American Goldfinch *Carduelis tristis*   *

___ Black Headed Grosbeak
      Pheucticus melanocephalus   ***

___ Blue Grosbeak *Guiraca caerulea*   **

___ Evening Grosbeak *Coccothraustes vespertinus*   *

___ Pine Grosbeak *Pinicola enucleator*   *

___ Rose Breasted Grosbeak *Pheucticus ludovicianus* *

___ Dark Eyed Junco *Junco hyemalis*   *

___ Horned Lark *Eremophila alpestris*   *

___ Chestnut Collared Longspur *Calcarius ornatus* ***

___ Lapland Longspur *C. lapponicus*   **

___ Smith's Longspur *C. pictus*   ***

___ Common Redpoll *Carduelis flammea*   *

___ Hoary Redpoll *C. hornemanni*   *** ?

___ Pine Siskin *C. pinus*   *

___ Green Tailed Towhee *Pipilo chlorurus*   ***

___ Rufous Sided Towhee *P. erythrophthalmus*   **

Weaver Finches:

___ House Sparrow *Passer domesticus*   *

Sparrows:

___ American Tree Sparrow *Spizella arborea*   *

___ Bachman's Sparrow *Aimophila aestivalis*   *** ?

___ Brewer's Sparrow *Spizella breweri*   ***

___ Cassin's Sparrow *Aimophila cassinii*   ***

___ Chipping Sparrow *Spizella passerina*   *

___ Clay Coloured Sparrow *S. pallida*   **

___ Field Sparrow   *S. pusilla*   **

___ Fox Sparrow   *Passerella iliaca*   *

___ Golden Crowned Sparrow
    Zonotrichia atricapilla   ***

___ Grasshopper Sparrow
    Ammodramus savannarum   ***

___ Harris' Sparrow   *Zonotrichia querula*   ***

___ Henslow's Sparrow   *Ammodramus henslowii*   ***

___ Lark Sparrow   *Chondestes grammacus*   **

___ LeConte's Sparrow   *Ammodramus leconteii*   ***

___ Lincoln's Sparrow   *Melospiza lincolnii*   **

___ Savannah Sparrow   *Passerculus sandwichensis*   *

___ Sage Sparrow   *Amphispiza belli*   ***

___ Seaside Sparrow   *Ammodramus maritimus*   ***

___ Sharp Tailed Sparrow   *A. caudacutus*   *

___ Song Sparrow   *Melospiza melodia*   *

___ Swamp Sparrow   *M. georgiana*   *

___ Vesper Sparrow   *Pooecetes gramineus*   **

___ White Crowned Sparrow   *Zonotrichia leucophrys* **

___ White Throated Sparrow   *Z. albicollis*   *

R
E
S
O
U
R
C
E
S

Here is a list of clubs and organizations that local birders may find interesting or useful:

Adopt a Park Program
Dartmouth Parks and Recreation
PO Box 817
Dartmouth, NS
B2Y 3Z3

American Birding Association, Inc.
PO Box 6599,
Colorado Springs, CO
USA
80934–6599

Animal Alliance of Canada
221 Broadview Avenue, Suite 101
Toronto, ON
M4M 2G3

Canadian Council on Ecological Areas
c/o Sustainable Development/ State of the
Environment Reporting Branch
Environment Canada
Ottawa, ON
K1A 0H3
(819)997–2320

Canadian Heritage Rivers Systems
Parks Canada
Ottawa, ON
K1A 1G2

Canadian Nature Federation
453 Sussex Drive
Ottawa, ON
K1N 6Z4

Canadian Parks and Wilderness Society
160 Bloor Street East, Suite 1150
Toronto, ON
M4W 1B9
(416)972–0868

Canadian Wildlife Service
Atlantic Region
PO Box 1590
Sackville, NB
E0A 3C0
(506)536–3025

The Clean Nova Scotia Foundation
1675 Bedford Row
PO Box 2528
Halifax, NS
B3J 3N5
(902)424–5245

Defenders of Wildlife
1244 Nineteenth Street NW
Washington, DC
USA
20036

Ecology Action Centre
3115 Veith Street, 3rd Floor
Halifax, NS
B3K 3G9

Federation of Nova Scotia Naturalists
c/o Nova Scotia Museum of Natural History
1747 Summer Street
Halifax, NS
B3H 3A6

Friends of McNabs Island Society
21 Willowdale Drive
Dartmouth, NS
B2V 1B9

Halifax Field Naturalists
c/o Nova Scotia Museum of Natural History
1747 Summer Street
Halifax, NS
B3H 3A6

National Audubon Society
PO Box 2667
Boulder, CO
USA
80321

National Bird Feeding Society
1163 Shermer Road
Northbrook, IL
USA
60062–4538

**The National Round Table on the
Environment and the Economy**
1 Nicholas Street, Suite 520
Ottawa, ON
K1N 7B7

The Nature Conservancy of Canada
Atlantic Regional Office
PO Box 8505
Halifax, NS
B3K 5M2

Nova Scotia Bird Society
c/o Nova Scotia Museum of Natural History
1747 Summer Street
Halifax, NS
B3H 3A6

NS Conservation Magazine
Nova Scotia Department of Natural Resources
PO Box 68
Truro, NS
B2N 5B8

Sackville Rivers Association
Superstore Postal Outlet
PO Box 45071
Lower Sackville, NS
B4E 2Z6

**School for Resource and
Environmental Studies**
Dalhousie University
1312 Robie Street
Halifax, NS
B3H 3E2
(902)494–3632

Sierra Club
PO Box 7959
San Francisco, CA
USA
94120–9943

Taking Action to Protect Animals (TAPA)
RR 2, Site 21
Box B-O
Porters Lake, NS
B0J 2S0

World Wildlife Fund
60 St. Clair Avenue East, Suite 201
Toronto, ON
M4T 1N5
(416)923–8173

I
N
D
E
X

D

R

V

W